SELLING
MICROSOFT

S E L L I N G
MICROSOFT

SALES SECRETS FROM
INSIDE THE WORLD'S MOST
SUCCESSFUL COMPANY

DOUG DAYTON

Adams Media Corporation
HOLBROOK, MASSACHUSETTS

Published by Adams Media Corporation
260 Center Street, Holbrook, MA 02343

ISBN: 1-55850-821-X

Printed in the United States of America.

J I H G F E D C B

Library of Congress Cataloging-in-Publication Data
Dayton, Doug
Selling Microsoft : sales secrets from inside the world's most successful
company / by Doug Dayton. — 1st ed.
p.   cm.
Includes index.
ISBN 1-55850-821-X (hardcover)
1. Selling—Case studies. 2. Selling—Computer programs—Case studies.
3. Computer software—Marketing—Case studies. 4. Microsoft Corporation. I. Title.
HF5438.25.D397   1997
658.8—dc21   97-24591
CIP

This book is available at quantity discounts for bulk purchases.
For information, call 1-800-872-5627 (in Massachusetts, 617-767-8100).

Visit our home page at http://www.adamsmedia.com

This book is dedicated to Terry Smith,
to my brothers Laurence and Alan,
and to my mother.

The unexamined life is not worth living.

—PLATO

MY STORY

I became a Microsoft millionaire by developing a selling methodology that works.

I was hired by Microsoft to be an OEM account manager. As an account manager, I closed more than 40 percent of Microsoft's OEM contracts.

So I was promoted.

I spent the next year of my life at Microsoft managing sales and contract support for Microsoft's OEM Division.

My job was to figure out how to explain the "who, what, where, when, and why" of my success to Microsoft's account managers.

This is my story.

I call my selling technology Client-Centered™ Selling because it focuses on the most important person in the selling process.

Right now, the most important person in my mind is you.

If you follow the step-by-step techniques I explain in *Selling Microsoft*, you will become a more successful salesperson. And if you master my Client-Centered™ Selling techniques, you will have a good chance of becoming a millionaire, too.

CONTENTS

ACKNOWLEDGMENTS

I would like to thank Bob Nelson, Murray Fish, Bob Maddocks, Randall Burrell, Bob Gendron, and all of my clients, business associates, and friends at Microsoft who have encouraged me to write this book.

I would also like to send a special thanks to Bill Gates, who convinced me to leave IBM and join Microsoft as employee number 169.

On the publishing side, I would like to thank Bob Adams and Edward Walters at Adams Publishing for their help and encouragement on this project.

PART ONE

TIME, OBJECTIVES, AND IDEAS

In this section you will learn how to use the Client-Centered™ techniques I developed at Microsoft to help you become a better salesperson.

You will also learn how to communicate more effectively with your customers, learn how to manage your territory using objectives and key results, and learn how to manage your time better by planning and prioritizing your selling activities.

CHAPTER ONE

OUR PRIMARY OBJECTIVE:
MARKET DOMINATION

*"Perfection of means and confusion of goals
seem—in my opinion—to characterize our age."*
— **ALBERT EINSTEIN**

Establishing technology standards—creating a "franchise"—in the
software business is the key to market domination and to financial success. Microsoft's Windows operating system is the best
franchise in the computer software business today. And it is the
most profitable one.

When Microsoft first introduced Windows back in 1984, we
realized that we needed to get virtually every hardware original
equipment manufacturer (OEM) to commit to our technology
if we wanted to ensure the viability of our operating systems
business. And we realized that we needed to have an overwhelming commitment from major independent software vendors (ISVs) to achieve the momentum we needed to drive the
Windows standard.

This is why Microsoft adopted a two-pronged OEM/ISV
strategy to sell Windows. Every OEM that bundled Windows with

their PCs made it that much more compelling for other OEMs to license our operating system. And every ISV that shipped a Windows product effectively raised the competitive bar in their application category.

It is certainly arguable whether Microsoft was the best company to develop and maintain the PC operating system standard. But in any case, PC-based computing advanced much more rapidly because Windows technology *standardized* so much of the PC's operating systems infrastructure.

If Microsoft had not done as good a job of selling Windows to its OEMs and ISVs, the entire PC business would have evolved in a completely different way. PC hardware manufacturers would need to support multiple operating systems, software companies would need to develop and support multiple versions of their products, and resellers would need to stock and resell many different solutions for the same application. PCs would cost more to purchase, and be more difficult to support and to use than they are today.

Which is why our objective of "total market domination" was both reasonable and *essential* for the viability of our operating system business.

In this chapter, I will tell you how we used management by objectives or "MBO" techniques to help us achieve our sales objectives.

MANAGEMENT BY OBJECTIVES

Jim Harris, my boss at Microsoft, was a firm believer in management by objectives. His previous position, in strategic planning at Intel Corporation, taught him that the most effective way to manage an organization was to build a reporting "infrastructure" based on setting and achieving carefully defined goals.

When he introduced us to management by objectives at one of our staff meetings, and tasked us with introducing goal-setting and MBO to everyone in our group, we weren't too concerned. The nine-step process he outlined seemed straightforward, and all of us had set goals for ourselves in the past.

We quickly learned that there is a great difference between setting goals, and then forgetting about them until the next planning cycle, and using goals to actually manage what we did with our time.

It took us two complete quarterly planning cycles to align our objectives with reality. At first we had a tough time defining goals that were both achievable and challenging; and we created too many goals for ourselves, which made it difficult to prioritize our selling activities. Then, after we became more realistic about defining our goals, many of us got lazy about tracking the performance criteria we had set up to monitor our results.

But once we integrated goal-setting into our planning cycle, and into our one-on-one meetings with our managers, we began to see how setting goals and managing our time with objectives could help us improve our productivity by helping us manage our most valuable asset—our time.

There is an old saying that "if you don't know where you're going, it doesn't make any difference what route you take; but if you have a destination, each move that you make will either take you closer to or farther from your destination."

Defining our objectives helped us work smarter. And it kept us focused on achieving our most important objective—total market domination.

It has taken me years to realize that each moment of the day, I make decisions about which activities I am going to work on and complete, and that these decisions, many of which I have given almost no thought to, ultimately determine what I do with my life and the level of success I can achieve.

STEP 1. **DEFINE YOUR GOALS**

Setting goals to help you prioritize your selling activities and make better use of your time makes good business sense, but setting goals also works at a psychological level. Before committing yourself to attaining a goal, you should evaluate whether your goal is achievable and challenging. Goals that cannot be achieved are demotivating; and goals that are not challenging will not motivate you to improve your productivity.

COMMON BUSINESS GOALS	EXAMPLE
• **Sales volume**	Produce $1 million in sales this year.
• **Market share**	Achieve 35% market share next year.
• **Profitability**	Maintain 15% pretax profits.
• **Number of customers**	Close fifty new customers this year.
• **Size of customers**	Sell to twenty *Fortune* 200 companies.
• **Number of employees**	Add twenty employees this year.
• **Market capitalization**	Do a $20 million IPO next year.

STEP 2. DEFINE YOUR KEY RESULTS

After you have defined your goals or objectives, you should define the performance criteria, or key results, that you will use as milestones to help you define progress toward your achieving your goal.

Key results should provide an objective measure of your progress toward your objectives. For example, to become a "top dog"—in the top 5 percent of salespeople in your company—you might need to sell $100,000 worth of products each month.

In this example, it would make sense for you to base your key results on specific sales activities. For example, you might define one of your key results based on the number of new accounts you close each month, or on the amount of time that you spend prospecting for new customers

Objective: Sell at least $100,000 worth of products this month.

Key results:

- Close two new accounts. (This represents the minimum number of new sales required to meet this objective.)

MBO: NINE STEPS TO IMPROVING YOUR PRODUCTIVITY

	EXAMPLE
1. Define your goals	My goal is to attain "top dog" status at my company by selling $100,000 worth of product each month.
2. Define your key results	I will close two new accounts each month.
3. Evaluate your strengths and weaknesses	I have a loyal install base, but my competitor's new product is less expensive than mine.
4. Determine a course of action	I will implement a telemarketing campaign to find new prospects, and will organize a "user group" to help me leverage my selling time.
5. Budget your resources (time, personnel, and capital)	I will spend 80% of my selling time with existing customers, and 20% of my selling time prospecting for new business.
6. Determine completion date	I will reach my sales objective by August 1.
7. Write down your plan	I have written my plan down, and I have scheduled blocks of time for activities that will help me achieve my goals.
8. Monitor results	I will review my progress with my sales manager once each week.
9. Implement rewards	When I make "top dog" I will take my family on a one-week cruise.

- Make twenty sales calls each day. This represents the minimum number of prospecting calls needed to identify at least four qualified prospects per month, assuming that you close 50 percent of your qualified prospects.

At Microsoft we defined objectives and key results for specific sales objectives such as closing new accounts and reaching our monthly sales targets. But we also set goals for personal training and development.

For example, an account manager who had difficulty demonstrating one of our products might set a goal of improving his or her demonstration skills by spending time with one of our support engineers or attending a training class.

STEP 3. **EVALUATE YOUR STRENGTHS AND WEAKNESSES**

Once you have determined what your goals are, and have defined your key results, you are ready to analyze your strengths and weaknesses to determine whether you have all of the resources, including time, personnel, and capital, that you will need to achieve your objectives.

For example, if your company's sales objective is to achieve 75 percent market share, you might need to invest in advertising and other promotions to build demand for your products. Or if you have a large customer base, but your competitor's new products are priced lower than yours are, you might need to offer additional services to maintain your market share.

Evaluating your strengths and weaknesses is often the most difficult phase of the goal-setting process, because in many situations you do not have enough information to be certain that your analysis is complete or accurate. For example, if you are selling a new untested product, or selling into a new sales territory, it can be very difficult to anticipate how much promotion will be needed to build awareness of your products so that you can achieve specific sales objectives.

In this situation, you may need to make your best "guess" about the type or amount of marketing resources that you will need to achieve your objectives. Then, after you begin marketing your products and gathering information about your market from your prospective customers, you can revise your objectives.

STEP 4. **DETERMINE A COURSE OF ACTION**

At this point, you should be ready to develop an action plan that describes how you will achieve your objectives.

The key to creating an effective action plan is to evaluate each activity that you are involved with, and then to prioritize the activities that you want to focus on to help you achieve your key results.

If, for example, one of your key results is to close two new accounts each month, you will need to budget some of your selling time to prospect for new customers. When you prepare your action plan, you might decide to budget one day each week to work on a telemarketing campaign or to launch a direct-mail promotion.

The important thing is to identify and prioritize the sales activities that you believe will give you the best chance of achieving your objectives.

STEP 5. **BUDGET YOUR RESOURCES** *(Balance)*

After you have put together your action plan, you will need to allocate the resources you are going to use to accomplish your activities.

For example, you might need to budget your selling time between working with your existing accounts and new account prospecting; or you might need to budget some of your sales assistants' time to help you coordinate a direct-mail promotion.

In most cases your resources, including your selling time, a budget for travel and marketing expenses, and whatever corporate resources you can engage to help you attain your business objectives will be limited. But you can use your most powerful resource—the power of your ideas—to help you achieve your sales objectives.

I have learned that when resources are slim, it's time to be creative!

STEP 6. **DETERMINE A COMPLETION DATE**

Defining completion dates for each activity you have planned provides an opportunity to test your conviction that you can achieve your key results by a specific date, and it also provides an opportunity to evaluate the relative priorities of different tasks.

To help me evaluate whether my goals are achievable, I block out time in my daily planner for each activity I plan to complete. If my plan calls for me to work twelve hours a day, six days a week, I know I am being unrealistic about how much I will be able to accomplish.

STEP 7. **WRITE DOWN YOUR PLAN**

Writing down your goals and outlining your action plan gives an opportunity for you to mentally commit yourself to attaining your objectives, and is an affirmation of your commitment to achieve your objectives.

Writing down your action plan can also help you communicate your plan with other people, and help you stay focused on the activities that are most important to reaching your goals.

When I was given my first multimillion-dollar sales quota at Microsoft, I had no idea of how I was going to achieve it. After reviewing my active accounts, I realized that the only way I could achieve my next quarter's sales quota was to close 95 percent of the contracts I was working on. And I knew that this was extremely unlikely, because the selling cycle with our larger OEMs was typically three to six months.

But when I began writing down my action plan, the solution to my dilemma became obvious: The easiest way for me to achieve my sales quota was to begin working with smaller OEMs that wanted to move through their purchase process very quickly. It turned out that our other account managers were as busy as I was, and that I had no difficulty taking on the additional accounts that I needed to achieve my objective.

STEP 8. **MONITOR YOUR RESULTS**

At Microsoft, we had one-on-one meetings with our manager two or three times a month, travel schedules permitting. We used these meetings to review our objectives and to discuss any problems or issues that might impact our ability to achieve our key results.

When events or problems outside of our control affected our ability to achieve our objectives, we could usually convince our manager to modify our objective or revise the due dates for our key results.

Most of our account managers had no problem meeting their revenue forecasts, but we were on the road so much that it was hard for everyone to stay current on paperwork, internal (I called these infernal) meetings, product training, and other departmental tasks.

In any case, our one-on-one meetings were good opportunities to review our action plans and to evaluate whether we still believed we would be able to achieve our key results by their due dates.

There is no rule about how frequently you should review your action plan with your manager. The important thing is to review your progress frequently enough to take corrective action if you begin to miss your key results—and, depending on why you are missing your key results, to reprioritize your selling activities, or develop an entirely new action plan that will enable you to achieve your objectives.

Sales Reports

At Microsoft we used several sales reports to help us monitor our sales performance.

We tracked our performance each month, using several indices, including:

- Sales by period/account manager/product
- Number of new accounts
- Profit by sales group/product
- Selling expense
- Results of promotions (such as trade show participation)
- Complaints and commendations
- Productive and unproductive selling activities
- Quarterly performance report

Creating sales reports is very important, but the time spent generating reports does not move business forward with customers. To help protect our selling time, we created Microsoft Excel templates for many of our reports. These templates enabled our account managers to fill in simple forms and then send their reports in Excel format to their sales managers. Our sales managers consolidated their account managers' reports, summarized the information, and then sent their own reports to our vice president. Our vice president (my boss) consolidated his sales managers' reports and created an OEM division monthly report, which was distributed at the senior management's executive meetings at the end of each month.

Sales Forecasts

A sales forecast is a prediction of what is expected to sell in a specified period of time. Sales forecasts are usually expressed in dollar volumes and number of units, and often include the names of specific customers who are moving through the selling process, and the degree of certainty that they will make purchase decisions during the forecast period.

Accurate sales forecasts enable a business to allocate its resources efficiently.

However, it is difficult for most salespeople to generate accurate sales forecasts, because they do not spend enough time qualifying their customers, they do not know how much competition they are facing from other suppliers, and they cannot be "objective" about their sales performance. Salespeople are, after all, paid to be optimistic!*

Sales revenues generated from established accounts, or from service revenues are usually much easier to forecast than new account sales. But in any case, the best way to develop accurate sales forecasts is to compile forecast data from multiple sources.

At Microsoft we based our sales forecasts on a combination of factors, including:

- Number of active prospects
- Outstanding sales proposals

---

* Overly conservative sales projections can lead to product shortages if production is scaled back to match an understated demand. And "blue sky" sales projections can lead to cash flow problems if a company purchases additional raw materials, ramps production, or increases overhead to support an overstated demand for product.

SALES FORECAST

SALESPERSON: Terry Smith, robotics account manager
TERRITORY: Western Washington
DATE: September 1997

Top 10 Prospects	$ Revenue	Date Close	% Confidence
Acme Corp.	$120,000	9/21/97	99
Blue Corp.	$80,000	9/21/97	95
Paper Supply	$74,000	10/30/97	90
Health Plus	$135,000	10/30/97	65
Johnson Tool	$35,000	11/15/97	75
Pencil Corp.	$63,000	12/1/97	60
Barbells Ltd.	$72,000	12/20/97	80
Elevator Corp.	$215,000	3/1/98	50
Desk Shop	$110,000	3/15/98	65
Lamp Store	$68,000	3/30/98	75
Lower-Priority Prospects			
Chairs Ltd.	$150,000	10/30/97	50
Lighting, Inc.	$80,000	12/15/97	50
Carpet All	$240,000	12/30/97	40

Total Forecast Revenue for Month of September: $200,000

Notes
*   We will lose Health Plus's business if we can't deliver an AX-600 to them by the end of the year.
*   Pencil Corp. expects us to honor the quote we gave them six months ago.

- Anticipated reorders
- Historical sales data
- Previous account sales history

Since each one of our OEMs' PCs required a copy of our operating system, our account managers could forecast their customers' operating system royalties almost perfectly—if they knew how many PCs their OEMs would be able to manufacture and sell each quarter. But the huge demand for PCs inspired many of our OEMs to forecast three to five times more PC sales than they were able to deliver. Needless to say, our account manager's sales forecasts were not very accurate.

Microsoft's product marketing managers learned to compile our account manager's sales forecasts with other data, such as planned corporate purchase studies published by independent market research companies, and sales projections from leading microprocessor and hard disk drive manufacturers. By evaluating all of these data points, they could get a pretty good idea of how many PCs would really be sold, how much OEM revenue we would generate, and, ultimately, how much profit would be generated from the OEM Sales Division to fund corporate growth.

STEP 9. **IMPLEMENT REWARDS**

Implementing rewards will help you motivate yourself to achieve your objectives.

At Microsoft, our account managers' bonuses and pay raises were based on achieving the objectives that they agreed to complete each quarter with their sales manager.

We also had an awards dinner for our OEM group every quarter, where we presented bonus checks to an account manager and a support person who had done the most exceptional job over the preceding three months. Of course before giving out the checks, we took the opportunity to verbally "roast" them, and one or two managers for good measure.

After leaving Microsoft, I realized that the financial compensation for account managers was modest, considering the demanding nature of the job, but the stock options turned out to be worth a great deal of money.

No one is immune—financial incentive and expressions of appreciation motivate people to make their best effort.

THE BOTTOM LINE

Studies have confirmed that people who set and track goals are more productive and more successful on the job. In addition to this benefit, people who set goals for themselves tend to be more positive, optimistic, and enthusiastic than people who live their life "one day at a time."

Once you've experienced the power of goal-setting, it will be hard for you to imagine organizing your time any other way. But don't wait to succeed—take the time right now to define your goals and start formulating an action plan to help you achieve success.

CHAPTER TWO

MAKING TIME TO ACHIEVE SUCCESS

"We must use time as a tool, not as a couch."
—JOHN F. KENNEDY

If people at Microsoft have one thing in common, it is that they are all very busy. Multitasking—doing more than one thing at the same time—is standard operating procedure.

Being very busy sounds impressive, but when you are working with customers, multitasking is not an option—you must focus your attention on your customers' needs and concerns to move business forward. So the only way to increase your selling productivity is to free up some of the time you spend on other activities. In that way you can have more time to devote to making sales calls and working with customers.

In this chapter you will learn how to *identify* your most insidious time wasters with a simple time audit, and then *eliminate* those time wasters, to recapture valuable selling time.

10 MAJOR TIME-WASTERS
Ranked by 10,000 U.S. Business Executives

1. Shift priorities
2. Telephone interruptions
3. Lack of priorities or objectives
4. Attempt too much
5. Drop-in visitors
6. Ineffective delegation
7. Cluttered desktop—lose things
8. Lack of self-discipline
9. Inability to say "no"
10. Meetings

WHERE DOES YOUR TIME GO?

All of us have felt at one time or another that there simply weren't enough hours in the day to accomplish our work, and still have enough time for our family and ourselves.

In fact, we really are running out of time!

According to a Harris survey, leisure time for the average American dropped 37 percent from 1973 to 1990, while the average workweek, including commuting time, increased from fewer than forty-one hours to more than forty-seven hours. At Microsoft, many of our account managers and support engineers stretched their workweeks to seventy or more hours.*

Most people are very optimistic about how much work they can accomplish each day. A recent study, for example, suggests that office workers believe that they can accomplish 48 percent more work in a day than they really can. But time cannot

---

* A recent study in *Worth* magazine (March 1997) said that men in the top 5 percent of income earners worked an average of 2,597 hours a year or about 50 hours each week, and that women in the top 20 percent of all households worked 1,434 hours each year.

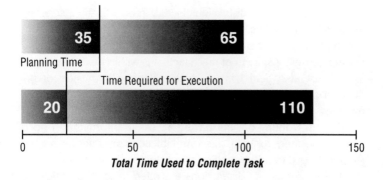

Planning Time

35   65

Time Required for Execution

20   110

0   50   100   150

Total Time Used to Complete Task

expand to meet our needs. To *manage* time we must make a *conscious effort* to control events in our life.

PLANNING YOUR WORKDAY

The secret to effective time management is learning how to plan events so that your high-priority tasks are handled first. But taking the time to plan your workday is a discipline that requires commitment and conscious attention.

Most salespeople can recite the advantages of planning activities, such as reducing wasted time, becoming better organized, reducing stress, avoiding crisis management, and having more time for personal activities. But most salespeople do not take the time to plan their workday.

The most common reasons why salespeople do not plan their workday are that they feel that they are too busy, that they do not feel like they are in control of their work, or that crisis situations come up too frequently—obviating the benefits of planning.

OVERCOMING DISTRACTIONS

I have found that the most difficult challenges to planning my daily schedule are distractions, which cause me to lose control of my daily schedule.

My "self-imposed" distractions include procrastination, selecting tasks with the wrong priorities, making mistakes, attempting to accomplish more than I can in a specific period of time, and social interruptions. Each of these factors is within my own control.

I must also deal with distractions that are outside of my direct control. These "business-imposed" distractions include interruptions, not having the decision-making authority to accomplish a task I am working on, not having access to information I need to move business forward, miscommunication, and not having the support I need to address all of my customers' concerns.

Business-imposed distractions are often difficult to anticipate and may be hard to overcome. However, I have found that if I am well organized, I can minimize their impact on my workday and on my productivity. And I have learned that despite the interruptions in my day, I must take responsibility for how I spend my time, and learn to budget my time with the same attention that I budget my money.

WHAT IS A TIME AUDIT?

Our perception of time is not a very good way to measure its actual passage. Most people, for example, believe that they work more hours than they do, and that they spend less time socializing than they actually do. Activities that are fun, such as vacations, seem to "fly by," while less desirable activities, such as telephone prospecting, often feel interminable.

The best way to find out where your day "really goes" is to do a time audit. To complete a time audit, you must track and record what you are doing each minute of the day.

The data you collect during your time audit will help you determine if your activities are consistent with your business objectives and will help you identify major time wasters that are decreasing your productivity. For example, if your time audit indicates that you spend most of your time socializing with customers, you might decide to schedule time for a telemarketing campaign to identify new prospects for future sales. By reprioritizing how you spend your time, you can focus your efforts on specific activities that can help you attain your business and personal objectives.

Most salespeople are reluctant to take the time to perform a time audit. They will agree that time is a precious resource and that a time audit could help them do a better job of managing the workday. But they often need a "push" to get themselves motivated.

At Microsoft, we used an outside training company to raise awareness of the importance of time management, and we encouraged each sales manager to complete his or her own time audit. Then, after our sales managers became time-audit "converts," we encouraged them to introduce the time-audit process in their one-on-one meetings with each account manager on their sales team.

SETTING UP YOUR TIME AUDIT

The first step in setting up a time audit is determining the basic task—categories you want to track.

When you set up your own time audit, you should limit the number of task categories you are tracking to the areas that are most important to your success. For example, at Microsoft I set up categories for Telephone Calls, Customer Meetings, Company Meetings, Socializing and Meals, and Travel Time. I used an Other Tasks category to record activities that did not fit into these categories.

It is best to track each activity in ten- or fifteen-minute blocks, and to record the activity in a daily planner that has space for each hour's activities. Then you can "credit" each block of time to an appropriate category in your time audit summary table.

The key to maintaining an accurate record of how you have spent your time is recording your activities right after they are performed, or at least once each hour.

Performing a time audit does not take very much effort. It takes most salespeople about ten to fifteen minutes per day, or fewer than one and a half hours per week to record their activities, based on spending ten to fifteen seconds per entry to record three to eight activities per hour.

Most salespeople are only patient enough to keep track of their daily activities for a week, but it is best to track your daily

DAILY TIME LOG	**ACTIVITY** T=Telephone, CM=Customer Meeting, CO=Company Meeting, S=Socializing and Meals, TR=Travel Time, O=Other Tasks	**ACTIVITY CODE**
7:00	Call AC Distributing	T
7:15	Meet with admin. ass't.	CO
7:30	Department meeting	CO
7:45	Department meeting	CO
8:00	Department meeting	CO
8:15	Department meeting	CO
8:30	Call home	S
8:45	Coffee break	S
9:00	Travel to Acme Corp.	TR
9:15	Meeting with Acme	CM
9:30	Meeting with Acme	CM
9:45	Meeting with Acme	CM
10:00	Travel to office	TR
10:15	Return telephone calls	T
10:30	Write up sales call report	O
10:45	Prepare sales forecast	O
11:00	Schedule demonstration for Acme Corp.	O
12:00	Lunch	S
	And so on...	

activities for two weeks, to get a more accurate "snapshot" of how you spend your workday.

Completing a time audit should be voluntary, and the results of your audit should be confidential, unless you choose to share your results with your manager. If you feel that your privacy is being compromised, you will be tempted to misstate your results to look more efficient or productive than you really are. And if you aren't honest about how you spend your time, your time audit will be a waste of your time.

EVALUATING YOUR RESULTS

Most salespeople find when they review their time audit results table that their perception of how much time they spend on different activities is very different from the time they have actually spent.

TIME AUDIT SUMMARY TABLE	TELEPHONE CALLS	CUSTOMER MEETINGS	COMPANY MEETINGS	SOCIALIZE AND MEALS	TRAVEL TIME	OTHER TASKS
Monday						
Tuesday						
Wednesday						
Thursday						
Friday						
Saturday						
Sunday						
Monday						
Tuesday						
Wednesday						
Thursday						
Friday						
Saturday						
Sunday						
Total hours						

In our example below, the perception (forecast) of how much time was spent socializing and eating meals was considerably shorter than was actually spent, and the perception of how much time was spent making telephone calls was considerably longer than the actual time spent on the phone.

TIME AUDIT RESULTS	FORECAST HOURS	ACTUAL HOURS
Telephone calls	20	11
Customer meetings	30	24
Company meetings	20	25
Socializing and meals	10	17
Travel time	10	7
Other activities	10	16

ACTIVITIES AND OUTPUT

It is important to distinguish between *activities*—the things you do during the day—and *output*, which is what you achieve. For example, a physician's output is helping to cure sickness, but his or her day-to-day activities include unglamorous activities, such as cleaning someone's ear, or looking in the person's nose. Output often appears important and worthwhile, while activities often appear trivial or insignificant.

When you examine the results of your time audit, it may be difficult for you to visualize how the composite of your daily activities leads to achieving, or failing to reach, your objectives.

Nevertheless, the keys to increasing your productivity and achieving your objectives are to determine which of your activities are the most important, and to prioritize those tasks.

This sounds easy, but you will not always have enough information to determine which activities are the most important, and at times you will need all of your will power to put aside enjoyable, low-priority tasks until your higher-priority tasks are completed.

THE PAYOFF

The primary purpose of a time audit is to make you aware of how you are spending your time, so you can reprioritize activities to help you achieve your objectives.

After you have completed your time audit, you will need to evaluate whether you are allocating time in a way that is consistent with attaining your objectives. You may find, for example, that you need to change some of your habits, such as socializing with coworkers or "surfing" the Internet, to free up blocks of time to accomplish your high-priority tasks.

Changing old habits takes an open mind, hard work, patience, and personal commitment. But the minutes you can save each day, by managing your time more carefully, can help you free up hours of time each week. And you can use these hours to accomplish more at work, and to enjoy with your family and friends.

OVERCOMING PROCRASTINATION

I think all of us have made excuses, at one time or another, for putting off what we felt was a difficult or unpleasant task. Unfortunately, some of us develop a habit of putting off these tasks.

Having too much work to do can overcome your will to complete your high-priority tasks; and doing nothing, or doing low-priority tasks, can result in important tasks piling up into "mountains" of work.

The key to overcoming procrastination is to prioritize your work, and then focus your efforts on completing your most important tasks before taking time to complete less important tasks or socializing.

Mountains to molehills: Break large projects into smaller tasks, and then complete each task before moving on to the next one.

Group similar tasks: Group similar activities together to save mental setup time and to enable you to accomplish more work in the same period of time.

Finish what you're doing: Finish the project you are working on before moving on to the next one.

Avoid distractions: Avoid distractions and interruptions, and keep inactive projects out of sight.

Start projects as soon as possible: It is usually best to begin a major project, even if all the materials or data you need aren't available. Otherwise you may experience further delays.

Get the worst over first: Get your most onerous project done first, while your personal energy is at its peak.

Set deadlines: Set deadlines for your work; and define specific milestones to help you track your progress.

Avoid pressure: Some people claim that they work best under pressure. But do-it-by-the-deadline habits backfire when tasks are put off to the last minute and there is not enough time left before the deadline to complete the task properly.

Don't chase perfection: One of the hardest things for many salespeople to learn is when to stop working on a project. In some cases you must force yourself to complete work before it is "perfect" so you can move on to your next project.

Use check lists: One of the easiest ways to organize projects is to use check lists to help you prioritize individual tasks.

Make a radical change: For many people, the best way to break the procrastination habit is to make a radical behavior change. For example, you may decide to postpone your morning coffee until you have updated your daily to-do list.

If you make this type of commitment, there are three things you can do to help ensure your success. First, start immediately; second, force yourself to keep your promise—don't allow any exceptions; and third, implement rewards that encourage you to stay on plan and achieve your goals.

ELIMINATING INTERRUPTIONS

Interruptions decrease your productivity by diverting your attention from high-priority activities to lower-priority activities and by requiring you to mentally "reorganize" your work.

This mental reorganization process takes most people three to ten minutes. So if you are interrupted six times in one hour, your productivity can decrease by more than 50 percent!

The best way to become aware of how interruption-driven your day has become is to keep a log of each interruption you have over a period of several days. Keeping an interruption log is, of course, an oxymoron. But if you maintain an interruption log for a few days, you will start to see interruption patterns emerge.

INTERRUPTION TRACKING DAY OF WEEK	SOCIAL INTERRUPTIONS	COWORKER INTERRUPTIONS	PHONE INTERRUPTIONS
Monday			
Tuesday			
Wednesday			
Thursday			
Friday			
Total number of interruptions			

Once you identify how and when you are being interrupted, you can change your work habits, retrain your coworkers, and reorganize your daily activities to help you stay focused on completing your highest-priority tasks.

---

6 TIPS FOR ELIMINATING INTERRUPTIONS

1. **Plan the workday**—don't wait for interruptions.

2. **Screen phone calls**—don't allow yourself to be interrupted.

3. **Schedule meetings**—avoid spur-of-the-moment meetings.

4. **Group similar activities**—focus on one type of problem at a time.

5. **Delegate responsibility**—don't micromanage delegated tasks.

6. **Retrain your coworkers**—break their interruption habit.

SELF-INTERRUPTIONS

Many salespeople develop "self-interruptions," such as wandering around their office to socialize, or making unnecessary sales calls, because they are bored or unmotivated by their work.

Most salespeople enjoy socializing. But spending too much time socializing will decrease your productivity, as well as the productivity of the people you work with.

THE OPEN DOOR

Most of our account managers at Microsoft had an "open door" policy. In principle this was a great way to build good relationships with their coworkers. However, many of our account managers worked extra hours every day to make up for the time they spent socializing.

The most effective way to limit interruptions is to set specific hours for your door to be "open." During other hours you need to resist interruptions so you can get your work done.

You can also use some of my "old tricks" to help you limit interruptions through the day. First, I ask my visitors how I can help them when they first arrive, to encourage them to get down to business immediately. Next, I give them my undivided attention, and verify that I understand the message they delivered, so they do not feel they need to repeat themselves.

I have found that the length of most visits is directly proportional to the level of hospitality I greet my visitor with. When people are comfortable, they don't mind taking the time to sit back and enjoy themselves. So when I am too busy to socialize, I don't invite my guests to have a cup of coffee or start serving cookies! And if my day is extremely busy, I ask unexpected visitors whether someone else in my office would be able to help them, or whether I can set up a specific time to meet with them later. Sometimes I have to be a bit tough—but the payoff is staying in control of my workday.

LEARNING TO BE ON TIME

Most of our account managers were extremely punctual, but some of our account managers never seemed to be able to keep appointments on time.

There are a number of reasons why people are chronically late.

Manipulation: Arriving late helps some people feel they are in control of a situation.

Feelings of importance: Some people feel important when they make other people wait for them.

Perfectionism: Some people will remain on one task, attempting to do a perfect job, despite the fact that this delay will make them late for their next appointment.

Anxiety or uncertainty: Some people arrive late for meetings because they are apprehensive about what will happen when they arrive.

Rebellion: Being late satisfies some people's desire to be rebellious or individualistic.

Desire for attention: Some people like the attention they get when they arrive late.

Most people who are chronically late get into the habit of leaving too little time between activities to arrive on time.

Fortunately, this is an easy habit to change. Paying attention to the time you should leave a meeting, rather than when your next meeting begins, will help you reserve your transition time, and help ensure that you have enough time to get to your next meeting on time.

You can also use your daily planner to keep track of when and why you were late for appointments. The next time you schedule a similar activity, you will have a better idea of how much time it will take you to get to your meeting.

Some people can trick themselves into being on time by setting their watch five or ten minutes early. But most people learn to "subtract" their extra time and defeat their own game.

MANAGING YOUR TRAVEL TIME

To be honest, I don't enjoy business travel anymore. The airlines have "engineered" the fun out of an airplane ride by decreasing the size of everything from seats and meals to carry-on luggage space. So before I commit myself to anyone's "friendly skies," I ask myself whether I really need to go. Then I ask myself five travel "qualification" questions to determine whether my planned trip is the best use of my time:

1. Is the trip absolutely necessary for me to achieve my business objectives?
2. What impact will travel have on my other business obligations?
3. Can I eliminate the need to travel by using electronic communications, such as electronic mail or videoconferencing?
4. Can I get the people I need to visit, to visit me?
5. Can I delegate the trip?

If after asking my five "travel qualification" questions I determine that I really do need to make a business trip, I spend a few minutes preparing my itinerary to help me determine whether I am making the best possible use of my travel time.

MY FAVORITE AIR TRAVEL TIPS

- Pack only what is needed for the number of days you will be gone.
- Keep a fully equipped toiletry bag in your suitcase.
- Don't check baggage unless it is absolutely necessary.
- Check in at the gate, or at a frequent-flier club, to avoid long lines.
- Avoid early morning, Friday afternoon, and holiday flying times.
- Call the airline to confirm flight times before leaving for the airport.
- Avoid overnight "red-eye" flights unless you can sleep on an airplane.
- Drink plenty of nonalcoholic liquids to avoid becoming dehydrated and to reduce jet lag.
- Bring reading materials, especially magazines you can read and then discard.
- If your trip is fewer than two hundred miles, consider driving, or taking a bus or a train to save travel time.
- Take food supplements to help you overcome jet lag. (You should check with your physician before taking any vitamins, or other nutritional supplements.)

My Travel Check List

- Have I prepared a list of objectives for my trip?
- What other tasks can I accomplish on my trip?
- Have I determined the most efficient routing between meetings?
- Do I have enough time between appointments?
- Do I have tasks planned for travel and waiting time?
- Have I reconfirmed my appointments and my travel arrangements?
- Do my assistant at work and someone in my family have copies of my itinerary?

City Guides

Many of my accounts at Microsoft were located in the technology corridors around Silicon Valley, Boston, and Dallas. And

I went to various computer shows in Las Vegas, Atlanta, New York, and Chicago every year.

To save time, I put together a folder for each city I visited, which included a street map, and the addresses and phone numbers of customer sites, hotels, and restaurants I frequented.

My system worked perfectly, as long as I remembered to bring my travel folders with me on my trips!

THE TIME YOU SAVE

Now that you have learned how to recapture some of your wasted time, you can decide how to "spend" the time you have saved. You may choose to invest your saved time in additional sales calls—to earn more money, or you can invest your saved time with your family—to enjoy the fruits of your work.

The best part of saving time is that in most cases you really don't feel like you've given anything up. Time, unlike most things in life, is "free." It just gets expensive if you waste it!

CHAPTER THREE

OUR NUMBER ONE PRIORITY: SELLING MICROSOFT

*"Time is the scarcest resource. Unless it is
managed, nothing can be managed."*
—Peter Drucker

It's easy to claim that your number one priority is selling, but it's hard to stay focused on activities that lead to sales.

At Microsoft we tried to spend as much time as possible working with our customers. But despite our efforts, it was not always possible to prioritize our day the way we wanted.

My "nemesis" was the time I spent traveling to and from customers' offices and industry sales events. I remember days when I was so busy trying to get somewhere, it was hard to take the time to return my customers' telephone calls!

But I soon learned that when there isn't enough time to accomplish everything you *want* to do, you must start prioritizing the things you really *need* to do. For me, this meant prioritizing the tasks that could help me move business forward with my customers, and then making a *conscious effort* to accomplish these tasks before beginning work on other, less important activities.

In this chapter you will learn how to prioritize your workday to help you stay focused on achieving your sales objectives.

PRIORITIZING YOUR TASKS

Not every task needs to be prioritized. Many activities, such as bathing, sleeping, and caring for your family, are "self-prioritizing." But most activities, such as watching TV, learning how to scuba dive, and making sales calls, can be prioritized, depending on your personal desires and your business objectives.

To prioritize your activities, you must first identify the tasks you need to accomplish to achieve your objectives. Then you must evaluate how important each task is in relation to the other tasks you must complete to enable you to reach your objectives.

The easiest way I have found to do this is to assign each activity an "A," "B," or "C" priority. Your "A"-level tasks should be your most important tasks and should have priority over your "B" and "C" tasks.

Ideally, you should accomplish your "A"-level tasks before moving on to your "B"- and "C"-level tasks. In reality, the resources (and personal energy) you need to accomplish a specific task may not be available when you are scheduled to begin working on it, so you will need to reprioritize different activities during your workday to maximize your productivity.

At Microsoft I considered any activity that was scheduled with a customer, such as a teleconference or sales meeting, to be an "A"-priority task. I also considered any appointment with my boss an "A"-priority task. My "B"-priority tasks were often just as important as my "A" tasks, but they weren't as time-sensitive—for example, contacting sales prospects or working on my income tax. My "C"-priority tasks were tasks I wanted to accomplish but I could "live without," such as taking time to see a competitive product demonstration.

SAMPLE TO-DO LIST FOR 8/13/99	PRIORITY	DUE/DONE
1. Prioritize tasks	A	8/13—done
2. Return telephone calls	A	8/13—done
3. Demonstration for Acme Company	A	8/13
4. Visit XYZ Company	B	8/13
5. Go to dentist	B	Reschedule for 8/21
6. Buy fax machine	C	8/13

PRIORITY OVERLOAD

When your schedule is full and you need to fit in new "A"-priority tasks, you will have to reprioritize and reschedule some of your other tasks.

Over time you will become better at estimating how much work you can accomplish each day. But when you have "B"- and "C"-priority tasks that are being rescheduled day after day, you may have to accept the fact that they are not going to get done unless you delegate them to someone else.

I have found that after I have rescheduled a "C"-priority task three times, I can be pretty sure I'll never get around to accomplishing it. If a demoted "C"-priority task is really important, I'll try to delegate it, or will move it to the time I reserve for myself on the weekend. I'm reluctant to give up my personal time. But sometimes there is no other choice.

After you have tracked your own priorities for a few weeks, you will begin to see patterns in how you prioritize your work. And you will learn when it's time to delegate tasks, or to commit some of your personal time to get them done.

SAVING TIME WITH YOUR DAILY PLANNER

One of the main benefits of using a daily planner is that you can review where you've been, and what you've accomplished.

I like to review my daily planner each week to determine whether I am making progress toward my objectives and whether I am using my time as effectively as possible. Most of the time I am "on track," but once in a while I discover that I have let myself get caught up in too much office work, or that I have been avoiding one or more unpleasant—but important—tasks. My daily planner helps keep me honest.

Some salespeople use palmtop computers (personal digital assistants) or larger notebook PCs to maintain their daily schedule and keep track of their prioritized action items. But most salespeople still rely on paper-based planning systems.

Perhaps it's because I have been in the computer industry too long, but I find that the easiest way to manage my personal schedule is with a Day Timer™, which fits in my coat pocket. It is easy to carry, and it helps me organize my day, maintain a to-do list, change the priority of my tasks, record the work I have completed each day, take notes, track my expenses, and maintain an approved record of my business activities for the Internal Revenue Service.

As palmtop computers and communications devices (smart phones) become smaller, less expensive, and more powerful, they will ultimately obviate paper-based planning systems. But in any case, the type of planning system you use isn't really important, as long as you adopt some type of planning system—and then use it religiously.

Daily Planner Abbreviations

Over the years I began using a few common abbreviations to help me save time when I record tasks in my daily planner. They may look confusing at first, but you'll get used to using them very quickly.

After you get used to working with these abbreviations you may want to think up some that make sense for your own business. For example, you might use (SP) for send proposal, or (OD) for on-line demonstration.

SYMBOL	DAILY PLANNER ABBREVIATIONS
A, B, or C	A-, B-, or C-level-priority tasks
✓	Task is completed
©	Telephone call
→	Item was forwarded to next day
⇨	Item was forwarded to next week
®	Reference item
*	Urgent or high priority
LM	Left message
NA	No answer
CB	Call back
M	Meeting
R	Report
T	Travel
TBA	To be arranged
ASAP	As soon as possible
SM	Sales manager
DM	District manager
OM	Office manager
GM	General manager
	Add your own codes

MAKING PARETO'S LAW WORK FOR YOU

Pareto's Rule suggests that 80 percent of a company's business will come from 20 percent of its customers. At Microsoft I

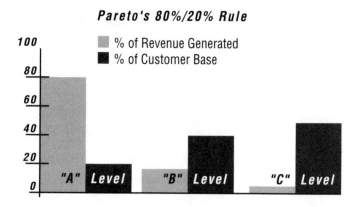

Pareto's 80%/20% Rule

considered the most productive 20 percent of my customer base to be my "A"-level customers.

I prioritized my selling time to ensure that I could spend at least 50 percent of my selling time with my "A"-level customers and about 50 percent of my time with my "B"- and "C"-level customers.

Depending on your own selling situation and on how many customers you are working with, you may be able to spend more or less of your selling time with your "B"- and "C"-level customers. But in any case, it is important to allocate your selling time very carefully.

If, for example, you are selling long-distance telephone services, your "A"- and "B"-level customers may account for more than 90 percent of your revenues, but you may not be able to grow your business unless you add many additional "C"-level customers. To accomplish this, you may need to spend 80 percent or more of your selling time with your "C"-level customers.

The key to prioritizing your selling time is to "spend" your time with the customers or prospects who provide the greatest return on your time "investment."

OVERCOMING PARKINSON'S LAW

Parkinson's Law states that work expands to fill the time allocated for its completion. By setting reasonable time limits for yourself to complete your projects, you can maximize your productivity.

For example, spending a few minutes each day prioritizing your tasks can help you focus your selling energy on accomplishing your most important goals. But spending an hour each day updating and rearranging tasks in a daily planner can become a time-wasting habit. The purpose of investing time planning your work in a daily planner is to *free up* time for your high-priority tasks.

If you are spending too much time on low-priority tasks, you will need to make a *conscious effort* to move through those tasks quickly so you can move on to higher-priority tasks.

At Microsoft we had one account manager who was extremely compulsive about writing detailed reports, and we had another account manager whose office looked like the "before" advertisement for a cleaning service. The meticulous account manager wasted time perfecting his paperwork, and the sloppy account manager wasted time "searching" for important papers that were lost in his clutter.

As you become more experienced at prioritizing your selling activities, you will get a "sixth sense" about how much time you should devote to each activity you work on during your workday.

MURPHY'S LAWS—GETTING A GRIP ON TIME

For thousands of years, mankind wondered why time was so difficult to manage. Then Murphy revealed his three laws:

Murphy's First Law: Nothing is as easy as it appears.

Murphy's Second Law: Everything takes longer than you think it will.

Murphy's Third Law: Anything that can go wrong will go wrong.

We have all experienced the effects of Murphy's laws, but the fact remains that the only way to gain control of how we spend our time is to plan our day and to prioritize our most important tasks. Then, when unexpected events derail our plans, we can blame it on Murphy, reprioritize our tasks, and take whatever steps are necessary to get back on plan.

COMMIT YOURSELF TO PLANNING FOR SUCCESS

At Microsoft I began a lifelong habit of taking a few minutes each morning to prioritize my list of open action items and plan my day. I believe that the time I take to plan my workday has been critical to my success. So I don't cheat myself. I respect my own priorities, and I visualize myself as an organized, energetic business professional.

You won't believe the difference that planning your day can make until you try it for yourself. Then you'll be hooked, too.

CHAPTER FOUR

TURNING OBJECTIVES INTO REALITY

"Eighty percent of success is showing up."
—WOODY ALLEN

In the past three chapters, you have learned the importance of setting goals, managing your time, prioritizing your activities, and improving your communication skills. In this chapter, you will apply the skills that you have learned to help you create territory and account plans that you can use to help increase your sales productivity.

The planning process that I developed at Microsoft is based on a simple step-by-step approach which begins with defining your company's primary business objectives. These objectives provide the basis for a *marketing plan* that defines the strategies, tactics, and resources that you can use to help you achieve your company's sales objectives.

Once you have defined your marketing plan, you can develop a *sales plan* that specifies how your sales force will achieve its objectives, a *territory plan* that specifies how individual salespeople will achieve their territory objectives, and

```
┌─────────────────────────────────────────┐
│     TERRITORY AND ACCOUNT PLANNING       │
│                                          │
│  1. Define Your Objectives (Goals)       │
│                  ⇓                       │
│  2. Develop a Realistic Marketing Plan   │
│                  ⇓                       │
│  3. Develop a Compelling Marketing "Story" │
│                  ⇓                       │
│  4. Develop a "Real World" Sales Plan    │
│                  ⇓                       │
│  5. Develop a Realistic Territory Plan   │
│                  ⇓                       │
│  6. Develop an Account Plan              │
│                  ⇓                       │
│  7. Develop a Sales Call Plan            │
│                  ⇓                       │
│     Achieve Your Objectives!             │
└─────────────────────────────────────────┘
```

account plans that specify how you plan to achieve your specific account objectives.

STEP 1: **DEFINE YOUR OBJECTIVES (GOALS)**

Before you can develop a marketing plan for your company and a sales plan for your territory, you will need to define your goals and specify the key results that you will use to monitor your day-to-day activities. If you don't remember why this is important, or how to do this, you should review the first chapter.

STEP 2: **DEVELOP A REALISTIC MARKETING PLAN**

If someone asked me for a formal definition of a marketing plan, I would say that it is a written statement that defines the strategies, tactics, and resources that a company employs to reach its business objectives. But I like to think of a marketing plan more simply as the "why" behind whatever I plan to do to achieve my sales objectives.

COMMON BUSINESS OBJECTIVES	EXAMPLE
Sales volume	$1 million in sales first year
Market share	10% market first year
Profitability	Increase product Z profits by 15%
Number of customers	Close 50 new customers this year
Size of customers	Sell into *Fortune* 200
Number of employees	Hire 22 new employees next year
Market capitalization	$18 per share valuation

In most cases, a company's marketing personnel or senior managers are responsible for developing a marketing plan for their company. But if you are given an opportunity to help develop your company's marketing plan, you should be sure that your plan addresses five key issues:

Product—Define the products and services that you will sell to meet your business objectives.

Place (Distribution)—Explain how you will contact and support your customers.

Price—Specify customer pricing and all other terms of sale.

Promotion—Describe how you will use advertising and other marketing activities, such as trade shows, telemarketing, and direct mail, to generate awareness of and preference for your products.

Competition/market intelligence—Evaluate what competitors in your market are doing, and how they will impact your ability to achieve your business objectives.

Product, Place, Price, and Promotion are the four "P"s of marketing. I like to throw in Competition, which changes the acronym to "PC," which is, of course, more politically correct.

I also like to spend some time comparing different *marketing opportunities* to determine whether I am making the best use of my selling time, and to identify the *purchase factors* that my customers will use to help them make a purchasing decision.

Market opportunities—To estimate the market potential for your products and services in different target markets, you will need to investigate who uses your products or services, where your prospects are located, and the rates of usage for your products or services by different types of customers.

You can use a simple equation to help you calculate your TOTAL MARKET OR TERRITORY POTENTIAL:

TOTAL MARKET OR TERRITORY POTENTIAL = [TOTAL NUMBER OF PROSPECTS IN MARKET OR TERRITORY] × [RATE OF USAGE OR QUANTITY OF PRODUCT NEEDED] × [AVERAGE REVENUE PER SALE]*

Using a "robotics company" as an example, its TOTAL MARKET POTENTIAL would be equal to $1.25 billion, assuming 2,500 (manufacturing prospects in the Western region) × 10 (the average number of robots needed per manufacturing site) × $50,000 (the average cost of a robotics system).

It is not always possible to estimate your TOTAL MARKET POTENTIAL accurately, but you should give it your best shot. Whether your estimate is high or low, you *are* betting your selling time and your marketing resources on your "guess."

At Microsoft I used historical, demographic, and market survey data to help me estimate the TOTAL MARKET POTENTIAL for different products in my territory. Sometimes I was right on the money, but other times I was way too conservative. To be honest, it was hard to believe that our business could sustain such a rapid rate of growth!

After you calculate the TOTAL MARKET POTENTIAL for each marketing opportunity in your territory, you can create a marketing opportunities table to help you prioritize your selling time among your different selling opportunities.

If the cost of marketing into each target market were roughly equal, it would make sense for you to focus your marketing efforts on products A and B, and services 1 and 2, in target market D.

In your market, specific factors, such as strong competitors or a competitive pricing advantage, may ultimately dictate your sales strategy. But it's still important to compare the different marketing opportunities that you have, to help you focus your sales efforts.

This process of comparing different marketing opportunities may appear too simplistic to be valuable, but the truth is, it's

---

* The rate of usage is simply the quantity of the product that you are selling that is required or consumed by each prospect.

MARKETING OPPORTUNITIES	TARGET MARKET A	TARGET MARKET B	TARGET MARKET C	TARGET MARKET D	TOTAL MARKET
Product A	10,000	30,000	10,000	**100,000**	150,000
Product B	20,000	30,000	80,000	**60,000**	190,000
Product C	2,000	2,000	6,000	10,000	20,000
Service 1	15,000	25,000	25,000	**85,000**	150,000
Service 2	20,000	40,000	10,000	**125,000**	195,000
Total Market Opportunity	67,000	127,000	131,000	380,000	705,000

much easier to reach your sales quota when there are lots of prospects for your products!

Purchasing Factors

Perhaps the most important issue to address in your marketing plan is your customer's purchasing factors. The better you understand your customer's buying concerns, the easier it will be for you to communicate your marketing story to them in a way that is in sync with their purchasing process.

Buying decisions are based on a constellation of factors, some of which can be measured objectively, and some of which are subjective. For example, on one day you might decide to purchase an expensive suit at a specialty shop, and on another day you might decide to shop at a discount warehouse. Your shopping preference might be based on an objective-purchase factor, such as your ability to afford a designer suit, or it might be based on a subjective-purchase factor, such as your confidence that your financial position will remain stable or improve.

Business decisions are usually based primarily on objective purchasing factors. But they are also influenced by subjective purchasing factors, such as a company's confidence that the demand for their products will continue to grow, or that they will be able to continue undercutting their competitors' prices.

Since customers' perceptions of their subjective purchasing factors change over time, the likelihood of your customer making a buying decision based on the sales information you provide may change from one day to the next.

In many situations there is nothing that you can do to overcome your customer's subjective buying concerns. But being aware of them can help you understand where your customer is in their purchasing process, and can help you move business forward when your customer's concerns shift to purchasing factors that you *can* influence or address.

Many salespeople make the mistake of thinking that buyers make purchasing decisions based on one or two factors, such as price or availability. But this is rarely the case. For example, customers who are looking for computer equipment might base their purchasing decision on any of these purchasing factors:

- Functionality and ability to solve problems
- Style of products
- Reputation of manufacturer and supplier
- Viability of supplier
- Range of products available from supplier
- Personal references
- Past experience with supplier
- Perceived quality of products
- Compatibility with existing equipment
- Acquisition, implementation, and support costs
- Financing terms
- Confidence in consultant or system integrator
- Availability of products
- Quality of sales personnel
- Quality of user support and training
- Product maintenance schedules
- Third-party support options
- Proximity to support services
- Warranties
- Personal factors

One company, for example, might purchase an IBM computer because of its confidence in a trusted local reseller, while another company might choose a computer system from Digital because of its compatibility with their installed computer equipment or an extended warranty program. In another situation, a company might choose products from Hewlett-Packard over Compaq, or vice versa, based on the availability of specific features.

At Microsoft, I found that most companies purchased our products because they believed that they offered the best solution for a specific application. But some OEMs purchased our products based on their confidence in our ability to enhance our products to meet their needs in upcoming product releases.

In any case, by taking the time to understand the purchase factors that are of concern to your customer, you can anticipate and address their concerns in your sales presentations.

The easiest way to qualify your customers' purchase factors is simply to ask them to list the purchase factors that are important to them!

Negative Market Factors

It is also important to identify and overcome any negative market factors that may impact your ability to achieve your sales objectives. For example, if economic conditions in your sales territory are poor, or if interest rates are very high, it may be difficult for your customers to obtain financing to purchase your products. In this situation, your selling success may depend on your company's ability to help your customers finance your products.

Similarly, if new competitors are moving into your market, new legislation is being proposed to regulate your marketing activities, or new technologies are changing how your customers manage their business, you will need to evaluate and respond to the impact that these factors may have on your customers' purchase decisions.

STEP 3: **DEVELOP A COMPELLING MARKETING "STORY"**

At Microsoft we had a small army of product-marketing managers whose primary mission was to create compelling marketing plans for their products and develop marketing programs for our retail sales channel.

When we met with our product-marketing managers to discuss our OEM customers' concerns, it became clear that they were not in touch with many of our OEM customers' needs. So I was given the job of coordinating the development of OEM sales support materials for our account managers.

I developed a simple "story" template, which addressed the "who, what, where, when, and why" of our OEM customers' concerns, to help me understand the purchasing factors that needed to be addressed in our marketing materials.

At first my colleagues were a bit skeptical, but the story concept was so intuitive and so compelling that we wound up using it to help us develop sales support materials for Windows and most of our other OEM products.

To create your own marketing story, you should start with all of the facts that a journalist would include if he or she were writing up a news event. You will need to describe *who* you are; *what* your mission is; *where* a customer can purchase your products; *when* your products will be available; *why* a customer should purchase your products; and *how* your products can help your customers save money, increase their profits, or develop new business opportunities.

The story elements you emphasize during a sales call or in a specific marketing brochure will depend on your business objectives, but your story should answer all of the basic questions that a prospective customer might ask about your company and your products.

For example, if your company manufactures industrial robots, and you are trying to recruit new resellers, you might focus on your company's leadership position in the industry (*who*), and the fact that your products offer a significant competitive advantage over other robotics suppliers (*how*). If your primary objective is the announcement of a new product, you might focus on the availability of your product (*when*) and its comparative features and benefits (*why*).

It is important to keep your story as clear, concise, and compelling as possible. Prospective customers will not ask for

STORY ELEMENTS	MARKETING "STORY" FOR A ROBOTICS COMPANY
Who?	We are the leaders in industrial robotics technology.
What?	We supply industrial robots to heavy equipment manufacturers.
Where?	Our products are available through regional equipment distributors.
When?	Our new Model 1000 is available now.
Why?	Our products can reduce our customers' production costs by more than 25%.
How?	Our pattern recognition systems enable our robots to perform tasks faster and more reliably than our competitors' robots.

your help unless it is obvious who you are, what you do, and how you can help them.

THERE IS NO "PERFECT" STORY

It is easy to be enthusiastic about your products when you are confident that they provide good quality and value. But it is important to understand that there is no "perfect" marketing story because there is no "perfect" product for every customer's needs.

In most cases, for example, customers must trade off some level of performance or quality against their desire to solve their problem as inexpensively as possible. One buyer may feel that a $50,000 robot is the right tool for his or her company, while another buyer with similar needs may feel that a $50,000 robot will provide $25,000 worth of features they will never need.

At Microsoft, most of our OEMs used a software development kit, which we provided, to help them interface our operating system with their hardware. But some of our OEMs paid Microsoft a great deal of money to do this "porting" work for

ELEMENTS OF MARKETING "STORY" FOR A ROBOTICS COMPANY	POTENTIAL CUSTOMER BENEFITS YOU MAY PRESENT
We are the leaders in industrial robotics technology.	It is less risky to work with an established company.
We supply industrial robots to heavy-equipment manufacturers.	Our products can meet your specific shop requirements.
Our products are available through regional equipment distributors.	We have local sales and support through authorized resellers.
Our new Model 1000 is available now.	We offer state-of-the-art products.
Our products can reduce our customers' production costs by more than 25%.	Our products are cost-effective and will provide a rapid return on your investment.
Our pattern recognition systems enable our robots to perform tasks faster and more reliably than our competitors' robots.	Our superior products will provide a competitive advantage to your company.

them. "Turnkey" or "do it yourself"—the "perfect" story depends on your customers' needs and concerns.

COMMUNICATING YOUR STORY'S ELEMENTS

No matter how compelling your marketing story is, it can provide only the *framework* for the information you want to present to your customers. You must use your communication skills to position and present the elements of your story in a way that is in sync with your customers' purchase process.

Salespeople are storytellers at heart—and the heart of Client-Centered™ selling is a clear, concise, compelling story.

STEP 4: **DEVELOP A "REAL WORLD" SALES PLAN**

Sales plans describe the "tactical" details behind a marketing plan and provide a road map to the specific sales objectives you have specified in your marketing plan.

If your company has developed a logical marketing plan, it should be relatively easy to formulate your sales plan. But if your company's marketing plan is based on flawed assumptions, it is unlikely that you will ever be able to create a sales plan that will enable you to achieve your business objectives in the "real world."

For example, if your marketing plan specifies that you will use outside sales representatives to market your products, your sales plan should specify the resources and incentive programs that will be available to support your sales representatives' selling efforts. If your company cannot budget enough money to support an outside sales force and to promote your products, it is unlikely that your salespeople will be able to achieve their sales quotas.

At Microsoft, our sales plans described:

- Size, organization, and geographical distribution of our sales force
- Alternate sales and distribution channels (including joint-marketing partners such as independent sales representatives and mail-order companies)
- Territory assignments
- Sales priorities (how our resources were focused to maximize sales)
- Recruiting plans for territory managers, sales representatives, and sales support personnel
- Compensation plans for sales representatives and sales support personnel
- Pricing for our products and services
- Sales training, motivation, and coaching
- Use of independent marketing resources and consultants

We used our sales plan to help us justify our head count and our departmental budget to upper management; but since our business was growing very rapidly, we had to update our sales plan and our budgets each quarter to reflect our growing customer base.

Very few businesses suffer from this "problem." But every business, regardless of their size or rate of growth, can use their sales plan to help them manage day-to-day operations and stay focused on achieving their primary business objectives.

Business/Marketing Partners

One of the best ways to leverage a limited marketing budget and "expand" your sales force is to join forces with one or more business partners.

Business partners can provide access to specific customers, product promotion, financing, technical expertise, and other resources you can use to help you market your products and meet your sales objectives.

Microsoft has developed business relationships with virtually every type of business partner. Our OEM group was especially interested in working with consultants who worked with our OEM customers; but Microsoft has committed significant marketing resources to ISV programs and to hundreds of standards committees, interest groups, and industry forums. These "developer" relationships are especially important to Microsoft because Microsoft's future success is contingent on creating demand for new products that are based on emerging technologies.

STEP 5: **DEVELOP A REALISTIC TERRITORY PLAN**

A territory plan is a subset of a sales plan. It defines the selling activities that will occur in a specific territory and specifies how and when those activities will result in meeting specific sales objectives.

Building a Prospect Database

I have always thought of my sales territory as a "prospect database" comprised of a finite number of selling opportunities.

As soon as I begin qualifying prospects in my territory, I categorize each prospect on the basis of how long I think it will take me to close their business. Then I enter this information into a database system to help me prioritize my selling time.

POTENTIAL BUSINESS RESOURCES	POTENTIAL STRATEGIC ADVANTAGE
Retailers	Access to customers Promotion
Value-added resellers	Technical expertise Access to customer base
Independent sales representatives	Commission sales Extremely motivated
Wholesalers and distributors	Help finance distribution Inventory management
Consultants	Provide leads Third-party expertise
Manufacturers' representatives	Extremely motivated Good contacts
System integrators	Technical expertise Access to customer base
Brokers	Contacts Expertise
National buying services	High volume Close-out specialists
Mail order companies	Low-cost distribution Pilot new programs
Government distribution (exchange stores)	Unique distribution High volume
Television marketers (infomercials, Home Shopping Network)	Promotion Close-out specialists
Superstores	High volume Large customer base
Internet, on-line services	Low cost of entry Add-on business
Professionals (physician, lawyer)	Referrals Expertise

I don't like complicated tracking systems, but I find it useful to divide the prospects I am working with into three categories: "A" (hottest—best-qualified), "B" (interested—needs work), and "C" (potential sale within some time frame, such as six months or one year).

Prioritizing Your Selling Opportunities

At Microsoft I prioritized meetings with my most important customers and prospects first, and then prioritized all of the other tasks I had to complete each month.

For example, if I had ten major accounts in my territory and was working on six new accounts, I might schedule ten days per month to work my existing accounts, and five days per month to work with my prospects.

Once I prioritized my selling activities, I "penciled" them into my daily planner. I knew that my schedule would change as the month unfolded, but I scheduled all of the sales meetings, demonstrations, interdepartmental meetings, training seminars, telemarketing programs, and any other tasks I had planned for the month.

Entering my schedule in my daily planner was a "reality check" on my ability to accomplish all of the activities I planned to complete to meet my business objectives and helped me reduce unnecessary travel and preparation time by helping me optimize my meeting schedule.

It is unlikely that your schedule will resemble my old schedule, unless you are working a small number of major accounts.

But in any case, taking the time to plan and track your sales activities in a daily planner is the most effective way for you to visualize how each activity that you invest your time in will impact your selling success.

If you don't prioritize your selling activities, and use some type of planning system to track what you are doing, your workdays will be interruption-driven, and you will not be able to leverage your selling time to maximize your sales territory's potential.

SALES CALLS	MONDAY	TUESDAY	WEDNESDAY	THURSDAY	FRIDAY
Week 1	Sales Meeting Office work	Account 1 Account 2	Account 3 Account 4	Account 5 Prospect 1	Account 6 Prospect 2 Prospect 3
Week 2	Sales Meeting Office work	Account 7 Account 8	Account 9 Account 10	Prospect 4 Prospect 5 Prospect 6	Sales Training
Week 3	Sales Meeting Office work	Account 1 Account 2 Account 3	Prospect Open	Prospect Open	Account 4 Account 5 Account 6
Week 4	Sales Meeting Office work	Account 7 Account 8	Account 9 Account 10	Prospect Open	Account Review Open

Finding New Selling Opportunities

A map can be a valuable tool to help you visualize new business opportunities, spot trends, and evaluate the importance of different market factors such as the location, size, and number of prospects in different marketing regions in your territory.

The easiest way to create a territory map is to purchase a map of your territory, and use colored markers or stickpins to indicate where your prospects and customers are located.

A more elegant way of creating a territory map is to use a PC-based mapping program to create a "digital" map of your territory, which can display different "views" of your customer database. For example, you might display a view of your customer database that highlights all of the active prospects in a major city, or one that shows each prospect who had a specific type of computer system installed in his or her business.

Then, you can use these different "views" of your sales territory to help you identify marketing opportunities, allocate your marketing resources, and leverage your selling time.

6 COOL TIPS FOR EFFECTIVE SEMINAR PRESENTATIONS

1. Invite the right people to your seminar by prequalifying your attendees.

2. Schedule rest breaks, snacks, Q&A sessions, and demonstrations to facilitate interaction with participants. You can't qualify your attendees unless there is an opportunity for them to tell you what they need!

3. Develop your follow-up program *before* scheduling your seminar.

4. Make sales seminars "win-win" by providing information that is of value to your attendees, whether or not they choose to do business with your company.

5. Schedule telemarketing to help ensure attendance.

6. Have each participant fill out a seminar review/follow-up form.

Seminar Selling

One of the most effective ways to communicate your story and to develop interest in your products is to present seminars that are targeted to your customers' specific interests.

At Microsoft we used seminars to reach new customers, introduce new products, and help our existing customers stay in sync with our product development strategy.

Leveraging Customer Relationships

Existing customers are your best prospects for new products and services.

If you can see how your products or services can fill your customer's needs, and if your customer is happy with your service, it is usually very easy to resell your "proven" solution.

Depending on your situation, you may be able to sell your products "horizontally," across an organization's companies, divisions, and work groups, or "vertically," within the company, division, or work group you are working with. For example, if you are selling laptop computers to an organization's sales group, you might approach their marketing personnel (horizontal) to see if they have any need for portable computers, or you could sell additional products, such as high-speed modems, to the sales group (vertical).

The most effective way I have found to leverage existing customer relationships at Microsoft was to "map" the products and services I was selling to my customer's business requirements.

For example, I "mapped" a need for Microsoft Word and Excel to OEMs that focused on the small business market. Bundling business software applications with their PCs enabled these OEMs to add value to their PCs that was compelling to business users and that helped differentiate their PCs from similar products from other suppliers.

At Microsoft I kept a list of all of Microsoft's products with me on my sales calls, to remind me to present different products to my customers whenever it was appropriate.

Requests for Information

It was easy for account managers at Microsoft to assume a "problem-solving" role in the selling process, because PC manufacturers typically called our department to request information about licensing our operating system software to sell with their PCs.

When we received a request for information from an OEM, we would send out an information packet, and have one of our account managers follow up the lead with a telephone call to qualify the OEM's interest in our products.

Then, depending on the situation, we would visit the OEM's company, set up a meeting with them at our corporate office, or just send them a copy of our standard OEM software license agreement.

You can use a customer's request for information as an "invitation" to qualify their needs and concerns, and to begin working together with them to develop a solution that meets their needs.

Referrals

Referral sales are usually the easiest sales to close because referred prospects usually grant you a problem-solving role early in the selling relationship. However, in most cases, referred prospects will not make a buying decision until they are convinced that you understand their concerns, that the solution you have proposed meets their needs, and that your proposed solution is cost-effective and competitive with solutions from other suppliers.

I have found that I can usually get a pretty good idea of how qualified a referral is by asking them how and why they have contacted me. A prospect who is referred by a respected colleague is, for example, much more likely to be qualified than a prospect who found my company's name in a trade journal or in the yellow pages.

On a Good Day, all You Have to Do Is Show Up!

Every salesperson has his or her favorite "from the trenches" story about prospecting for new customers. My favorite took place at Comdex, a major computer show in Las Vegas.

I was standing in a booth, looking at a new accounting software application, when a man behind me asked the man he was standing next to if he had read Doug Dayton's book on automating small businesses. The other man said he hadn't seen it.

Normally, I don't eavesdrop, but I couldn't resist mentioning that I was in fact Doug Dayton. The gentleman who had not read my book was the president of a major PC accounting software company. I told him about my training business and sent him a copy of my book. The next month his company asked me to help them train their resellers.

Developing Inactive Prospects

I like to contact my active prospects at least once every two months. I have learned that if my contact is less frequent, my prospects will tend to forget about me, and I will lose some of the advantage of my initial contact.

The easiest way to maintain contact with inactive prospects is with a newsletter or other direct-mail piece; however, seminars, user group meetings, and telemarketing calls are also good ways to build "mind share."

Whenever I contact prospects, I like to provide something of value to hold their attention and to build good will. For

10 REALLY GOOD TIPS FOR DEVELOPING REFERRAL SOURCES

1. My favorite way to cultivate referrals is to meet my customers for "power breakfasts" or for lunch.

2. The more experience a customer has with your company's products and services, the more credible he or she will be as a referral.

3. Verify that your customer is satisfied with your products and services before using him or her as a reference.

4. Confirm that your referral is willing to talk to prospective customers.

5. Don't overuse your referral sources.

6. Don't publish your referral list; competitors may use your list to market into your customer base.

7. Direct prospective customers to a referral who is using your products in a way that is similar to their intended use.

8. Follow up contacts between your prospects and your referrals to verify your prospects' level of interest.

9. Ask the person who referred a prospect to you for help moving business forward with his or her business associate.

10. Reward referral sources with special services or purchase terms.

example, when I send out a newsletter, I like to include ser-vice and support ideas that may be of value to my customers.

Information Packets

If you think that the marketing materials you send out to your prospects are anything less than compelling, throw them away!

As the old saying goes, "You only have one chance to make a first impression." If your marketing materials don't com-municate your story effectively, they will not help you move busi-ness forward.

A Fresh Perspective

After you have worked a territory for a long time, you may feel that you have qualified every selling opportunity. At this point it is helpful to mentally partition or "segment" your sales territory on the basis of different market factors, such as your prospect's current supplier, the type of business they are in, or their need for a specific solution. The trick is to use one or more market factors that will enable you to "view" your selling opportunities from a fresh perspective.

At Microsoft I challenged myself to look at my territory from as many different points of reference or "views" as possible. This process helped me understand my customers' needs and helped me motivate myself to continue mining new business opportunities.

One of my objectives before I left Microsoft was to generate new business from OEMs that were developing computers based on non-Intel microprocessors. There wasn't a great deal of business potential in this segment relative to our Intel-based PC business. But a few large OEMs, such as Commodore and Atari, were developing home computers that could run "skinny" versions of Microsoft office applications, such as Word and Multiplan.*

It was challenging selling to companies in the consumer electronics business, and my "view" of the computer industry was literally redefined when I realized the sales potential for home computers running games and home office software applications.

A salesperson's most overlooked resource is the power of his or her creativity!

STEP 6: **DEVELOP AN ACCOUNT PLAN**

Once you have determined how you want to prioritize the different selling opportunities in your territory, you are ready to develop an account plan. An account plan defines your objectives for a specific account and describes how and when specific sales activities will occur.

At Microsoft I created a simple account analysis form I could use to help me analyze my accounts. You can tailor this form to meet your own business requirements.

---

* Multiplan is an MS-DOS-based electronic spreadsheet that competed with Lotus 1-2-3. Multiplan was replaced by Excel, which requires Microsoft's Windows operating system.

ACCOUNT ANALYSIS FORM

Account/customer name: Acme Corporation
Contact information: Tom Brown
Date: 9/18/97
Sales representative: Terry Smith
Prior sales representative: Linda Gray
Sales manager: Don Richard

CONTACTS
Buyer: Sally Smith
User: Peter Thomas, Judy Sell
Technical influencer: Richard Jones
Other advocate: Melinda Robertson
Gatekeeper: Marsha Johnson
Manager: Sue Norman
Decisionmaker: Ann Tanner
President/Principal: Bob Backer

ACCOUNT HISTORY
Type of business: Component manufacturer
Account priority: A
Products installed: Competitors BY-300
Special deals: N/A
Buying practices/cycles: FY begins in January. All budgets must be approved by December 1.
What? Purchase Department approves all purchase orders.
When? POs are approved monthly.
How much? POs over $50,000 require executive-level review.
How often? N/A
Past Problems: N/A
Reference Account: Yes No
If not a good reference, describe why: N/A

SITUATION ANALYSIS
Objectives for account: Sell AX-600 to Production Department
Account potential/percent of quota: 50,000/5%
Percent of account's business: 100%

COMPETITION
Action Robotics' BY-300

OUTSTANDING SALES OPPORTUNITIES
Introduce AX-600 to support Production Department's requirements

SPECIAL ISSUES/OTHER NOTES
Customer will not move forward without seeing an in-house demonstration.
Be prepared to demo AX-600 robot and to leave an evaluation unit.
In the past Acme has preferred to lease all manufacturing equipment.

LAST MANAGEMENT REVIEW
Date: July 15, 1995   **By:** TBL

Account Reviews at Microsoft

At Microsoft we scheduled formal OEM account review meetings each quarter. Our account reviews were facilitated by our sales managers and by the vice president of our business unit. At the meetings, which ran for two or three days, each account manager would present each one of their major accounts.

The account manager would describe their customer's account history, including any joint marketing and development projects, and any outstanding technical issues. The account manager would also describe their objectives for each one of their accounts, including new contract and revenue potential.

This account review process was a great way for our account managers to communicate the status of their accounts and for management to get a top-down picture of the entire division's sales activities. However, it was not a good forum for sales coaching or for brainstorming about how to handle difficult selling situations.

To meet those needs, we needed to develop a process that was less formal and that had a more tactical emphasis.

I developed a meeting format, which I called *focus groups*. Our focus groups were usually facilitated by one of our sales managers. Our account managers were invited, but were not required to participate in focus groups; if they wanted help, it was there for the asking.

The "power" of our focus group meetings was the synergism of working on an account manager's problem together, and from the group's ability to look at each selling situation objectively.

If, for example, an account manager was having difficulty communicating with one of his or her customer's technical managers, outside consultants, purchasing managers, lawyers, or decisionmakers, the account manager would have an opportunity to solicit feedback from the group on how to work more effectively with that individual. Similarly, if an account manager was having difficulty overcoming a competitive challenge, the group would brainstorm about how he or she could more effectively demonstrate the value of a Microsoft solution.

The meetings were not always successful, but most of the time the group was able to help the account manager develop one or more unique approaches or solutions to address his or her problem.

Account managers at Microsoft knew that they could rely on the experience and moral support of their managers and their peers.

STEP 7: **DEVELOP A SALES CALL PLAN**

At Microsoft I learned that one of the most effective ways to help our account managers stay focused on achieving their objectives on sales calls was to encourage them to write up a brief sales call plan or meeting agenda *before* leaving their office to meet with their customer.

In some cases, our account manager's primary sales call objective was getting approval on a contract; however, in most cases their primary objective was solving a technical problem, delivering marketing materials, soliciting referrals, exploring new business opportunities, or resolving some other issue.

Regardless of their reasons for making a sales call, our account managers had a much greater chance of meeting their objectives if they knew exactly what they wanted to communicate, and exactly what they wanted to accomplish, before leaving their office.

SAMPLE SALES CALL PLAN

Customer: Acme Corporation

Meeting location: Acme's offices

Date/time: September 18, 1997

Primary objective: Introduce AX-600 to support Production Department's requirements.

Secondary objective: Meet new purchasing manager.

Special action items: Be prepared to demo AX-600 or to leave an evaluation unit.

Special materials/equipment: Bring AX-600 and special power adapter.

Other:

Sales Call Reports

After each sales call I made at Microsoft, I wrote up a brief sales call report that specified where I went, who I saw, what was discussed, what actions were taken, and a list of follow-up tasks I needed to attend to before my next customer contract.

After completing my sales call report, I would copy any open action items from my report into my daily planner, to help me schedule my follow-up activities.

The process of completing a sales call report provides an opportunity for me to review my sales call, plan my strategy for my next customer contact, and communicate what I was doing "in the field" to my manager.

Your sales call reports may provide detailed information on every aspect of your sales call, or just contain summary-level information, such as how many sales calls you made, how many demonstrations you gave, how many proposals you delivered, and how many products you sold during a specific selling period.

What is important is that your sales call reports include all of the information that you and your sales manager need to help you track your selling activities and manage your territory.

Planning for Success

Sales planning is a valuable activity, but planning how you will spend your selling time should not become a burden. You do not need to be compulsive and write down everything you plan to do. The trick is to spend just enough time developing sales plans to maximize your effectiveness.

It will take time to find this balance. Less experienced sales-people usually spend too much time developing sales plans and reports, and more experienced salespeople often want to skip the planning and reporting process altogether.

I have learned that the key to finding this balance is using a month-at-a-glance planner to get a top-down view of your territory plan, and your daily planner to get a top-down view of your sales call plan. Once you become comfortable switching

COMPANY DATE TIME CONTACT	PRODUCTS AND ISSUES DISCUSSED	REQUIREMENT ANALYSIS SPECIAL PROBLEMS	DEMONSTRATE SOLUTION WRITTEN PROPOSAL * = Action Items	CUSTOMER COMMITMENT DELIVERY SCHEDULED
Company A 5/10/96 11:00–12:00 Bill Jones	Ancillary Processor chip Pipeline Memory	Will work in OEM board Good fit	* Send prototype kit * Send copy of magazine review	Expect commitment within 15 days
Company B 5/10/96 2:30–5:30 Vela Richard	Model 6400 Memory chip Training Program	Expect prompt delivery of all components	Demonstrated evaluation board Delivered contract	Expect signed agreement by Friday
Company C 5/11/96 9:00–1:00 Mr. Fisher	Gamma Processor chip	Needs 24-pin package	* Discuss packaging with sales support engineers	Evaluation process will take 60 days
Company D 5/11/96 2:00–6:00 Theresa Lee	Delta Processor chip Inline memory	Picked up sample of their new PC boards	* Send prototype kit * Check power output on sample board	Evaluation process will take at least 90 days

between these two "views," you will be able to visualize exactly what you need to do to achieve your business objectives.

Be patient with yourself; make an effort to understand every step of your selling process; and don't fool yourself into thinking that you can know the outcome of a selling situation before you qualify your customer and verify that you have addressed all of his or her needs and concerns. Life is full of surprises!

CHAPTER FIVE

MICROSOFT'S SECRET WEAPON

"The past twenty years have been an incredible adventure for me."

—Bill Gates, *The Road Ahead*

Microsoft is the most successful company in the computer industry today. And the secret weapon behind Microsoft's success is effective communications.

Microsoft has not always been able to deliver the best product on the market, although after one or two product updates they usually come out on top. But there is no doubt that Microsoft has the best marketing team in the business. And there is no doubt that the "secret" behind Microsoft's marketing success is their ability to package Microsoft's story in a way that is extremely compelling.

In this chapter you will learn how to use the Client-Centered™ communication techniques I developed at Microsoft to help you become a better communicator and to work more effectively with your customers.

CLIENT-CENTERED™ SELLING

My first priority as Microsoft's manager of OEM sales and contract support was to help Microsoft's salespeople become more effective account managers. But I soon learned that my own success as an OEM account manager did not prepare me for my new job. Before I could explain what I had been doing right, I had to analyze exactly *what* I had been doing, and *why* it moved the selling process forward.

Since I could not climb into my customers' heads to find out what I was doing to help them move through their purchasing process, I decided to analyze exactly how I made my own purchasing decisions. I reasoned that by determining the factors that influenced my purchasing process, I would be better able to understand the purchasing factors that influenced my customers.

Although it sounds easy, it was actually very hard to analyze my own purchasing process. But one technique I found helpful was to try to make myself aware of all of the promotions and appeals that were used to catch my attention, to compel me to enter a store, to talk with a salesperson, and ultimately to make a purchase.

During my shopping expeditions at our local shopping mall, I tried to pay careful attention to every aspect of the selling process by "observing" myself shop. I learned that when I talk with salespeople, I expect them to make an attempt to find out what I am looking for, and to be concerned about satisfying my needs. And that I am more comfortable with salespeople who are polite, and who have good verbal skills and product knowledge, than I am with less mature salespeople who don't know much about their products and who appear impatient to make a sale.

I also learned that while I consider myself to be practical and logical, my purchasing decisions are heavily influenced by emotional factors. For example, I prefer to shop at Nordstrom rather than JCPenney, which targets less status-oriented shoppers, and I sometimes buy things I don't need if they are on sale.

It was easy to make observations about the salespeople I worked with at the shopping mall, but it was hard for me to accept the fact that my purchase process was not at all consistent with the image I had of myself as an unemotional buyer.

But after a few visits to the shopping mall, my step-by-step analysis of my purchasing process—from my first contact with a salesperson, to the moment I decided to make a purchase, to the feeling that I might have found a better deal if I had visited another store—paid off.

I finally learned how to put myself in my customers' shoes and how to see the world through their eyes.

The ability to mentally put yourself in your customer's position is the most important step on the path of Client-Centered™ selling.

THE SECRET TO EFFECTIVE COMMUNICATION

People often say that the key to effective communication is being a good listener. Being a good listener is certainly the hardest communication skill for most salespeople to master, but the real secret to effective communication is learning how to establish an open, productive dialogue.

Dialogue means sharing ideas without trying to change the mind of the person you are communicating with, and without trying to prove that their position is right or wrong. Opening this type of dialogue with your customer creates an environment that is conducive to honest, straightforward communication.

When you and your customer are open to discussion, you are well on the way to working cooperatively. And when you and your customer are working cooperatively, you can move the selling process forward by identifying and responding to your customer's needs and concerns.

It is easy to see how the dialogue between you and your customer is the foundation of the selling process and why you cannot move the selling process forward until you establish a productive dialogue with your customer. But in the "real world" some customers are easy to communicate with and some aren't.

I have learned that the most effective way for me to establish a productive dialogue with my customers is to communicate precisely, verify my communications, and avoid making assumptions that may confound my ability to view the selling process, and my customer's needs and concerns, objectively. In the next section I will explain how you can master these essential communication skills.

Effective communications begin with a conscious effort to understand the communication process, and to create an open dialogue with your customer.

THE COMMUNICATION CYCLE

Most people do not communicate very precisely. The way they present ideas and information requires a great deal of interpretation by the person they are communicating with. In fact, different customers often interpret the same message differently, depending on their state of attention, their prior experience with their salesperson, and their "openness" to considering their salesperson's views. Political debates and arguments in which neither side is open to considering opposing points of view epitomize ineffective communication.

When you analyze a communication between two people, you can break it into a five-step "communication cycle." Understanding the five steps that comprise this communication cycle will help ensure that your communications are transmitted as accurately as possible:

What You Intended to Say

Learning to think before you speak is the first step toward communicating effectively. Before you speak, you must determine exactly what you need to communicate, and then present it in a logical, easy-to-understand way.

What You Actually Said

What you think you are saying is often quite different from what you are actually communicating. Most people, for example, do not communicate clearly when they become emotional.

What Your Listener Heard

You cannot control what your customer hears. Customers can misunderstand a communication when their attention wanders, when they do not understand specific words or references, or when they "tune out" their salesperson because they think they already know what he or she is going to say.

What Your Listener Thought He or She Heard

After receiving a communication, a customer must interpret the communication. This evaluation process may result in an interpretation very different from what was originally intended. If, for example, a customer is prejudiced against the salesperson's point of view, the communication may be polarized to support the customer's prejudice.

Feedback from Your Listener to Verify the Communication

A customer may or may not respond to your communication. This lack of feedback may make it difficult to determine whether your communication was received as you intended it.

VERIFYING COMMUNICATIONS

In selling situations it is important for you to communicate as clearly as possible. But successful communication can be undermined at each step of the communication cycle. And miscommunication can lead to a constellation of problems, including wasted time and poor interpersonal relationships with your customers. In other words, no sale.

Since you can control only your side of the communication process, the most effective action you can take to help ensure a successful communication is to *verify* that your message was communicated clearly.

There are several ways to verify your communication. The easiest way to verify a communication is to paraphrase it in the form of a question. For example, you might say to your customer, "If I understand correctly, you are saying that..." Or you might say, "Am I correct that you need to have our product do . . . for your company?"

Another way to verify a communication is to ask your customer a question to "test" whether that person has understood your communication. For example, if you have just discussed the need for your client to purchase your product, you might ask whether the client can think of anything you haven't covered in your needs analysis that might impact the effectiveness of your proposed solution. Depending on your customer's answer, you should be able to evaluate whether he or she understood the logic behind your recommendation.

As you move through the selling process, it is also important to verify that your customer is in agreement with your recommendations or proposed solution. To do this you might ask your customer whether he or she felt that your proposed solution could, for example, "handle your company's requirements for the next six months."

If you forget to verify your communications, you can fall out of sync with your customer's purchase process, and you may propose a solution before you have properly qualified your customer, or before you have presented compelling reasons for your customer to accept your recommendations.

ASSUMPTIONS—BREAKING THE HABIT

The more experienced a salesperson is, the more assumptions they tend to make about their customers, the selling process, and their ability to communicate without misunderstandings. Although it is easy to place customers in categories, and to make assumptions about their needs and concerns, different customers have unique concerns, and they may not perceive what is presented during the selling process in the same way.

Unfortunately, it is almost impossible to break the habit of making assumptions about different customers' needs and concerns. Most salespeople are comfortable relying on their previous experience, and they don't realize that some of their assumptions are hindering their ability to communicate with new customers.

COMMUNICATION CYCLE	YOUR COMMUNICATION
Step 1: What you intended to say: *The network computer I am proposing will satisfy all of your company's requirements.*	Before you speak, determine exactly what you need to communicate, and then present it in a logical, easy-to-understand way.
Step 2: What you actually said: *We think that our network computer will work for your company.*	What you think you are saying is often quite different from what you are actually communicating.
Step 3: What your listener heard: *We think that our server will work for your company.*	You cannot control what your listener hears. Listeners often misunderstand your communication.
Step 4: What your listener thought he or she heard: *You are not confident that your company's product is a good fit for our company.*	After receiving a communication, your listener must interpret what he or she heard. This evaluation process may result in a communication very different from what you intended.
Step 5: Feedback from your listener to verify the communication: *We appreciate your time, we'll call you next week.*	Lack of feedback from your customer may make it difficult to determine whether your communication was received as you intended it.

The most effective technique I have found to avoid the problems that arise from making incorrect assumptions is to make a *conscious effort* to ask my customers questions with an open mind, and to *verify* that my assumptions are true. In other words, I have learned to be confident of my selling skills and my intuitions, but to be suspicious of any assumptions I make about my customer's needs or concerns until I verify them.

Taking this Client-Centered™ approach helps me ensure that I am communicating clearly with my customer and that we are moving in step toward agreement on a solution to my customer's problem.

SELL YOURSELF FIRST

You cannot move the selling process forward until you qualify your customer's needs and concerns. And you cannot qualify your customer's needs and concerns until your customer feels comfortable enough with you to discuss his or her business.

To resolve this dilemma, you must open a dialogue with your customer, and then establish rapport by being open, honest, and nonjudgmental, and by maintaining a positive, enthusiastic attitude about your work.

The old sales adage "sell yourself first, then sell your company, and finally, sell your products" makes good sense, because customers who are "sold" on you, and on your company, will be receptive to hearing about how your company's products can help them solve their problems.

At Microsoft I realized that the "secret" to opening a productive dialogue with my customers and "selling myself first" was to put myself in my customers' shoes, to listen to my customers and focus on their needs, and to ask for my customers' help in moving the selling process forward.

See Yourself Through Your Customers' Eyes

Be sincere: People are very sensitive to other people's sincerity. If your customers suspect that you have a hidden agenda, they will be reluctant to open a dialogue and to share their ideas and opinions with you.

Be friendly and optimistic: Creating a positive atmosphere at customer meetings is the best way to ensure that your customers will interact with you in a positive, constructive way. I make it a habit to open every sales meeting with a greeting and a smile. I tend to be influenced by and do business with people I like and trust, and I believe that my customers feel this way, too.

Don't use inappropriate language or humor: What is funny to one person may be insulting to another. If you make jokes, make them at your own expense. If you are in doubt about the propriety of a joke, don't tell it. Over the years I have listened to hundreds of jokes told at other people's expense. I don't pass them on.

Avoid personal criticism: Regardless of whether you feel justified in making disparaging remarks to a customer, or gossiping about another customer—don't do it! The individual who is attacked will become less cooperative and may work at getting even.

It took me years to learn that the key to enjoying my work was giving up my expectations about how other people should behave. Most people are doing the best they can. And if you try to change other people's behavior, or try to get even with everyone who disappoints you, you'll have no time left for joy.

Don't make your customer feel defensive: Very strong statements or opinions may make your customer feel defensive, and customers who feel defensive do not make buying decisions; they look for new salespeople.

If your customer takes a strong position about something, the best course of action is usually to be as agreeable as possible and to try to minimize the differences in your opinions. This will enable you to maintain a productive dialogue with your customer and to continue to influence his or her purchasing process.

Harassing people to encourage them to change their minds rarely works outside of Hollywood courtroom dramas. Being courteous and patient is the best way to encourage your customers to keep an open mind and to remain receptive to implementing your suggestions.

Balance aggressiveness and being too timid: The key to finding the right balance between aggressiveness and not pushing hard enough to move business forward is understanding your customer's objectives and concerns.

If you feel that you are moving through the sales process faster than your customer, take time to verify that you agree about the key issues you are discussing before presenting any new information. And if you sense that your customer is uncomfortable with your personal selling style, take time to reestablish an effective dialogue.

If you are an impatient person, it will be hard for you to overcome your natural tendency to "push" your customer through the purchasing process. But if you put yourself in your customer's position, you will realize that when you are too aggressive, your customer's natural reaction will be to move away from you, by dismissing your recommendations or by seeking out another salesperson he or she is more comfortable working with.

Listen to Your Customers

Pay attention to your customers' concerns: If you stop "listening" to your customers, they may feel that you are only interested in making a sale and that you do not have their best interests in mind.

I have actually been on a sales call where my client interrupted me to say, "Oh, I guess you know what I'm thinking!" Fortunately, I was not oblivious to my customer's sarcasm, and got back in step with the purchasing process.

If you are an outgoing individual, as I am, you will have to resist the temptation to dominate your sales meetings, or to position your opinions as facts. If you think you are talking too much, stop talking—and ask your customer a question to help you get back in step with the purchasing process.

Selling is like dancing: You have to stay in step with your customer. If you do all the talking, you will not have an opportunity to identify all of your customer's concerns, and you will fall out of step with your customer's purchasing process.

Don't interrupt your customer: Interrupting people is rude and makes people feel that their ideas are not valued. If your customers are long-winded, encourage them to summarize their main points so that everyone at your meeting can consider them and so you can help them move through the selling process.

Write down your customer's ideas: Taking the time to write something down communicates in a nonverbal way that you believe the information is important enough to remember and to act on. Writing down your customer's ideas and concerns demonstrates your interest and helps you establish an open dialogue.

Ask for Your Customers' Help

Your customers are experts: One of the best ways to open a dialogue is to ask for your customers' help in qualifying their needs. Customers are the foremost "experts" on their problems, and they usually love to talk about their business if they feel comfortable with you.

Acknowledge contributions: Public acknowledgment of contributions is one of the most effective ways to build trust, good will, and positive working relationships. I make it a rule to thank my customers and coworkers for their time and their contributions whenever it is appropriate to do so.

At Microsoft I often sent E-mail "thanks" to people who worked with me on sales calls, and then carbon-copied the thank you to their managers, with a note thanking *them* for having their people support my selling efforts.

Don't become a teacher or evangelist: When you are a salesperson, your mission is to make sales, not to be a teacher or an evangelist. Stay focused on solving your customer's problems, not on demonstrating your knowledge or your wit.

Microsoft maintains its lead in the competitive software business by staying focused on addressing its customers' needs and concerns and by articulating how and why its products and services are of value to its customers.

If you "shoot from the hip," shoot straight: When I made sales calls at Microsoft, I usually worked with my customer's senior marketing and technical personnel. In many cases, my customers had a much deeper understanding of the topics we discussed than I did.

After my very first "executive briefing," I realized that I had two clear choices when I responded to my customer's questions. I could shoot from the hip and hope that I did not make a complete fool of myself; or I could be straightforward about what I did and didn't know.

I probably lucked into being straightforward because it was a whole lot less work. But it was effective. My customers respected me for being honest about my limitations, and they trusted me because they knew I would never lie to them.

Don't be arrogant about your success: It is easy to become arrogant about success, arrogant about knowing more than your customers know, or even arrogant about your customer's need to do business with your company, if you supply products that are difficult to second-source. But people who behave arrogantly make it difficult for other people to work with them. And customers who are uncomfortable working with a supplier will try to find a new supplier as soon as possible.

BODY LANGUAGE

Studies have shown that people express themselves with hundreds of nonverbal signals. Nonverbal communication, or "body language," can help you understand what your customer is thinking and can help you uncover hidden concerns when your customer's nonverbal signals are inconsistent with his or her verbal communications.

Some nonverbal body signals, such as avoiding eye contact or smiling, are almost universal and are easy to recognize. But deciphering more subtle nonverbal signals is a very inexact science. For example, a customer who rubs his or her nose may be considering what you are saying, or may be suffering from allergies or dry skin.

In rare instances, people will display negative nonverbal signals when they are positive and vice versa, but usually you can rely on the following table to help you interpret your customer's nonverbal messages.

However, before you *rely* on a nonverbal communication, you should *verify* what you think your customer is communicating. For example, if your customers cross their arms, you might suspect that they disagree with what you are saying. But if your customers disagree with something you are saying, you must still find out what they disagree with, and why they disagree with it.

Most salespeople I have worked with do not pay too much attention to their customers' body language. But I find that after I have met with a customer several times, and made a conscious effort to observe his or her body language, I find it quite easy to gauge whether the customer agrees with what I am saying by observing that person's nonverbal communications.

POSITIVE SIGNALS	NEGATIVE SIGNALS
• Appears interested	• Appears distracted, impatient
• Good eye contact	• Poor eye contact
• Nods	• Shakes head
• Leans forward	• Leans back
• Arms and hands are relaxed	• Arms are folded
• Smiles	• Frowns
• Talks freely, asks questions	• Not responsive

MOVING BUSINESS FORWARD

Once you have established a dialogue with your customer, you can use Client-Centered™ interview techniques to help you communicate effectively and to move business forward.

Ask General Questions to Encourage Creative Thinking

The best way to encourage creative problem-solving is to ask general questions, such as "How else can we overcome this problem?" or "Do you have any ideas about how we can make this work?"

At Microsoft I would often ask my customers if there was anything we could do to "help your company get your products to market faster."

Ask Specific Questions to Test Ideas

The best way to explore specific ideas and evaluate different solutions is to ask specific questions. For example, you might ask, "Could you use Excel to generate that report?" or "Can you use a third party to source your printers?"

Stay Focused on Key Issues

At Microsoft many of my customer meetings lasted four to eight hours and covered a wide range of technical, marketing, and contractual issues. With such busy agendas it was difficult to stay focused on covering my original objectives.

In most situations, I could handle new concerns that came up during our meeting time, but sometimes I had to schedule a teleconference or another meeting to address my customer's new concerns.

When I followed up on these concerns, I realized that many concerns that seemed very important at the time were of much less importance to my customers once they had an opportunity to put their concerns in the perspective of their overall business objectives.

The key to moving business forward is to be as responsive to your customer's concerns as possible, but to stay focused on achieving your primary sales objective, which is helping your customer move through their purchasing process.

It's Only Business

There is nothing wrong with conflict. The process of resolving conflicts often leads to innovation and effective solutions. However, when people become emotionally involved or upset, it is hard for them to be good listeners or to be receptive to new ideas.

I have found that focusing on business issues, rather than on personal opinions, enables me to maintain a productive dialogue with customers who hold widely differing opinions.

It doesn't make sense to have a disagreement, or to try to "win" an argument with a customer, if in the process you lose the opportunity to win the customer's business.

The best way to reestablish a productive dialogue with an upset customer depends on the situation. In one situation it might make sense to redefine your own position; in another situation you might try to find an area of mutual agreement, or try to reach a compromise.

If your efforts to calm your customer down seem to be making the situation worse, you might ask your sales manager or someone else from your company to help you reestablish a dialogue with your customer.

Anticipate Your Customers' Concerns

By "thinking ahead" of your customers you can communicate your empathy for their needs and concerns and help them feel that you are sympathetic to their way of thinking.

For example, if you sense the point that your customers are trying to make, and make it clear that you agree with them before they make it, they will feel that you are in "sync" with their ideas or beliefs. However, when you use this technique, you must be careful not to interrupt your customers' train of thought.

Simplify Technical Details

Technical buzz words and jargon that are not understood by your customers can lead to misunderstandings and confusion and can make your customers feel uncomfortable. If your customers don't understand what you are telling them, they may feel compelled to meet with another salesperson who can communicate in "plain English."

At Microsoft I learned that a great deal of the information I felt was self-explanatory needed to be explained during my sales presentations, and that it was necessary to explain many of the technical terms, acronyms, and industry references I used to describe our products and technologies. I also learned that it took less time to provide written step-by-step directions and instructions when I needed to describe a complex process than to deliver long-winded verbal explanations.

When you communicate information in a simple enough way to ensure that your customers understand exactly what you are saying, your sales meetings will become shorter, and it will be easier for you to stay in sync with your customer's purchasing process.

The shortest route to a sale is paved with clear communications!

SALES TRAINING AT MICROSOFT

As busy as we were at Microsoft, we scheduled at least one week of sales training every six months. We tried to cover as many selling skills as possible, including communication skills, time management, negotiation techniques, and account management. Sometimes we used internal personnel to facilitate our training, but most of the time we brought in outside training specialists.

Most of our account managers felt that our training sessions were very valuable, but a few of our account managers always complained that our training was a waste of their time. Surprisingly, our "complainers" were often the most enthusiastic participants, and invariably gave our seminars very positive reviews!

It is hard to identify a specific training program that had the most impact on our effectiveness as a sales organization, but there is no question that role-playing was the single most effective tool we used to help our account managers improve their communication skills.

My favorite communication exercise is what I call the "good, better, best" communication game.

1. First, choose an idea you would like to communicate.
2. Then think of at least three different ways to communicate this information.
3. Role-play each approach with a partner.
4. Don't forget to verify your communication!
5. Finally, analyze what impact each approach has on your ability to move business forward.

For example, you might use one of the following approaches to communicate the idea that "automating your inventory control system will help you manage your inventory more efficiently."

Approach 1: "I am an expert on automation. In my opinion, you should automate your inventory control system...."

Approach 2: "Our company has automated several companies that are in your business. Each one has been able to lower their operations costs. If your business is similar to theirs, I am confident you will experience the same success...."

Approach 3: "The first step toward determining whether automation makes sense for your company is to analyze your current inventory control system. If your current system is working well, you may not need to automate; on the other hand, if your current system is inefficient, you may be able to save money by automating...."

Customers will respond to *what* you communicate, and to *how* you communicate your ideas.

Approach 1 assumes that your customers believe you are an expert and that they will follow your expert advice. However, in many selling situations, customers discount their salesperson's "testimonial" because they believe their salesperson cannot be completely objective.

Approach 2 assumes that your reference account is similar to your customer's business. If it is, this approach can help support your proposed solution. However, this approach is risky, because many customers feel that their business requirements are unique and that what works for "similar" businesses may not work for them.

Approach 3 does not assume a conclusion. It suggests that the customer's problem needs further analysis. This approach makes it easy for your customer to get in sync with the ideas and recommendations you present during the selling process.

While each of these approaches could help you move the selling process forward, the third approach is the most compelling because it makes the fewest assumptions about your customer's needs and concerns; helps position you as your customer's advocate; and most importantly, helps you open a dialogue with your customer.

SELLING SUCCESS—A STEP AT A TIME

As you experience different selling situations, you will have an opportunity to develop your selling skills. However, the opportunity cost of learning on the job can be very high.

You will improve your selling skills much faster if you identify one selling technique at a time that you would like to improve, and then practice it until you have mastered it.

One week, for example, you might pay special attention to verifying communication during your sales calls. Another week, you might challenge yourself to create a multimedia sales presentation based on suggestions that are presented later in this book. As the weeks roll by, you will improve your selling skills, and you will gain confidence in your ability to close business and manage your territory.

Success doesn't come overnight. Even Microsoft took more than ten years to become a billion-dollar company! So be patient with yourself, and have faith that your persistence and hard work will pay off.

*The hardest part of learning a new skill is learning how to stop doing things the old way. Client-Centered™ communication techniques are simple, but you will need to make a con*scious effort *to integrate them into your selling process.*

CLIENT-CENTERED™ SELLING

Account managers at Microsoft have four resources they can use to meet their sales objectives: their time, a budget for travel and marketing expenses, whatever corporate resources they can engage to help them attain their business objectives, and the power of their ideas.

Selling is a "business," and as with any business, your resources must be carefully managed to achieve the greatest return on your investment. In this section you will learn how to use Client-Centered™ selling techniques to help you better manage your selling resources.

CHAPTER SIX

CLIENT-CENTERED™ SELLING

"Successful salesmanship is ninety percent preparation and ten percent presentation."
—BERTRAND R. CANFIELD

Many books on sales claim that "persistence and confidence" or "good listening skills" are the keys to successful selling. But while reducing the complexity of the selling process to a sound bite is enticing, it really isn't very useful.

At Microsoft I began to think of the selling process as a sequence of logical steps. Breaking the selling process into logical steps made it easier for me to analyze the effect that different factors had on my selling efforts.

I learned that different factors, some of which I could control, such as the way I qualified my customers, and some that I could not control, such as competitive market pressures, could help me move business forward or could derail my selling efforts.

By analyzing the selling process and evaluating the specific activities and sales tactics I used during each step, I created a selling technology or "infrastructure" that enabled me to move business forward *regardless* of my customers' specific purchase concerns, or where they were in their purchase process.

THE CLIENT-CENTERED™ SELLING PROCESS

Client-Centered™ selling is based on an intuitive, five-step process that begins with *prospecting* for new customers using direct and indirect prospecting techniques.

After you have identified prospective customers, you must *qualify* the possibility that they will purchase your products, by asking them questions about their need, their budget, their buying authority, and their time frame for making a purchasing decision.

If your prospective customer is qualified, you can *present* information about your company's products and services, and propose a solution that addresses your prospect's needs.

It is important to *verify* that your prospective customers understand how and why your proposed solution is appropriate for them and that they do not have any concerns that will make them postpone their buying decision.

And finally, you must *ask your prospective customers for their business.*

As you read through the next two chapters, you should try to plug your own selling situation into the Client-Centered™ selling process and to think about how you can apply different Client-Centered™ selling techniques to help you leverage your selling opportunities.

Then, after you have analyzed each step in your selling process, you can experiment with different Client-Centered™ selling techniques to determine which ones work best for you in different selling situations.

STEP 1. PROSPECTING

Before you can sell your products, you will need to identify and contact prospective customers. This step is called prospecting.*

---

* A *qualified lead* is often referred to as a *prospect*, and the words *prospect* and *customer* are often used interchangeably, although prospects do not really become customers until they make a purchasing decision.

Prospecting is time-consuming, and it isn't always fun. But, of course, you're not going to have anyone to sell to until you find prospective customers who want to communicate with you about the products you are selling.

Depending on your selling situation, you may use both *direct* prospecting methods such as direct mail, telemarketing, advertising, cold calls, and trade shows, and *indirect* prospecting methods such as referrals, seminars, articles, and networking with business contacts, to help you identify new customers.

Everyone wants to use the "most effective" prospecting method. But the best way to identify new customers depends on a constellation of factors:

- Number of prospects in your territory
- Geographical distribution of prospects
- Type of products or services being marketed
- Your company's market position and strategy
- Marketing budget
- Number and capabilities of sales and support personnel
- Outside marketing resources
- Competitors' marketing strategies
- Joint marketing opportunities

Depending on your situation, you may need to use more than one prospecting technique to help you identify qualified prospective customers.

At Microsoft, our OEM account managers spent very little time prospecting for new accounts, because virtually all of our OEMs contacted us about licensing our operating system software when they were ready to release a new PC.

But our corporate accounts sales representatives were very proactive about identifying and qualifying new selling opportunities for our office productivity tools. They used trade shows, direct mail, telemarketing, and other prospecting techniques to reach PC software buyers. And, of course, they worked with national distributors who supplied our products to PC retailers and system integrators.

The effort you will need to invest in prospecting for new customers will be directly related to the demand for your products. The higher the demand is for your products, the less effort you will need to make to secure new customers.

If your company is just starting out, or if your products are new or rely on a new technology, you may need to invest a great deal of effort communicating your Story to generate demand for your products.

EVALUATING PROSPECTING TECHNIQUES

When I am deciding between investing my time and marketing resources in two different prospecting activities, such as a telemarketing campaign and a direct-mail response card promotion, there are four questions I try to answer about each prospecting opportunity:

1. Will the prospecting activity enable me to communicate with my targeted marketing opportunities?
2. How much will the prospecting activity cost in terms of time and money?
3. What is my best estimate of the number of leads that the prospecting activity will generate?
4. Based on prior experience, what is the likelihood of closing the leads that are generated?

Then, to help me evaluate the pros and cons of each prospecting activity I am considering, I construct a simple decision table. I use my decision table to help me select the prospecting activity I believe will have the best chance of generating the number of qualified prospects I need to work with to meet my sales objectives, at the lowest cost (prospecting time and market development funds) per lead.

Is Your Prospecting Program Working?

It is very difficult to predict how successful a specific prospecting activity will be. A direct-mail solicitation, for example, may generate 500 responses or 5,000 responses, depending on how

DECISION TABLE	
TELEMARKETING	**DIRECT-MAIL RESPONSE CARDS**
Can use SIC codes to target best prospects	Can use SIC codes, contact names, and titles to target best prospects
Cost is equal to opportunity cost of my selling time	Costs $10,000 to create and distribute mailers
Requires 200 hours of telemarketing time to generate 50 leads	Requires 10,000 mailers to generate 100 leads
Requires 50 telemarketing leads to generate 10 sales	Requires 100 mailer leads to generate 10 sales

effectively you have communicated your Story. But in any case, once you begin using a prospecting technique you will be able to evaluate whether it is effective in your selling situation.

Prospecting activities that have worked in the past may not be as effective when they are reused. And, depending on your selling situation, you may need to pursue additional prospecting activities to identify enough qualified prospects to meet your sales goals.

For example, a direct-mail piece that has had a response rate of 4 percent the first time it was sent out, may have only a 1

PROSPECTING METHOD	NUMBER OF LEADS GENERATED	COST PER LEAD (TIME AND MONEY)
Direct mail		
Telemarketing		
Cold calls		
Tip/referral club		
Advertising		
Trade show		
Industry directories		
Yellow pages		
Other		

or 2 percent response rate the second or third time it is mailed to prospective customers in your territory. On the other hand, a direct-mail piece that includes a discount coupon or some other appeal may be more effective during subsequent mailings.

Focus, Focus, Focus

If the number of prospects in your territory is very small, you can spend more time qualifying each prospect than if you have a very large number of prospects to work with.

For example, if you have 100,000 prospects in your territory, you might do a direct-mail promotion to generate "semiqualified" leads, and then follow up those leads with a telemarketing program to generate better-qualified leads and to schedule sales calls. But if you have only 200 prospects in your territory, you might skip the direct-mail step and try to qualify every prospect in your territory with telemarketing calls.

The key to effective prospecting is to focus your marketing efforts on identifying prospects as cost-effectively as possible; to focus your selling efforts on qualifying your prospects as quickly as possible; and to focus your personal energy on moving business forward with every prospective customer you work with.

Sales Formulas and Real-World Results

One of the most common mistakes salespeople make is assuming that they can take a sales "formula," apply it to their business, and achieve a predictable outcome. The world is not so kind!

Several years ago I consulted with a software company that had developed a Windows-based word processor. Their product competed with word processors from Microsoft, Lotus, and WordPerfect—the three most successful companies in the PC software business. Their company was not doing well, and they asked me to help them evaluate their prospects for success.

My client's marketing people informed me that the market for word processing software was enormous and that they

EXAMPLE OF A PROSPECTING "FUNNEL" USING DIRECT MAIL AND TELEMARKETING	NUMBER OF "QUALIFIED" PROSPECTS
Total number of prospects in territory	Unknown
Initial contact: Direct mail	100,000
Initial response: 5% of recipients request additional information	5,000
Second contact: Direct mail—send detailed product information	5,000
Third contact: Telemarketing qualification by sales assistant after prospect receives second mail piece to verify need and time frame for purchase	4,700 (300 leads did not provide telephone number or asked not to be called)
Fourth contact: Sales call—detailed needs assessment	3,000
Fifth contact: Product demonstration	2,500
Sixth contact: Proposal—90% of prospects who see a demonstration are sent proposals	2,250
Sales: 70% of proposals lead to a sale	1,575

needed to win only a 2 percent market share to meet their sales objectives.

I told my customer that achieving a 2 percent market share might be easy in a "normal" selling situation but that it was virtually impossible in *their* situation. I explained that sales formulas can provide insight into how a "normal" market might respond to a specific appeal but that any assumptions that are based on "normal" markets must be verified before you could rely on them. Depending on the situation, ten "qualified" prospects may lead to one sale, to ten sales, or to no sales at all.

I pointed out that my client's initial marketing efforts had demonstrated that they could hardly give their product away. And I recommended that they "downsize" their application and reposition it as a page layout tool for business users, rather than go head-to-head against virtually insurmountable competition.

My client didn't like my advice, and hired another consultant who agreed to help them "target" prospective customers. Eight months later I heard they were out of business.

I hope this story will remind you to do a reality check on any sales assumptions you make that are based on a "conservative" sales model you have heard about somewhere.

Before you bring a product to market, you must figure out exactly why a prospective buyer would want to purchase it. Then, when you think you have developed a compelling marketing Story, you should test it with prospective customers before assuming that you have the right "formula."

The most reliable "sales formula" you can use is one based on your own market research and prior sales experience.

STEP 2. **QUALIFICATION**

Once you have identified potential customers for your products or services, you will need to *qualify* their need for your products and their level of interest in moving toward a purchasing decision.

The earlier in the selling process that you qualify your customer, the less time you will waste with unqualified prospects, and the more time you will be able to spend helping well-qualified prospects move through their purchasing process.

The most direct way to qualify your customers' need and interest is to ask them four basic questions:

1. Do you *need* our product?
2. Do you have *money* budgeted to purchase our product?
3. Do you have the *authority* to purchase our product?
4. When (*time*) do you plan on making a buying decision?

Although it seems like it would be easy enough to get straightforward answers to these questions, it is often very difficult to do so. For example, your prospective customers may suspect that they need your company's products, but they may not feel they are informed enough to make a purchasing decision, or they may be unsure about whether their personnel will be able to use them.

In fact, most prospective customers cannot answer these "simple" questions until they begin to move through their purchasing process.

The primary value you can bring to your customers' purchasing process is to help your customers resolve their purchasing concerns through the qualification process.

NEED

In most selling situations the first question you should address is whether your prospect needs your products or services.

The easiest way to qualify your prospects' need, is to ask them general questions to establish a dialogue about your prospects' problem and to help you reveal specific purchase concerns.

For example, you might ask your prospect:

- How would you like to improve your operations?
- What do you like and dislike about your current system?
- Are there any bottlenecks in your operations?
- What would you like your current system to do that it is not doing?
- Are your costs of operation in line with production?
- Are you outsourcing this work?
- Are you having problems getting your old system serviced?

If I don't know very much about my prospects' business I usually ask how they are solving their problem now; what they like and dislike about their current system or solution; and, most importantly, what they think they need. If I can provide exactly what my customer wants, I know I have a good chance of making a sale.

I also like to ask questions that help me determine my prospects' product and industry knowledge. If my prospects are familiar with the type of products I am selling, it will take much less time to move through the selling process with them. Conversely, if my prospects have little or no information about my products or about my industry, I need to budget more selling time to provide the information they will need to make an informed purchasing decision.

In any case, my qualification questions must provide enough information for me to determine what actions, such as scheduling a product demonstration or meeting with someone else from my prospect's company, I will need to take to move business forward.

Identifying Personal Concerns

Both business and personal concerns impact corporate purchasing decisions. For example, customers who are shopping for office automation equipment are usually focusing on business issues such as price, performance, compatibility, quality, service, and support. But in addition to these concerns, customers are often concerned about personal issues that may be very emotional, such as potential loss of their job, reassignment to another department, loss of status, not having adequate job skills to adapt to new business operations, or just having additional work to do.

The most effective way to address your customers' personal concerns is with specific explanations and examples. For example, if your customers are concerned about their job skills, you might discuss your training programs or provide examples of your documentation to prove that they are easy to read and understand. Or if your customers are concerned about job security, you might point out how learning new technologies can improve their competitiveness in today's job market.

Customer Requirements Analysis

In high-tech sales it is often necessary to prepare a detailed customer requirement analysis to qualify a prospect's need.

I have found that the most effective way to prepare a customer requirement analysis is to ask lots of questions, to try to make as few assumptions as possible about my customer's business, and to verify that I have not overlooked any factors that may affect my proposed solution.

If my customer requirement analysis is very detailed, I prefer to document my findings in a written report that I review with my customer *before* making any recommendations or proposing any solutions.

Using this Client-Centered™ approach helps me communicate my concern, stay in sync with my customer's purchase process, and ensure that I understand the totality of my customer's problem before I commit myself to a specific product recommendation or solution.

Money

The next qualification step is determining whether your prospect has budgeted money to purchase a product that addresses his or her need.

The easiest way to qualify your prospect's budget is to ask your prospect general questions to establish a dialogue about your prospect's business operations and objectives. For example, you could ask:

- How large is your company?
- How many employees do you have?
- What is your current system costing each month?
- How much do you pay for system maintenance and support?
- When is your next budget cycle?
- Have you discussed this with your financial officer?
- Do you have a budget for this purchase?
- Do you plan to lease or finance this purchase?

Over the years, I have learned that it is unwise to assume that a company I am qualifying, regardless of their size, has a budget for my products or services until I ask them.

And if I am at all concerned about my prospective customers' ability to qualify for financing or to pay their bills, I check their creditworthiness with my banker or finance company before I invest my selling time helping them move through their purchasing process.

Authority

The more time you spend with the people in your prospective customers' organization who are responsible for making or influencing their purchasing decision, the less time you will waste with unqualified prospects.

Lower-level people in an organization are usually easier to reach than higher-level decisionmakers. But selling to higher-level personnel makes it easier to establish relationships at multiple levels within your customer's organization; and having multiple contacts makes it easier to influence your customer's purchasing process.

Time

Most prospects will respond honestly to a direct question about when they will be making a buying decision. However, prospects often need to move through part of their purchasing process before they feel that they have enough information to evaluate the pros and cons of purchasing a product or service.

If, for example, your prospects do not know how much money or time they can save, or how much additional revenue they can generate by investing in your products, you may need to justify your proposed solution *before* you can assess your prospects' readiness to make a purchasing decision.

Most organizations operate on periodic budget cycles. Corporate budgets usually have some flexibility; however, when government agencies do not have funds budgeted to make a specific purchase, they usually have to postpone their purchase until their next departmental budget is approved.

I have made it a rule to ask my customers, at our very first sales meeting, when they are planning to make a purchasing decision. It is not absolutely necessary for them to have a timetable for their purchase. But I have learned that when customers have "no idea" about when they will be making a purchasing decision, they are often on a fact-finding expedition that

QUALIFICATION FACTOR	GENERAL QUALIFICATION QUESTIONS
Need	• Are you using our products now? • Have you evaluated our products? • What other products have you evaluated?
Money	• How large is your company? • Are you an independent department? • Do you have a budget for this purchase?
Authority	• What do you do at your company? • Are you in charge of product evaluations? • Are you the decisionmaker for this purchase?
Time	• When are you planning to upgrade your system? • Have you evaluated the return on investment for this type of equipment? • How soon do you plan to install your new system?

can waste a great deal of my selling time. Sometimes it's worth investing time to move a customer through the initial stages of their purchasing process, but in other cases, it isn't.

Customers' time frames for making a purchasing decision often change as they move through their purchasing process; however, you should not use your prospects' purchasing concerns as an excuse to not attempt to qualify their purchasing plans.

Qualification Questionnaire

Qualifying your prospects with a qualification questionnaire or contact form will help you save time and will help you remember to ask all the questions you need to ask to qualify your prospect's *need, money, authority,* and *time* and to update your customer (contact) database.

Contact Forms

It is very difficult to remember all of the qualification information that is communicated by prospects at seminars and other large

---

SAMPLE QUALIFICATION QUESTIONNAIRE

Contact Information
Company:
Contact:
Address:
Telephone:

Qualification Questions
Use more than 10 telephone lines?
Use ISDN services?
Use T-1 or T-3 lines?
Use telephone lines for both voice and data?
Use a local area network?
Use, or plan to implement, videoconferencing?
Use, or plan to implement, an Internet server?

Qualification Priority
No interest—no need/no money/referred to:
No interest—competitive system installed/satisfaction level:
Low interest—call back in __months/send information:
Interested—invite to seminar on:
Very interested—schedule meeting on:

---

meetings. The easiest way to manage this information is to record it on some type of sales contact form.

If you do not feel comfortable filling out a qualification form at your sales meeting, you can tuck a list of qualification questions between a few sheets of the paper tablet you are using to take notes at your meeting. Then, periodically, or at least once before you finish your meeting, you can check your list to remind yourself to ask your customer all the questions you need to qualify their needs and concerns.

STEP 3. **PRESENTATION**

When I first began developing my Client-Centered™ approach to selling at Microsoft, I realized that the ability to view the selling process from my customers' perspective enabled me to get much closer to my customers and to be much more persuasive.

It is hard to explain exactly why this is so, but I believe it is because making an effort to understand the selling process from

SAMPLE SALES CONTACT/QUALIFICATION FORM

Priority of lead: <u>A</u> B C No interest

Meeting location: Seattle Trade Show

Date: February 11, 1999

Salesperson: Terry Smith   **Sales assistant:**

Contact: Kerry Smith

Title: Vice president of sales   **Decisionmaker?:** <u>Y</u> N

Company: Good Way Industries

Address: 456 Northern Road

Phone: 555-7890

Fax: 555-7891

CONTACT PROFILE

End user/Retail/Distributor/<u>Manufacturer</u>/Professional

Government/Education/Nonprofit organization

Product interest: Product: T-600

Time to purchase: Next 60 days

Need/interest: Production Department

Budget: $125,000

Action required: Schedule product demonstration

Product: Y-200

Time to purchase: 6 months

Need/interest: Accounting Department

Budget: $25,000

Action required:

Follow-up

Send product information

Press kit

Reseller kit

<u>**Schedule sales call:**</u> February 22

Best time to call: Afternoon

✔**Action item:** Review account with technical support manager to determine requirements.

✔**Action item:** Reserve demonstration room.

✔**Action item:** Confirm meeting before next Tuesday.

my customer's perspective makes it easier for me to anticipate my customer's concerns. And once I understand my customer's key concerns, I can present my proposed solution in a way that my customer can understand and appreciate.

Learning how to present sales information in a way that will arouse your customer's interest and create a preference for your products is a cornerstone of Client-Centered™ selling.

Information on making effective sales presentations will be covered in the chapter on sales presentations.

Your Customer's Purchasing Process

The better you understand your customer's purchasing process, the easier it will be for you to anticipate your customer's concerns and influence his or her purchasing decision.

At Microsoft I used this ten-step purchasing process as a template to help me analyze my customer's purchase process and to think creatively about how I could move the selling process forward.

As you review the ten-step purchasing process, you should try to identify opportunities for you to influence your customers' purchasing decision at each step of their purchasing cycle. For example, you might advertise in a trade publication to help

THE 10-STEP PURCHASING PROCESS

1. Define specific characteristics of need
2. Anticipate or recognize need
3. Search for supplier
4. Qualify supplier
5. Analyze and evaluate available solutions
6. Request proposals from suppliers
7. Analyze proposals
8. Select supplier
9. Order solution
10. Evaluate performance (feedback to purchasing)

potential customers "anticipate or recognize need" for your products; and schedule a product demonstration at a trade show to help your customers "analyze and evaluate available solutions."

Studying this ten-step purchasing process will only be of value to you if you take the time to "plug in" your own selling situation, put yourself in your customer's position, and think about the things you can do to move your customer toward a purchasing decision.

Identifying Customer Concerns

The key to overcoming customer concerns is getting in touch with how you manage your own concerns when you are the buyer. In other words, you must put yourself in your customers' position to help them through the selling process.

For example, before you purchase a new car, you need to qualify your own needs and desires. If your family enjoys going out together on camping trips, you might have to choose between a practical sedan and a more expensive sport utility vehicle.

Once you decided on the type of vehicle you wanted to purchase, you would have to decide how much time and money to devote to shopping for your vehicle. If you were in a hurry, you might just evaluate one or two vehicles. But if you had more time to spend shopping, you might evaluate every vehicle in your price range before making a final decision.

After choosing the type and model of vehicle you wanted, your purchasing process would still be far from over. You would still need to select the options you wanted, choose a dealer, and negotiate a price.

Each step of the purchasing process requires patience and compromise. For example, if your favorite color was out of stock, you might have to decide between the immediate gratification of driving home a vehicle in a less desirable color, or the frustration of waiting for a car to be delivered in your favorite color.

The salesperson you work with can help you through your purchasing process and can influence your decision if he or she understands your concerns and maintains an open, productive dialogue with you.

I have found that most customers share the vast majority of buying concerns and objections. For example, many of Microsoft's MS-DOS customers were concerned about compatibility problems they might experience integrating Microsoft's operating system software with their PC hardware.

The easiest way to overcome these common customer concerns is to address them directly in your sales presentations.

Overcoming Customer Concerns

Customers who express a number of concerns or objections often trouble inexperienced salespeople. But handling customer concerns is a normal part of the selling process. When customers express concerns, it suggests that they are serious about the purchasing process, that they value your opinion and counsel enough to share their concerns with you, and that they want you to help them reach a purchasing decision.

The most important step in overcoming a customer's concern or objection is *verifying* that you understand what you have been told. Unless you are absolutely sure you understand what your customer has communicated, you should verify his or her concern before presenting any new information.

If your customer has expressed several concerns, you can write them down to ensure that you remember them, and to nonverbally communicate your attention, and your appreciation that your customer is willing to share his or her concerns with you.

Then you should verify that your customer does not have any other concerns.

It is not necessary to "overcome" every concern your customer has, and in fact it is often impossible to do so. Most purchasing decisions require the buyer to make some compromises. However, the better you are at addressing your customer's concerns, the more help you will be to your customer, and the farther along you can move the purchasing process.

For example, if you were selling a sedan, and your customers were vacillating between purchasing a sedan and a more expen-

TYPICAL OBJECTION	POSSIBLE REASON FOR OBJECTION
We need to think about it.	I am not convinced your solution will work for us.
We need to discuss it.	I do not have enough information to make a buying decision.
We like our current supplier.	I don't see the advantage of doing business with you.
Your product is too expensive.	I am not convinced your product is worth the price.
We don't need it now.	You have not made me want your product.
You need to discuss this with someone else (purchasing, engineering, etc.)	You have not captured my interest.
We want to see other products.	I am not convinced this is the best solution.
My boss wouldn't authorize it.	I don't want to sell this for you.
I don't see how it could work.	I am afraid of change.

sive sport utility vehicle, you might suggest that they purchase a tent and rent a Jeep several weekends each year to enable them to enjoy camping holidays. This would enable your customers to purchase a more comfortable sedan, enjoy their recreation, and save thousands of dollars in vehicle acquisition and fuel costs.

STEP 4. **VERIFICATION**

Before you finish a sales call, you should verify that you have addressed all of your customer's purchasing concerns and that your customer has received all of the information needed to help him or her make an informed purchase decision.

If you do not verify your communications, and verify that you have addressed all of your customer's purchase concerns, you will never know why a prospective customer has decided to postpone their buying decision, or to give his or her business to one of your competitors.

When I consult with sales professionals, I find that virtually every problem-selling situation can be traced back to incorrect assumptions about their customer's needs and concerns, and a failure to verify communications with their customers during the qualification process.

STEP 5. CLOSING THE SALE

If you ask your customers for their business before you have addressed all of their purchasing concerns, you will get out of sync with their purchasing process. But if you stay in sync with your customers' purchase process and *verify* that you have addressed their purchasing concerns before trying to "close" the sale, your customers should be ready to make a purchasing decision at the *exact moment* you ask them for their business.

There are many different ways to "close" a sale. And as you will see in the next chapter, the "closing" process can be absolutely painless.

PROACTIVE FOLLOW-UP

When you are busy working with customers and closing new business, it is easy to neglect customer follow-up. But if you don't take care of your customer's needs, your competitors will have an opportunity to win your customer's business by providing better customer service.

I have learned that the key to effective customer follow-up is to take responsibility for every outstanding action item that must be completed to move business forward. To help me keep track of outstanding action items, I create "to-do" check lists for each account, and write down time-sensitive tasks in my daily planner.

CLIENT-CENTERED™ SELLING

The Client-Centered™ selling process begins with prospecting for new customers using direct and indirect prospecting techniques.

After you have identified a prospect, you can use the Client-Centered™ communication skills you have learned to qualify the

SELLING PROCESS	OBJECTIVES
1. Prospecting	• Attract prospect to company • Display high personal energy • Build confidence and trust • Qualify reason for interest
2. Qualification	• Qualify need • Qualify money • Qualify authority • Qualify time • Complete contact form
3. Presentation	• Arouse interest • Provide new information • Create preference • Propose solution
4. Verification	• Verify communication • Develop follow-up action plan • Verify solution
5. Ask For Business	• Close sale • Support customer's buying decision • Value-added selling

prospect's need, budget, buying authority, and time frame for making a purchasing decision.

As your customers move through the purchasing process, you can use the marketing story you have developed to help you present information to your customers that will help them make an informed purchasing decision.

It is important to present a solution that addresses your customers' needs and purchasing concerns and that provides a *compelling* reason to do business with *your* company.

And finally, it is important to *verify* that your prospect understands your communications at each step of the selling process; to *verify* that your customer understands your proposed solution; and to *verify* that your customer does not have any outstanding concerns that will make him or her postpone the purchasing decision.

CHAPTER SEVEN

CLOSING HIGH-DOLLAR SALES

*"When you are skinning your customers you
should leave some skin on to grow again so that
you can skin them again."*
—NIKITA KHRUSHCHEV

Selling is a profession—it is not an act of aggression. If you are honest about your products and services, and your company is ethical in its business relationships, selling can be a win-win process for you and for your customer.

When I worked at Microsoft I was proud of the products I represented, and I believed that my company was ethical in its business relationships. It was easy for me to ask for my customers' business, because I believed that a decision to do business with Microsoft was the best decision my customers could make. But I was not foolish enough to *ask* for my customers' business until I had earned the right to do so, by identifying my customers' need, proposing a viable solution, justifying my proposed solution, and addressing any concerns my customer had about partnering with Microsoft.

If you try to close a sale prematurely, before you have addressed all of your customers' concerns, your customers may feel that you are more interested in "selling them something" than in helping them solve their problems. But if you follow the Client-Centered™ approach outlined in the preceding chapter, you will be able to move business forward almost effortlessly—which, of course, is exactly how the selling process should move forward!

Customers expect salespeople to put their needs and concerns first and are reluctant to do business with salespeople they feel are only interested in earning commissions.

ASKING FOR YOUR CUSTOMER'S BUSINESS

I have never had any difficulty closing sales. My secret is that I never ask for my customer's business until I have put myself in my customer's position, by asking myself five "keep myself honest" questions:

1. Have I identified a real need?
2. Have I verified that my customers recognize this need?
3. Have I established the value of my product or solution? Will our products or services help my customers:
   - Improve operations?
   - Generate new business?
   - Reduce expenses?
   - Develop new business opportunities?
4. Have I verified that my customers recognize this value?
5. Have I verified that my customers do not have any outstanding concerns that must be handled before they will be in a position to make an informed purchasing decision?

When I worked at Microsoft, I got my customers excited by presenting and demonstrating new technologies, but I closed business by explaining how Microsoft could provide reliable solutions that could help my customers achieve their business objectives.

BUYING SIGNALS

After you have had an opportunity to go through your sales cycle a few times, you will realize that the main reason why it is so difficult to anticipate when a customer will be ready to make a purchasing decision is that every customer has unique buying concerns.

One prospect may, for example, be ready to make a purchasing decision after seeing a product demonstration or reviewing a cost justification analysis, while another prospect may require a trial use period before they feel that they have enough information to make an informed purchasing decision. When customers are ready to buy, they will usually signal their interest with both verbal and nonverbal "buying signals."

However, when your customers are ready to make a purchasing decision, they may:

- Appear relaxed and be especially glad to see you.
- Nod, smile, and act more agreeable than usual.
- Say they checked your references and that they were impressed.
- Take you to meet their boss, or other high-level personnel in their organization.
- Agree that your proposed solution would satisfy their needs.
- Ask detailed questions about installing or implementing your solution.
- State that their objections have all been answered.
- Ask you if it is possible to get special pricing or to negotiate a better deal.

When you observe these buying signals, you should be ready to ask for your customer's business.

You can use the closing/buying signals worksheet to help you evaluate where your customer is in the purchasing process.

CLOSING/BUYING SIGNALS WORKSHEET

Company: Acme Corporation

Primary contacts: Alan Brown, MIS director
T. L. Smith, executive vice president (decisionmaker)

Requirements analysis: AX-600 Communications System

Demonstration: Demo of AX-600 9/16/97 to MIS director

Proposal: Sent proposal 9/25/97; MIS director said it answered all of their concerns.

Initial concerns: Interoperability with existing PBX

Outstanding concerns: Price and delivery date

Buying signals observed:

- Asked about training for their system administrator
- Introduced us to vice president of operations
- Seemed anxious about delivery dates
- Asked about finance options

Trial close: Asked whether we should schedule system administrator training. Customer agreed.

Close: Asked if we should put a system on order for delivery in 6 weeks. Customer agreed.

Outcome: Sold AX-600 with all communication options for pilot installation.

Follow-up:

- If AX-600 system works as specified, customer will order system for all 23 of their branch offices.
- Work with technical support personnel to ensure smooth implementation of pilot installation.
- Follow-up with contract personnel to ensure rapid order processing.

THE PURCHASING PROCESS IS STRESSFUL

The larger a purchase is, the more stressful it is for a customer to make a purchasing decision.

Customers' stress levels are usually very low during the early phase of their purchasing process, because they do not need to make any decisions. But their stress levels increase as the selling process moves forward, bringing them closer to a purchasing decision, and peak right before they commit themselves to their purchasing decision.

After customers make their purchasing decision, their stress level will usually decrease. But they will continue to experience some stress until they are satisfied they have made the best decision for their company and that they have earned their manager's approval.

The best way to understand this emotional cycle is to observe your own purchasing process. Once you learn how to "see the world through your customers' eyes," it will be easy for you to empathize with your customers' purchasing concerns and know when to provide the reassurance they need to feel comfortable about their purchasing decision.

TRIAL CLOSES CAN MOVE BUSINESS FORWARD

After you have proposed an appropriate solution for your customer, you can do a "trial close" to help you uncover any hidden concerns or objections your customer may have to making a purchasing decision.

When your customers respond to a closing question such as "Would you like to schedule a product training class?" they must either agree, leading to a sale, or provide reasons why they don't agree, revealing their concerns and objections.

In either case, you can use your customer's response to your trial close to move the selling process forward.

The trial close is a powerful selling tool, but you should not use a trial close until you have earned the right to ask for your customer's business. If you do a trial close too early in the selling process you will appear to be overly anxious to close the sale and may make your customer uncomfortable.

CLOSING STYLES

The best way to ask for a customer's business depends on how you were introduced to your customer, how formal or informal your relationship is, the type of product that you are representing, and your own personality.

I am a very direct person, so I have always been most comfortable asking for my client's business with a direct question. However, over the years I have had an opportunity to use many different closing techniques.

Surprisingly, I have found that the closing technique I use doesn't make much difference—if my customer is far enough along in the selling process to feel comfortable making a purchasing decision. So before I ask my customer for his or her business I ask my five "keep myself honest" closing questions. And then I use one of these "classic" closing techniques:

Direct Question

The most common way to ask for your customers' business is to ask if they would like to order your product or use your services. For example, you might ask, "Would you like us to install our XYZ product next month?"

I think this is the most effective technique to use with business managers.

Partnering

The partnering approach is useful when the sales process has been long, enabling you and your customer to "partner" together to solve a complex problem. For example, you might ask, "When should we get started?" or "Have you selected a liaison person to interface with our implementation team leader?"

I like to use this technique when I sell to technical or operational personnel.

Assumptive Close

In an assumptive close, you "assume" that your customer has already made a purchasing decision, and move business forward as if your customer had already made their purchasing decision, until you get an objection from your customer.

For example, you might ask your customer when they would like to schedule training on their new system, knowing there is no need to get trained on a system they do not plan to install. Or you might ask a question such as "Do you want to order a six-pin, or a twelve-pin model?" or "Did you want to lease this equipment, or to finance it yourself?," to which either choice assumes a purchasing decision.

The assumptive close is difficult for many salespeople to master. If your customer is not ready to make a buying decision, you may appear to be subsuming your customer's decision process, and if you are out of sync with your customer's purchasing process, you may appear to be insensitive to their concerns.

As a rule, less experienced salespeople should avoid using assumptive closes in professional selling situations.

Cost-Justification Close

The cost justification close is based on the assumption that your customer will make a purchasing decision if it can be cost-justified.

In a cost-justification close, you present a cost/benefit analysis, and then ask your customer for agreement that your proposed solution makes good financial sense.

Cost justification is a powerful tool; however, if competitive products will also meet your customer's needs, cost justification may help you move your customer's purchase process forward, but it will not be an effective technique for asking for their business.

When I sell "high ticket" items, I can often overcome a customer's concern about the total cost of my proposed solution by breaking the price down into a cost per period of time, per location, or per employee. Presenting my cost benefit analysis this way makes it easier for my customer to relate the cost of my solution to the benefits they will receive over time. For example, I might ask my customer if implementing a $2,000 word processing system is "worth the $5 per day it will cost to improve your office assistant's productivity."

Time Out Close

In a time out close, a deadline is used as an incentive to make a buying decision. For example, you might use a sale period, a scheduled price increase, or the limited availability of a special model to "force" your customer to make a decision "while there is still time."

Everybody likes bargains, which is, of course, why the media are full of time-sensitive promotions.

Ben Franklin "Ledger" Close

In the classic Ben Franklin close, you draw a line down the center of a piece of paper and then list all the reasons not to purchase on the left side of the paper, and all the reasons to make a buying decision on the right side of the paper.

If you have made a good case for your proposed solution, the overwhelming number of reasons to buy your product on the right side of the page will help convince your customer to make a purchasing decision.

The Ben Franklin close is a good technique for moving your customer toward a purchasing decision, but you should verify that you have addressed as many of your customer's concerns as possible before making your case. Customers often think of new objections while you are preparing your list of pros and cons, and any purchasing benefits you list as "pros" may be difficult to cost-justify without prior preparation.

Benefits Summary Close

Customers who are "sitting on the fence" often need to be reminded of the reasons why it is beneficial to make a buying decision.

I have found that reviewing the benefits of a buying decision is often all it takes to help my customers overcome indecision if they are convinced that my proposed solution makes good business sense.

Personal Appeal

Some customers are susceptible to personal appeals such as "If I make one more sale this month, I will win a trip to Hawaii." However, in most business-to-business selling, using personal appeals to help you close sales will alienate your customer and tarnish your image as a problem-solver.

Referrals Close

You can use referrals and customer testimonials to help you close sales by describing the benefits your customers have realized after implementing your proposed solution, and then proposing that your new customer adopt the same solution to achieve the same benefits.

Many salespeople are comfortable using a referrals close; however, I prefer to use referrals earlier in the selling process, to build credibility for my proposed solution.

Downsizing Close

A less common technique, often employed in consumer sales, is to suggest a solution that is way too complex or too expensive, and then "downsize" the solution to fit your customer's real needs.

Customers, relieved that they can "get by" with an affordable solution, may appreciate the opportunity to solve their problems for an affordable price. However, a downsizing close can easily backfire in a professional selling situation. If your initial proposal is way out of line, your customers may conclude that you don't have the expertise to solve their problem, and they may not give you a second opportunity to reevaluate their need or propose an alternative solution.

I've Earned Your Business

One of the most popular ways to ask for your customer's business is to summarize all the work that you have done for your customer, such as performing a needs assessment, demonstrating your products, and developing an implementation plan, and then to suggest that you deserve your customer's business because of all of the work you have done to "earn it."

I have used this closing technique with established customers. However, I have always felt awkward reminding new

6 COMMONSENSE TIPS
TO MOVE BUSINESS FORWARD

1. Make sure that your customers know that your time is as valuable as theirs is.
2. Be prepared to provide references.
3. Talk about past successes.
4. Don't gossip about your other customers.
5. Be prepared to explain your fees or prices.
6. Insist on using a written contract or work order.

prospects of the work I have invested "earning their business." It is, after all, my job!

I have always enjoyed asking my customers for their business, because a "yes" means that I have done my job well and that I have helped my customers solve their problem!

THE REAL WORLD

Trust Your Feelings

One of my favorite sales adages is: "When your gut tells you a deal is fishy, cut your line and try casting in clearer waters."

One of the most interesting (and fishy) accounts I worked with at Microsoft was with one of the leading home computer manufacturers.

At our first meeting, my customer told me they were interested in bundling a copy of our Multiplan spreadsheet with every computer they sold if we were willing to sell our product to them at a "reasonable" cost. They also told me that they had sold more than a million home computers and that they expected to sell more than three million more computers over the next eighteen months.

The revenue potential of this opportunity certainly got my attention.

Unfortunately, things looked much brighter going into our contract negotiations than they actually were. I quickly learned that my customer practiced hardball negotiation tactics and specialized in "take it or leave it" ultimatums. My customer's management team had a *very* strong personal need to feel they were "winning" our negotiations.

The strategy I devised to move business forward was to befriend the vice president who was responsible for negotiating with me. I explained to him that I did not have any experience selling to consumer electronics companies and that I would appreciate any advice he could share about how his company did business. I also promised him that I would do everything I could at Microsoft to ensure that we were able to come to an acceptable business arrangement. Of course, that was my job.*

Despite the rapport we developed, I faced a new ultimatum each time I visited their offices. My favorite was "If you can't give us a better deal we'll develop our own spreadsheet!" Of course, I took these "threats" with a grain of salt. And after a while I actually got a kick out of the high-energy dialogue that my customer's managers appeared to thrive on.

After about five or six meetings, we agreed to a minimum royalty of $7 million paid over the term of our software license.

Although our negotiations took several weeks, we had agreed at Microsoft to offer my customer these terms after our first internal meeting about their deal. We also agreed that we should be flexible in our contract terms because we did not want to lose the deal to a competitor. We realized that the revenue stream from an OEM deal of this size could fund a tremendous amount of software development, and we didn't want it to be targeted at our core businesses.

After our first meeting, I knew instinctively that if I offered my customer our "best" deal, they would simply push me for better terms. So I let them "beat" me down to our internally agreed price. It cost me a few travel days and an amazing drive down an expressway that was under renovation during a thunderstorm, but it made my customer happy.

---

* When a customer is confrontational, the easiest way to "disarm" their aggression is to be as agreeable as possible without giving up your own negotiating position. It doesn't cost anything, it helps put you on "their side of the table," and it can help you qualify their needs and concerns.

I believed that our agreement was on pretty solid ground until I had my first, and as it turned out, last meeting with my customer's CEO. Our contract was literally on his desk to be signed when he informed me that his company might not honor their agreement with us unless he felt it was in his best interest!

At this point I went from "concern" about my customer's negotiation style to having a "very uneasy feeling" about entering into an agreement to supply products to his company. I sent E-mail to Jim Harris and Bill Gates advising them that I did not believe that my customer was negotiating in good faith and that I was concerned about their honoring the agreement we had reached.

We had another meeting but decided that, despite these concerns, it would be a mistake to turn down their business. So we went ahead with the deal.

My customer broke our contract a few months later, and we had our lawyers beat each other over the head for a while.

To be honest, I don't think anyone at Microsoft was too surprised by my customer's actions. But I learned an important lesson. I realized that I had not yet learned to *trust my intuitions*. I gave notice to my bosses that I smelled a fish, but I should have been more earnest about cutting the bait.

If you are uncomfortable working with a customer or are concerned about their integrity, there is a good chance you are going to have problems after the sale. It is almost always more profitable to walk away from bad business than to deal with the aftershock.

Don't Argue with Your Customer

Microsoft does not normally put source code for their products into escrow accounts for their OEM customers.* Microsoft's products are so widely available that this "insurance" is unnecessary. In fact, none of my customers had ever asked us to do this, until a young attorney from a *Fortune* 100 company informed

---

* Source code for an application is sometimes put into an escrow account that is held by a third party to ensure that a customer will be able to get support for their product in the event the software developer goes out of business.

me that he would not accept our contract unless we set up an escrow account for the operating system software that his company was interested in licensing.

I explained to the attorney why this was unnecessary, but he was convinced that setting up an escrow account was essential to protecting his company's interests.

I could have argued with my customer's attorney, and may have been able to convince him to accept our standard licensing terms. Instead I agreed to modify our contract for a five-figure fee.

My customer's attorney immediately agreed to my terms, feeling he had won a major concession. I felt pretty good, too. I had earned enough extra profit on the sale to cover my bonus for the year.

By putting myself in my customer's position and accepting their view of the selling situation, I was able to engineer a win-win contract, which enabled my customer to feel they had won a major concession and which enabled me to close a very profitable million-dollar contract.

Stay in Sync with Your Customer's Purchasing Process
After we established MS-DOS as the de facto industry standard operating system for IBM-compatible PCs, virtually every PC manufacturer in the world was anxious to license our software.

These OEMs were interested in learning about Microsoft's future product strategy, but their primary concern was moving through our software licensing process as quickly as possible so they would have an operating system to ship with their computers.

Some of our less experienced account managers wanted to schedule technical presentations with these OEMs before completing software license agreements. I think this helped them feel they had "earned" their customer's business. But I encouraged them to stay in sync with their customer's purchasing process, and to address product strategy issues after their customer had licensed our software.

When you meet with customers who are ready to make a purchasing decision, it is important to get in sync with their purchasing process, and to move forward as quickly as possible.

Presenting new information may arouse additional purchasing concerns and can derail your sales efforts.

WHY WON'T THEY MAKE A PURCHASING DECISION?

Several years ago I had an opportunity to work with a leading computer systems integrator in the Midwest. They asked me to help them evaluate why one of their senior account managers was having difficulty selling an advanced client-server accounting system in her territory.

I began my sales "audit" by reviewing my client's sales and marketing programs, and I determined that their sales plan was very well thought out. I agreed that whatever problems my client's account manager might be having, they were not from a lack of marketing support.

I scheduled a meeting with my client's account manager and was pleased to discover that Terry was bright and well informed about her products and the markets she was selling to. She was also well organized and had a professional appearance and a good sense of humor.

Terry told me that she was very excited about selling her company's products but that she was discouraged about her territory; she confided that she had sent proposals to more than twenty prospects over the past four months but that she was able to close only two deals.

Over the years I have learned that the most effective way to diagnose sales problems is to go out in the field with my client's salespeople to watch how they interact with their customers. (Salespeople behave very differently when their customers are around!)

Terry agreed to take me with her on a sales call later that afternoon.

On our sales call, Terry did an excellent job of introducing herself, her company, and her products. And she did a good job of qualifying her customer's business needs. However, I was very surprised when, as we were about to leave her customer's office, she offered to send them a "proposal."

After we got back to her car, I asked Terry why she wanted to send her customer a sales proposal so early in the selling process. She replied that she had been taught that the next "step" in the selling process, after qualifying her customer's business needs, was to send them a written proposal.

In that moment I realized that Terry was having difficulty closing business because she was out of sync with her customer's purchasing process. She was out of sync because she failed to verify that her customers understood and agreed with her recommendations before suggesting that they review her recommendations in a written proposal.

Terry assumed that her customer was ready to move their purchase process forward when in fact they were still in a preliminary information-gathering stage. And to complicate matters, Terry assumed that a written proposal would "push" her customer toward a purchasing decision. But Terry's proposals were not *compelling*; they simply restated the information she had presented during her sales calls.

My "prescription" was to have Terry revisit every account she had sent a proposal to, to requalify their needs and concerns. I reminded her to *verify* that she had addressed all of her customer's concerns and to discuss her recommendations *before* hand-delivering revised proposals that included her new system recommendations.

Fortunately, my prescription paid off. Terry began closing sales at an extraordinary pace, and my client met their quarterly sales targets.

In most selling situations, assumptions about the selling process and failure to verify communications hinder salespeople from seeing the world through their customer's eyes. It is impossible to know where a customer is in their purchasing process if you are too involved with your own sales process.

WORKING WITH UNMOTIVATED PROSPECTS

If several purchasing decision deadlines have come and passed, and your prospect still has not made a buying decision, it is usually time to reevaluate your customer's buying qualifications.

Your customer may not recognize the need for your products; they may no longer have money budgeted for a purchase;

they may not have purchasing authority; or they may not have the resources in place to support a purchasing decision. In any case, it is necessary to uncover the real reasons why the decision process is being delayed.

There is no formula that can help you determine when you should stop investing your selling time on an unmotivated customer—you will need to use your intuition, or ask your manager to help you evaluate your situation from a more objective perspective. But I have identified several clues you can look for to help you identify whether you are *ever* going to be able to do business with your prospective customer.

Student Prospects

Many people work with vendors to help them learn about things of interest to them. For example, I had several prospects while I was at Microsoft who acted as if they were interested in licensing our software, when in fact their real interest was learning about the PC business.

To be honest, I have convinced myself on more than one occasion that my student prospect was moving toward a purchasing decision when in fact they were simply moving up their learning curve.

It is hard to recognize "student" prospects because they are sincerely interested in hearing your story. And once you get into a complex selling process with them, it is reinforcing to have them agree with almost anything you say to keep the education process rolling along.

The best way I have found to identify "student" prospects is to observe their stress level during sales meetings. "Student" prospects' stress levels remain very low throughout the selling process because they are not concerned about making a purchasing decision.

Prospects Who Won't Accept Obvious Facts

Many businesspeople are curmudgeons; and their stubbornness can be a virtue. But if your prospects are unwilling to recognize the value your products and services can provide, they may spend time with you, but it is unlikely that they will ever spend their money.

In my experience, when a prospect continues to deny obvious benefits, there is no way to move the purchase process forward until they are willing to share their hidden concerns or agenda.

I like to ask unmotivated prospects general questions, such as what is "holding them back" from making a purchasing decision to get them to disclose their hidden concerns.

HANDLING DISHONEST OR UNETHICAL PROSPECTS

It can be extremely frustrating, and very expensive, to work with a customer who lies, has a hidden agenda, reveals confidential information, or is dishonest.

I have learned to trust my intuition about the people I work with. If I suspect that a prospect is dishonest or unethical, or that I will have problems with them after making a sale, I will walk away from their business.

I believe that in the long run, it is far more profitable to do business, and build my success, with customers I am proud to work with.

COMMITMENT TO CHANGE

Implementing new solutions often requires companies to change their operations, their management style, or their fundamental business model. For example, a company that is automating their purchasing system might need to revise their purchasing policies, redesign their purchase order forms, and reengineer their manufacturing process to take advantage of a just-in-time inventory management system.

When you propose a solution, you need to be sensitive to the impact and changes your solution is going to have on *all* aspects of your customer's business.

A recent study conducted by Deloitte & Touche revealed that only 9 percent of senior-level financial executives at 221 surveyed companies felt that the client-server accounting systems their companies had implemented were "world class," and that 85 percent felt their systems "fell short of expectations."

If these products didn't work properly, none of the surveyed executives would have been satisfied; in fact, 9 percent of the companies overcame a constellation of technical and people-related problems to achieve a "world class" implementation.

If you sell complex products such as computer systems, you must be prepared to help your customers visualize how they will be able to integrate your proposed solution with their existing business operations.

The only way to do this is to invest enough time in your presale requirements analysis to understand these issues, and then to disclose exactly what you believe your customers will need to do to achieve a successful outcome.

SALES AGREEMENTS AND CONTRACTS

There are three things that I have learned about sales contracts over the past twenty years. The first thing I learned is how difficult it is to develop a sales contract that balances your desire to protect your company's interests with your desire to make it as easy as possible to close new business. The second thing I learned is that it is essential to have your sales contract drafted or at least reviewed by an attorney to ensure that it protects your interests. And the third thing I learned is to insist that my sales contracts be as straightforward and easy to understand as possible.

This "balanced" approach will help you close business, will help you collect your receivables, and will help keep your company out of court.

When I first joined Microsoft, negotiating OEM deals often took months as our account managers, their customers, and our respective corporate attorneys battled over specific terms and conditions in our software licensing agreement.

Some of our account managers were comfortable negotiating contracts, but many of our account managers found it difficult to negotiate "legal" issues. I was given the task of restructuring our software licensing process to make it easier for our OEMs and our account managers to move business forward.

Needless to say, our attorneys had a great deal to say on the subject, but eventually we agreed to use a "standard boilerplate" contract, which was written in plain English. We tried to cover as many of our customer's licensing concerns as possible in our contract. And we compiled a list of terms and conditions, which had been preapproved by our legal department, that our account managers could use as guidelines if their customer wanted us to change any of the terms in our standard agreement.

Our account managers were allowed, for example, to negotiate payment terms, depending on the minimum royalty commitment their customer was making. But some terms, such as any modification to our limitation of liability clause, were "dealbreakers." If a customer insisted that we remove this clause, we would pass on their business.

Our new OEM contract made it easier for our account managers to close business, and it helped our OEMs feel they were being treated fairly. Our new contract also helped us avoid legal complications that might have arisen if we offered more favorable business terms to some of our customers than to others.

PRICING STRATEGIES

Another of my jobs at Microsoft was to coordinate pricing for our OEM products.

I learned that pricing depends on a constellation of factors, including costs of development and manufacture, marketing expenses, and, of course, the amount of profit a supplier wants to earn on each sale. At Microsoft we liked to earn a lot of profit.

Our OEM customers were price-sensitive. But the cost of our operating system software was a very small percentage of the overall cost of producing a PC. Our larger OEM customers viewed our software royalties as a "cost of doing business" in the PC business. But our smaller OEM customers were concerned that we could offer significantly lower pricing to higher-volume OEMs, making it difficult for them to compete.

We overcame this concern by providing relatively small discounts for large volume commitments, and by providing aggressive discounts to OEMs who agreed to bundle our operating systems on every Intel-based PC they manufactured and sold.*

Price sensitivity is related to a customer's sense of value, which depends on a constellation of factors and which can be very subjective. But I have learned that the key to overcoming a customer's price sensitivity is ensuring that they feel they are being treated fairly.

To win a sale, you must justify the price of your product with the value it provides. If you are not convinced that your products are worth their price, it will be very difficult to convince your customers to purchase them.

SELLING QUALITY AND SERVICE

Price, quality, and service are interrelated. To lower a product's selling price a company must lower their quality or service, or reduce their profitability. So when a customer expresses concern

---

SELLING QUALITY AND SERVICE

- Save money
- Reduce operating expenses
- Save time
- Last longer
- Provide greater ease of use
- Higher reliability
- Increased security
- Better performance
- Better service and warrantee
- Other factors

---

* Although our bundling policy limited our OEMs' operating system options, it really wasn't much of an issue at the time. Our OEMs' PCs required an operating system, and Microsoft's operating system was the product that their customers demanded to run industry-standard "IBM-compatible" software applications.

about the price of your products, or you are forced to compete against a lower-priced competitor, you must sell your company's quality and service.

JUSTIFYING PREMIUM PRICING

To justify premium pricing, you can explain how your products can help your customer solve their problems, save money, reduce operating expenses, save time, last longer, and provide greater ease of use, reliability, and security than competing products. You can also review your costs, to highlight your investment in producing high-quality, high-performance products and providing superior customer service.

MEETING YOUR COMPETITORS' PRICE

Lowering your price to meet competitors' bids can be justified if you are selling commodities and providing virtually identical terms of sale. However, in business-to-business selling, reactive price cutting often results in lost credibility and lost sales.

I have found that the best way to overcome my customer's concerns about price is to use creative pricing strategies. For example, you might agree to lower your price—if you can take out your support costs; or hold your price—but provide more favorable payment terms; or match your competitors' prices—if your customer agrees to single-source products from your company.

At Microsoft we offered more favorable pricing terms to OEM customers who were willing to bundle our operating systems software with every PC they sold. This bundling strategy was a win-win situation, because it helped our OEM customers lower the selling price of their systems, and it helped us build market share for our products.

THE "MARRIAGE" BEGINS AFTER THE SALE

By putting yourself in your customer's position, you can make your customer's transition from prospect to partner as stress-free as possible.

After I receive a sales order, I always thank my customer for their business and for their confidence in my recommendation. Then, if I have not already gone over the details of the sale, including installation and implementation issues, I do so at this time.

I also like to joke around a bit with my customers after making a deal, to help relieve tension, and to help rebuild any rapport that may have been lost during a prolonged negotiation.

OVERCOMING BUYER'S REMORSE

Many customers experience "buyer's remorse"—the feeling that they could have found a better solution or made a better deal if they had delayed their purchasing decision—after making a major purchase.

Buyer's remorse arises from purchasing concerns that have not been completely addressed before a purchasing decision is made. So customers who are "pushed" through the purchasing process are more likely to experience buyer's remorse than customers who have taken more time to evaluate their options.

Buyer's remorse is less common in business-to-business selling than in retail consumer sales, because the purchase process is generally more objective. But business customers do experience buyer's remorse. For example, businesses that have purchased a new computer system often have "second thoughts" about their purchase decision if they encounter unexpected difficulty implementing their new system, or if they have trouble getting technical support.

I have found that the most effective way to help my customers overcome buyer's remorse is to remind them of the benefits they will realize from their purchasing decision and to provide a high level of ongoing after-sale support.

VALUE-ADDED SELLING

The cost of generating a sale to a new customer is far higher than making a repeat sale to an existing customer, so it makes good business sense to keep your customers satisfied.

Over the years I have learned that the easiest way to keep my customers satisfied is to treat them the way I would like to be treated if I were in their place.

The Golden Rule is the real secret behind Client-Centered™ selling.

PERSONAL SATISFACTION

Some of the account managers I worked with at Microsoft got a great deal of personal satisfaction out of closing contracts. But many of our account managers mentally pushed themselves into their next selling situation before taking any time to appreciate their success.

The danger of becoming a "selling machine" is that you may stop caring about your customers, and you may fall into a routine that kills the creative spark in your selling process.

I have learned that taking time to appreciate my selling success helps me prevent job fatigue, and the stress that can lead to career burnout. Plus, it's always nice to have an excuse to celebrate!

CHAPTER EIGHT

TELLING MICROSOFT'S STORY

"Inequality of knowledge is the key to a sale."
—ROBERT W. HAACK

The easiest way for us to get our OEM customers' attention was to bring Bill Gates to our sales meetings. All of our customers wanted to meet with Bill, because they knew that his insights about the computer industry could help their companies become more successful. And we loved to bring Bill to our meetings—because meetings with Bill were never boring.

I asked Bill to attend a meeting with one of my major OEMs because their CEO felt that it was important to establish a personal relationship between himself and Bill; and because, as I later learned, he felt that he was a consummate negotiator.

When Bill Gates, myself, and another account manager arrived, we were seated around a large conference table with Bill Gates at one end, and my customer's CEO at the other end.

I suspected that my customer's CEO had just returned from a trip and was suffering from jet lag. In any case, after our introductions, he slept through the first hour or so of our meeting, breathing rather noisily. When he woke up, he put a finger in the air and announced twice in a revelatory tone that "MS-DOS is PC-DOS!"*

Following this revelation, he argued with Bill that his company could be just as successful supplying Digital Research's CPM-86 operating system with their PCs as they could supplying our MS-DOS operating system. At the time, MS-DOS held more than 75 percent market share and was widely regarded as the industry's de facto standard PC operating system. Digital Research's CPM-86 operating system held less than 5 percent market share.

Bill, who was obviously getting impatient with their CEO, grabbed the table with white fingers, leaned forward out of his chair, and asked him, "What planet are you on?"

Actually no one at the table could be sure at that moment exactly what planet the CEO was on, but he agreed later that afternoon to bundle MS-DOS, for our standard royalty, on every PC his company shipped.

Sometimes the most effective way to move business forward is to "break the rules"—and when, like Bill, you control an emerging industry, you can afford to be as honest and direct as you like when you want to make a point.

In this chapter you will learn how to present your story.

TELLING YOUR STORY

At Microsoft we developed sales support materials such as product specification sheets, application guides, and slide presentations, to help our account managers present our story. But despite our efforts, some of our account managers had a difficult time making effective sales presentations. They could tell our story, but they did not do a good job of building rapport with their customers, and they did not create any sense of urgency to help them move the selling process forward.

One objective of a sales presentation is to provide the information a customer needs to make a purchasing decision. A

---

* IBM marketed Microsoft's MS-DOS operating system with a few minor modifications as PC-DOS.

TYPE OF COMMUNICATION	EXAMPLE	COMPLEXITY OF MESSAGE	POTENTIAL FOR MISCOMMUNICATION	TIME TO PREPARE
Informal sales presentation	Phone call Impromptu meeting	Simple	High	Low
Formal sales presentation	Speech Videoconference	Moderate	Medium	Medium
Informal written materials	Note E-mail	Moderate	Medium	Medium
Formal written materials	Proposal Newsletter	Complex	Low	High

second, equally important objective is to build rapport, and to communicate urgency, excitement, and concern about satisfying your customer's needs.

TEN STEPS TO EFFECTIVE CLIENT-CENTERED™ SALES PRESENTATIONS

Sales presentations can be more persuasive than written communications because you can use your customer's comments and their nonverbal cues, such as nodding their head or looking away, to verify their understanding and acceptance of the ideas you have presented. And, when necessary, you can modify your presentation as you are delivering it, to better address your customers' interests and concerns.

Over the years I have learned that there are five keys to making effective Client-Centered™ sales presentations:

1. Take the time to plan and organize your presentation before meeting with your customer.
2. Use your presentation as an opportunity to develop and maintain an open, productive dialogue.
3. Provide the information your customer needs to make an informed purchasing decision.
4. Verify your communications to move the selling process forward.

5. Use your sales presentation to introduce and support the recommendations you make to your customer.

I used these five key concepts at Microsoft to develop a simple ten-step process you can use as a template to help you develop and deliver *compelling* sales presentations.

STEP 1. **DEFINE YOUR PRESENTATION OBJECTIVES**

The first and most important step in planning a presentation is to define your presentation's objectives.

The easiest way to define your objectives is to write down the reasons that you are making your presentation as specifically as possible.

Presentations should be targeted to meet your customer's specific needs. For example, presentations that are targeted to retail consumers might provide an overview of product features and benefits, while presentations that are targeted to resellers might focus on your company's reseller support programs.

If you are not clear what your objectives for making a sales presentation are, you are not far enough along in the selling process to be making a sales presentation. You need to slow down, and open a dialogue with your customer to qualify their needs and concerns.

Salespeople often forget that their primary objective for making a sales presentation is to move business forward, not *to educate their customer. If you confuse your primary objective, you will lose track of your customer's purchasing process, and you will present information that may make it more difficult for your customer to make a purchasing decision.*

STEP 2. **OUTLINE YOUR MAIN POINTS**

Starting with your main point, which is often your conclusion, recommendation, or a generalization about your presentation, you should create an outline that includes each main point you want to make, and every subpoint that you want to make to support your main points.

PRESENTATION OBJECTIVE	SPECIFIC EXAMPLES
Arouse Interest	• Advertise success • Demonstrate product • Point-of-sale promotion
Provide information	• Discuss product features • Discuss product benefits • Present needs analysis • Propose solution
Create preference	• Describe past successes • Present competitive analysis • Propose cost-effective solution

The only trick to organizing the points you plan to make is that you should be careful not to assume that your customer knows something at the beginning of your presentation that you plan to cover later on.

Perception

People translate what they hear into images and concepts that are based in part on their own personal experience. By taking your customers' previous experience or "profile" into account, you can make your presentation more compelling by addressing specific concerns that are important to them. For example, operations managers tend to focus on operational issues, financial managers focus on costs and potential earnings, and marketing managers focus on the features and benefits of a proposed solution.

I find it helpful to ask myself, as I am developing my presentation objectives, if there is any way I can position my presentation to take my customer's previous experience into account. Doing this helps me take a Client-Centered™ view of the presentation process and helps me verify that I understand my customer's primary purchasing concerns.

Anticipating Your Customer's Response

I have found that predicting how decisionmakers will respond to a presentation is very difficult. However, I can often anticipate my customer's reaction to specific ideas or recommendations, based on previous experience with other customers I have worked with who have had similar interests and concerns.

For example, at Microsoft, when I introduced Windows to a new customer, I would always mention its ability to support both DOS and Windows-based applications, because many of our customers depended on specific mission-critical DOS applications to support their business operations.

Emotional Appeals

Sales presentations that are designed to influence your customer's thinking or opinions can employ both factual and emotional appeals.

For example, a fire alarm salesperson can use a factual appeal, such as lower insurance premiums, and an emotional appeal, such as a picture of a family running out of a burning house, to help him or her close a sale to an apartment building owner who is also a parent.

Although most salespeople are uncomfortable using emotional appeals to "manipulate" their customers, many common sales tactics are based at least partially on emotional appeals. For example, telling a customer about a successful competitor who has used your company's products to improve their operations or increase their sales is an emotional appeal, because most customers have a competitive ego response to any competitor who is beating them in the market.

Handling Sensitive Subjects

The best way to present sensitive or potentially embarrassing issues in the most positive light during your sales call is to discuss them *before* they come up as customer concerns. Unfortunately, in the real world, you cannot always anticipate the problems that will arise.

One of the most difficult customer situations I handled at Microsoft was explaining why a custom version of one of our programming languages, which we were developing on contract for one of our largest OEMs, was going to be delayed at least nine months. It wouldn't have been quite as painful to deliver this news if I hadn't met with this customer the previous week to inform them that the software would be ready for them to test in two weeks.

Our program development manager told me that the reason for the setback was that our programmers wanted to rearchitect their code base so it wouldn't run bug slow. There was no "silver lining" behind this cloud.

I decided to pass along this information at a face-to-face meeting, and to try to put a positive spin on our delay by emphasizing Microsoft's commitment to performance.

At our meeting I told my customer that we wanted to put "extra effort" into the project to meet their performance expectations. My sugar-coated message didn't make my customer feel very much better about the situation. But my customer was impressed by our insistence on delivering a quality product, and probably respected me for showing up in person to deliver the bad news.

STEP 3. **INTRODUCE YOURSELF**

Before you begin a presentation, you should introduce yourself, state your qualifications, and describe your relevant experience.

How you introduce yourself is very important. A positive, enthusiastic introduction can help you build rapport with your customer, and develop the credibility you need to accomplish your presentation's objectives.

If you are being introduced, you should provide the person who is introducing you with a résumé, or background notes about your previous experience. This will make their job easier and will help ensure that you are introduced properly.

Selecting a Presenter

If you are selecting a presenter, you should choose someone who has a good knowledge of the material being presented, or who can easily learn the material. It is also best to choose a presenter who has credibility with your customer, who can make an objective presentation, and who has good presentation skills.

INDIVIDUAL PRESENTATIONS	GROUP PRESENTATIONS
• Informal	• More formal than individual meetings
• Easy to build rapport	
• Candid	• Can deliver a consistent message to
• Undivided attention	group
• Easy to control the agenda	• Can waste time if not well planned
• Can speak "off the record"	• Agenda is needed to cover material
• Easy to miss important issues and difficult to handle all concerns	• Higher expectation for preparation for problem resolution
• Low opportunity cost	• High opportunity cost
• Easy to "shoot from the hip"	• Require more planning and practice

At Microsoft we often had our product-marketing managers make technical presentations to our OEMs. In many cases one of our account managers could have delivered these presentations, but our product-marketing managers were more credible when they discussed their products than our account managers were.

Personality

If your customers do not like you, they will be less accepting of your factual arguments. If you have an abrasive personality, are difficult to understand, or if you do not have appropriate business credentials, you will need to put extra effort into developing a well-structured presentation with compelling arguments to support your conclusions.

STEP 4. **INTRODUCE YOUR TOPIC**

The way you introduce your topic sets the tone for the rest of your presentation. If your introduction is positive, you can begin building support for the ideas you will present through the rest of your presentation.

I like to base my introduction around three classic openings:

"I Have Important Information"

For example, I might begin a presentation by saying: "Microsoft has just made an important announcement about its Internet Information Server."

This introduction works extremely well if your customers agree that your information is important to them.

"I Understand Your Concerns"

I might begin my presentation by describing one or more concerns I believe are important to my customer, such as a concern about "the impact that the Internet is going to have on your company's distribution channel."

After describing my perception of my customers' primary concerns, I usually ask my customer to verify (raising their hands works well in a large group) that the problems I plan to address are, in fact, their primary concerns.

This "prepresentation qualification" works like a trial close. If I have done a good job of qualifying my customer's concerns, my customers will appreciate the effort I have made to understand their purchasing process. And if I learn that I have missed one or more issues that are important to my customers, I will have an opportunity to address them during my sales presentation. Either way, I have a better chance of moving business forward.

"I'm Here to Help"

One of my favorite ways to introduce a sales presentation is to ask my customers to describe their concerns, and then "piggy-back" my presentation on their concerns by describing how my company's products or services can help my customers overcome their problems.

For example, I might begin my presentation to a small group by asking my customer to "describe the key features you need in your inventory control system," and then proceed to explain how my company's products can meet my customer's specific requirements.

The advantage of this type of introduction is that it enables me to maintain an open, productive dialogue throughout my presentation. By maintaining this dialogue, I have the best chance of moving business forward.

Regardless of how you introduce your presentation, you should try to stay close to your discussion topic. Focusing on your customer's needs and interests will help you build rapport and will help you capture and hold your customer's attention.

INEFFECTIVE INTRODUCTIONS

Many presenters undermine their own credibility by employing ineffective introductions.

Negative or Derogatory Statements

Introducing your presentation with a strongly negative statement or forecast can polarize your audience if there is disagreement, and may impact your perception of objectivity. Employing a positive introduction can have just as much impact as a negative introduction, and it sets the stage for you to be seen as a problem-solver.

When I introduce a presentation, I try to present a glimpse of a potential solution to a major problem rather than a pessimistic view of the current situation.

Rhetorical Questions

Rhetorical questions can give the impression that you know something your customer doesn't know—but should.

Are rhetorical questions a good way to build rapport? I think not!

Overused Quotations

It is difficult to use quotations without appearing pedantic. If you include quotations, be sure they are on point and entertaining.

Jokes

If you have a gift for telling jokes, feel blessed and go for it; but avoid any joke that is told at anyone's expense but your own.

Apologies

Unless you have had logistical problems, such as being late due to a snowstorm, you should avoid apologies. If you are poorly prepared, you will not make anyone feel better about wasting his or her time to hear your presentation by apologizing first.

Irrelevant Stories

Anecdotes or stories that relate to your past experience can be effective icebreakers and can provide an easy transition to the body of your presentation. But it is usually best to avoid any anecdote that does not tie into your presentation material, or refer to people or situations that are of specific interest to your customers.

Lengthy Introductions

If you are doing a long presentation, it is usually appropriate to spend a couple of minutes introducing yourself and describing your expertise. However, if you are making a short presentation, you should make your personal introduction as brief as possible.

STEP 5. INTRODUCE YOUR MAIN POINTS

After introducing yourself, you should summarize the main points you will be making. This helps your customers remember these points and sets the stage for the rest of your presentation.

If your presentation will include a question-and-answer session, or if you are trying to encourage participation, your introduction is also a good time to state the "ground rules" for open dialogue. For example, you might ask your customers to hold their questions until you have finished speaking, or to feel free to interrupt your presentation if they have a question.

If your customers are well informed about the history behind your presentation, you should try to move through introductory information as quickly as possible so you can spend your time presenting new information.

Stay on Your Customer's Wavelength

People tend to trust people who hold the same beliefs they do. This is why most experienced presenters (at least since Shakespeare) begin their presentations with ideas or principles that are shared with their audience.

I have found that people tend to stop listening and begin to think about counterarguments if their basic beliefs are questioned or threatened. So I try to present my ideas in a non-threatening way.

For example, I might suggest that "doing this is *one way* to overcome this problem" rather than saying "doing this is the *only way* to overcome this problem." Or I might *ask* my customers if they would "consider this solution" rather than *telling* my customers to "just do this."

The best way to move business forward is to maintain a dialogue with your customers that enables them to move toward your proposed solution in their own way, at their own speed.

Selling Solutions

Customers are primarily interested in finding solutions to their business problems. So the most effective way to make a sales presentation compelling is to focus on solutions and benefits rather than on features and statistics.

Since I know that customers are influenced by benefit-oriented statements that focus on solutions far more than by feature-oriented statements, I spend most of my selling time presenting benefit-oriented statements, and a minimal amount of time presenting feature-oriented information.

Help Your Customer Visualize Benefits

The easier it is for your customer to understand and "visualize" your product's benefits, the easier it will be to move business forward.

For example, if a gardening tool's main selling point is that it has a long handle that "saves your back," you could help your

EXAMPLES OF FEATURE-ORIENTED SELLING	EXAMPLES OF BENEFIT-ORIENTED SELLING
Our product produces 6 different kinds of charts.	Our charts are easy to generate and will enable your managers to have the information they need at their fingertips.
Our software generates an ABC inventory report.	You can use your ABC inventory report to identify slow-moving inventory items and improve your inventory turn ratio.
Our machine can create 4 different shapes.	We can reduce your milling costs by 35%.

customer visualize the benefit of using your tool by pretending to use a short-handled competitor's tool and then straightening up and grabbing your "sore back."

Testimonials

Testimonials are a great way to support the conclusions you make in your presentation. But the authority of expert testimony is directly proportional to the credibility and objectivity of your expert.

The best way to present testimonials is to be specific about *who* made the statement, *what* the statement was, *when* the statement was made, *why* your expert is considered to be an authority, and *how* the person's statement relates to your conclusion or recommendation.

When we announced new products at Microsoft, we tried to align and partner ourselves with as many well-known, influential companies and industry "gurus" as possible. For example, when we announced Windows, we simultaneously announced that scores of independent software vendors and PC manufacturers had agreed to support our new technology.

STEP 6. DEVELOP YOUR PRESENTATION LOGIC

Logical presentations are easier to follow and to understand and are more compelling than presentations that just present "facts."

Most sales presentations are built around seven classic arguments:

Inductive Argument

Many presentations are structured around an inductive argument, where several specific statements share a common characteristic and suggest an obvious conclusion.

For example, your presentation might propose that the only way to build a state-of-the-art notebook computer is to use an active-matrix screen and a lithium battery. Since your company's notebook computers use active-matrix screens and lithium batteries, your computers must be as good as any other notebook computers on the market. If your customers accept your underlying premises, they can reasonably conclude that you have developed a leading-edge notebook computer.

Cause and Effect

In cause-effect presentations, your conclusions are justified on the basis of a causal relationship between different factors or issues.

For example, you might argue that since vitamins are required for good health, people who take vitamins will stay healthy.

The weakness of cause-effect arguments is that it is often difficult to prove that a relationship is causal, rather than just correlated in some way, and that it may be impractical or impossible to identify or isolate all the factors that are related to a specific effect.

For example, if you argue that taking vitamins will make a person healthy, your logic would be compromised, because good health is related to many factors, including an individual's genetics, the amount of exercise they get each day, and their stress level. Taking vitamins is just one of many factors that are related to an individual's health.

Deductive Argument

Deductive arguments are based on supporting a major premise with a minor premise that refers to the major premise and suggests a conclusion.

For example, your presentation might suggest that your products are of high quality because they were developed using the C++ programming language, based on the fact that other high-quality software applications were developed in C++.

Pros and Cons

Pros and cons or "advantages vs. disadvantages" arguments are useful when it is necessary to generate discussion, and when several similar alternative solutions are available.

Of course, if you already have a solution in mind, you should be sure that its pros clearly outweigh its cons.

Process of Elimination

You can use the process of elimination to support your presentation logic if there are specific issues that will eliminate other possible choices.

For example, if your customer is interested in purchasing a portable computer, you could easily eliminate any competitive products that required a connection to an AC power source.

Yes...but

"Yes...but" arguments create an apparently sound case for one conclusion and then eliminate it, by showing a flaw or weakness in some key point.

You can use a "yes...but" argument to convince your customer that you have analyzed their problem carefully and eliminated alternative solutions before finally presenting your own "no buts" solution.

The problem with presenting "yes...but" arguments is that if they are overdone, your customers may become impatient or annoyed before you present your "no buts" solution.

Thesis, Antithesis, Synthesis

In a thesis, antithesis, synthesis presentation you first present the reasons for doing something, then the reasons for not doing it, and finally a comprehensive solution based on combining the best parts of each of the preceding options.

Thesis, antithesis, synthesis presentation logic is often used to build consensus in meetings where customers are comprised of factions that hold strong disparate views, and during complex negotiations.

I use the thesis, antithesis, synthesis technique during most of my contract negotiations.

STEP 7. **DEVELOP A CLOSING STATEMENT**

The beginning and ending of your presentation are especially important, because people tend to be most attentive during the first and last few minutes of a presentation.

In your summary or closing statements, you should review the main points you have presented, and assuming you have time, summarize the presentation logic you used to support your conclusion or recommendation.

Then you can describe the steps you believe are required to move toward a purchasing decision, or present a "call for action," which may be a trial close.

The more compelling your presentation has been, and the more committed your customer is to your plan of action, the more succinct your closing statement can be. But regardless of your presentation logic, the best way to ensure that your customer understands and remembers your most important points is to:

1. Introduce your main points.
2. Cover your main points in a clear, logical, and reasonable way.
3. Summarize your main points one more time in your closing statement.

STEP 8. **FLOW-CHART YOUR PRESENTATION**

After you have created a structure for your presentation and decided how you will introduce yourself and how you will close your presentation, you are ready to flow-chart the body of your presentation.

The easiest way to flow-chart your presentation is to make an outline of all the main points and subpoints you will be discussing.

Then, you can decide how you want to transition from one major point to the next, and when and where to introduce audiovisual materials such as charts and diagrams.

Transitions from one major point to another are critical in presentations because they provide a link between ideas and provide an opportunity to summarize the points you have already covered.

Create Storyboards

If you are doing a complex presentation, or if multiple presenters will be involved, you may want to create storyboards.

You can use your storyboards to "talk through" your presentation, to ensure that transitions between your major points are logical and convincing, and to determine how much time it takes to cover each topic.

If other people are involved with your presentation, your storyboards can help everyone "visualize" the presentation and can provide a framework to discuss how specific information should be covered.

STEP 9. **MAKE YOUR PRESENTATION AS UNDERSTANDABLE, CREDIBLE, REASONABLE, AND SIMPLE AS POSSIBLE**

Most customers are uncomfortable making purchasing decisions until they have heard a compelling argument backed up with convincing data. The better your presentation logic is, the easier it will be for your customer to accept your proposed solution.

However, regardless of the presentation strategies you employ, your presentation should be understandable, credible, reasonable, and as simple as possible.

Storyboard 1

Introduces Presenters
Overview of Microsoft
Corporation's OEM Division

Storyboard 2

Describe previous
approaches to graphical
computing

Storyboard 3

Discuss need for a standard
Graphical User Interface
to support multimedia
PC applications

Storyboard 4

Describe Microsoft's
innovative approach to
designing a Graphical User
Interface

Storyboard 5

Present marketing video on
Microsoft Windows

Storyboard 6

Summarize advantages of
implementing standard
application programming
interfaces

Storyboard 7

Present OEM Pricing Discuss
Cost vs. Benefit Analysis

Storyboard 8

Summary of Key Points Call
to Action Questions

SAMPLE STORYBOARDS

Title: Microsoft Windows Supports Graphical PC Computing

Presenter: Terry Smith, account manager

Time and place: Microsoft Office, Room 306, August 15, at 9:00 A.M.

Presentation materials: Notebook PC, PowerPoint presentation, PC viewer, overhead projector (screen in room), laser pen, VCR, cables

Understandable

If your customers do not understand your presentation, they will not be able to use the information you present to support the conclusions that you are making.

If, for example, you use obscure technical terms, or make unfamiliar references, your customers may not be able to understand how you have justified your proposed solution.

Credible

If your presentation is not credible, your customers will tend to discount your conclusions.

For example, if you claim to have developed a perpetual-motion machine, people will be skeptical because such an invention would contradict widely accepted physical laws.

Reasonable

The easiest way to get your customers to agree with your ideas is to make a reasonable presentation.

It would be difficult to argue, for example, that someone should use a sledgehammer to drive finishing nails, or that a sixteen-bit application is going to perform as well as a thirty-two-bit application—even if it does.

Statistics can help you support your presentation logic. However, you should be very cautious about using inferential statistics, where conclusions about the general case are drawn from the results of a small sample. Most people are suspicious of statistics unless they reflect a representative sample size and unless a reputable, objective investigator compiles them.

Simple

People cannot remember everything they hear during a presentation, so it is important to make your presentation simple and easy to follow.

At Microsoft, when I had too much material to cover during my allotted time, I would use my presentation time to emphasize

---

PRESENTATION PLANNING WORKSHEET

Customer: Acme Corporation

Presentation/date and time: September 14, 9:00 A.M.

Objectives of presentation: Discuss integration, licensing, and production issues for Microsoft Windows

Participants (decisionmakers): Darlene Smith, VP of Engineering; Sam Almond, Director of Marketing; Sandy Johnson, VP of Operations

Participants' background/interest:

Smith: Discuss integration of Windows and PC hardware

Almond: Discuss licensing terms and joint PR announcement

Johnson: Discuss production issues, serial numbers for disks

Expected concerns or objections:

Smith: Needs recommendation/support for BIOS

Almond: Concerned about dual-boot option for Windows NT work stations

Johnson: Wants to know formats for all deliverables, wants help integrating product updates and setting up on-line software distribution

Presentation style (formal or informal):

Informal presentation—may need to meet separately with Sam Almond

Some of Darlene Smith's software engineers may attend the presentation

Presentation materials:

Technical backgrounder on Windows integration with PC hardware

Beta-code from next-generation Microsoft Office for demonstration

Special arrangements:

Check with Sam Almond to see if we need to bring an overhead projection system to display notebook output.

Next step/action plan:

- Verify meeting date and time with Sam Almond.
- Confirm reservations with Travel Center.

---

my most important points, and then cover the rest of my material in "take-home" handouts.

If you are tempted to cram details into your presentation, just remind yourself that most of those "important" details will be forgotten by the time your customers get back to their office.

EIGHT HOT TIPS ON PRESENTATION STYLE

1. Keep your sentences short and simple.
2. Use your normal speaking vocabulary.
3. Avoid passive constructions (e.g., you "may").
4. Don't overdo repetition to emphasize important points.
5. Read your presentation aloud to check grammar and style.
6. Try not to speak in a monotone.
7. Use normal hand gestures.
8. Speak loudly enough to be heard.

STEP 10. PRACTICE YOUR PRESENTATION

Before you make a presentation, you should practice it at least once, to make sure you can complete it in your allotted time and to verify that it is interesting, informative, and entertaining.

Most presenters are comfortable speaking at about 150 words per minute. If you speak much faster, you may overwhelm your customers; and if you speak much slower, your customers may lose interest in your presentation.

Whenever possible, you should run through your presentation in front of one or two friends or coworkers, to get feedback on whether they understood the information you presented and whether they can make any suggestions to help you improve your delivery.

Turn On the Video

At Microsoft we encouraged our account managers to use our videocameras and recorders to refine their presentation skills.

Some of our account managers were self-conscious about how they appeared on video. But we found that videotaping our account managers' presentations was the most effective way to help them identify bad habits, and to improve their confidence about speaking in front of groups.

Fear of Public Speaking

A recent study identified public speaking as the most frightening personal situation that most businesspeople can imagine.

If you suffer from stage fright, or feel you need additional practice developing and delivering presentations, you should consider joining your local Toastmasters™ club. Toastmasters can help you improve your presentation skills and overcome your fears about public speaking.

YOU'RE ONSTAGE NOW—PERFORMANCE TECHNIQUES

Handling Questions and Interruptions

Many people are reluctant to interrupt a presenter to ask questions, or to clarify a point, because they believe it is impolite, or that it will make them appear ill-informed or stupid.

You can help your customers feel more comfortable about asking questions by "inviting" them to ask questions during your presentation and by being respectful to everyone who asks a question or makes a comment.

When a customer asks me a question, I let him or her finish the comment or question before jumping in with a reply. Then I restate the question or comment if it was difficult for other people to hear, and acknowledge the contribution.

I have learned to not take my customers' questions or concerns personally. If I become defensive, I will lose credibility and may lose control of my presentation; but if I maintain an open dialogue, I can almost always move my sales presentation toward consensus and positive action.

Spontaneous Invention

When I used to go out on sales calls with our OEM account managers, I was surprised by the number of times I heard them make up answers to questions they were not prepared to answer, and use technical jargon incorrectly.

Most of the time our salespeople got away with their "spontaneous inventions," but occasionally their customers caught them.

Over the years I have learned that it is much more productive and much less stressful to use my energy to *prepare* for my sales calls, than to hope I can "wing it" when I meet with customers.

Handling Difficult Customers

The rambler: In most cases, customers who ramble on without coming to any relevant point can be "redirected" by thanking them for their comments, and then asking if anyone else at the meeting has had a similar experience or insight. With a bit of luck, someone at your meeting will pick up the conversation and move it back to a relevant topic.

Nowhere man: Customers who carry on private conversations during sales presentations, often in an annoying whisper, can generally be brought back into the meeting by pausing, at which time they may realize they are causing a distraction, or by asking them if they have something to contribute (they usually do).

The bully: If one of your customers' representatives is being abusive or intentionally divisive, you should acknowledge and address their concerns immediately, if you can do so, or schedule another meeting as soon as possible to discuss their concerns.

Mr. Unconcerned: When you lose your customers' attention or interest, it is almost always because you have gotten out of sync with their purchasing process.

The best way I have found to get back in sync with my customers, and to regain their attention, is to adopt a more enthusiastic presentation style, and to reestablish a dialogue by asking my customers questions to find out what they are really concerned about.

IF YOU DON'T KNOW YOUR PRODUCTS, WHAT CAN YOU SAY?

Many salespeople believe they do not need to understand how their products work to sell them. But taking the time to understand the underlying technologies behind your product will help you differentiate your product from similar products offered by your competitors.

I have gone on many sales calls with salespeople who can't demonstrate their products or explain how they work. To be honest, I am embarrassed for them.

At Microsoft my training group organized seminars every month to help our salespeople learn exactly what our products did; how they worked; and most importantly, how they provided useful solutions to meet our customers' needs.

The better prepared you are to answer your customers' questions, the more comfortable you will be making sales presentations, and the easier it will be for you to move business forward.

ARMED AND DANGEROUS

If you cannot address a customer's concern on your sales call, you will need to "get back to them." This delay increases the amount of time you will need to invest to attain your business objective—closing the sale—and may cause you to lose the sale if the delay enables a competitor to penetrate your account.

The most valuable sales tool we provided our account managers at Microsoft was a basic *sales kit* in a three-ring binder. Our account managers used the information in this kit to help them organize the information they needed to respond to their customers' concerns when they went out on a sales call.

The key to putting together an effective sales kit is to think through each step of your sales process, and then to assemble all of the information you will need to address your customers' concerns about your products and services.

For example, if you were in the computer business, your sales kit might contain the materials listed in the "Sales Kit for a Computer Salesperson," and a local area network configuration guide. The configuration guide might be a form, or it might be a program that was stored on an Internet server that you could access with a modem connected to a portable computer from your customers' offices.

If you don't already have your sales kit put together, it's time to get "armed and dangerous"!

SALES KIT FOR A COMPUTER SALESPERSON

- Company information
- Company history
- Company's mission statement
- Success stories
- References
- Company policies
- Product information (e.g., published on an Internet Web site)
- Pricing
- Availability
- Delivery and installation information
- Equipment leases
- Contracts and other forms
- Your business calendar (e.g., desktop information manager)
- Sales brochures
- Demonstration materials (e.g., auto-demo on Web site)
- Product samples
- Competitive information
- Customer interview (requirements/analysis) form
- Calculator, tape measure, or other tools
- Personal information
- Other information (e.g., a network configuration guide)

PRESENTING COST JUSTIFICATION INFORMATION

Before customers make a purchasing decision, they must justify the total expense for their purchase, including the costs of implementation, maintenance, support, and disposal.

Depending on your selling situation, you may need to present cost justification, and a payback analysis to support your recommendations.

For example, if you are selling a computer, and your customer asked you to explain the financial impact of purchasing a computer system, you might prepare the cost justification:

COST JUSTIFICATION FOR AUTOMATED ACCOUNTING SYSTEM *

Cost of Implementing Proposed System

Hardware and software costs	$ 30,000
System support and service costs	$18,000
Training costs	$ 15,000
System planning and acquisition costs	$ 1,000
Total cost of system	$ 64,000

After-tax Cost of System Depreciated Over 5 Years

Total cash out	$ 73,642
Recoverable cash	$ 28,457
Five-year cost	$ 45,185
Average monthly cost	$ 753

Payback Analysis

Improved billing cycle	$ 658
Reduced A/R labor	$ 11,440
Reduced warehouse labor	$ 9,360
Reduced sales labor	$ 26,900
Reduced bookkeeping labor	$ 11,220
Expected first-year savings	$ 59,798

Cost Justification

First-year cost savings	$ 59,789
First-year system cost	−$ 15,060
First-year savings	$ 44,738
Five-year cost savings	$298,990
Five-year system cost	−$ 19,460
Five-year system savings	$ 279,530

Secrets of Presenting Cost Justification

Many customers prepare their own cost justification analysis using the product acquisition and support costs supplied in their vendor's sales proposals. But in some cases it is necessary to present a formal cost justification for your proposed solution.

Unfortunately, cost justifications that are prepared by vendors are often ineffective in the selling process, because the assumptions that are used to justify financial payback, such as employee

---

* Adapted from Doug Dayton, *Computer Solutions for Business* (Redmond, Wash.: Microsoft Press, 1987).

productivity gains, are derived from hypothetical numbers, which, depending on a specific customer's situation, might or might not be valid.

I have found that the most effective way to present a cost justification is to *verify* that my customer agrees with all of the assumptions about costs and benefits that I plan to use to justify my proposed solution *before* I present my financial justification to them.

Verifying assumptions in your cost justification will enable you to stay in sync with your customer's purchasing process.

PRESENTING TECHNICAL INFORMATION

One of the many challenges our account managers at Microsoft faced was avoiding their customers' requests to do minitechnical seminars every time they did a sales presentation.

If you find yourself presenting detailed technical information, do a reality check and ask yourself if providing this information is necessary to move business forward, and if you are really the best person to provide this information.

I have found that when I start listing my product's features, or providing very detailed technical explanations to simple questions, I am usually getting out of sync with my customer.

The best way to get back in sync with a customer is to ask them questions to verify that you understand their needs and concerns, and then refocus your presentation on how your proposed solution can meet their specific needs. Then, if you have made any recommendations, you can verify that your customer understands and agrees with your recommendations before attempting to move the selling process forward.

The Devil Is the Details

When I first started making technical sales presentations, I tried to cover every detail I could think of. But as I became more confident of my own understanding of technical issues, I felt less compelled to demonstrate my knowledge by presenting a "core dump" of information to my customers.

And after presenting thousands of sales presentations, I realized that, in most cases, customers don't want to sit through exhaustive sales presentations; they want to learn just enough information to make them feel that they are prepared to make an informed buying decision.

Unfortunately, my revelation hasn't made my job any easier, because it is harder to deliver a simple, compelling executive-level presentation, and then be prepared to answer your customer's questions, than it is to deliver a detailed, scripted technical presentation.

When I thought about why this was the case, I realized that when I do an executive-level presentation, I create a dialogue with my customers, in contrast to simply presenting information without being aware of how my communication is being received.

Each customer has a unique personality, unique concerns, and a unique view of the world. And each customer will "hear" what you are saying in a different way. These differences are what makes sales an "art" and what will keep your sales presentations from ever getting boring.

PRESENTATION HANDOUTS THAT KEEP ON SELLING

At Microsoft, we used two types of handouts to summarize and reinforce the information we presented to our customers: *working handouts,* which were used during our presentation; and *background handouts,* which were distributed after our presentation, so they did not distract our customers.

Working handouts can obviate the need to take notes during a sales presentation, which is especially important when you want to be as persuasive as possible and when you want your customers' complete attention. Background handouts are useful for communicating lengthy, detailed information.

When I make formal sales presentations, I create my slides or transparencies using Microsoft PowerPoint, and then use PowerPoint to create a working handout. This technique works especially well if I include enough information on my slides (or in my handout notes) so they can be understood—and so they

VISUAL MEDIUM	STYLE	SIZE OF AUDIENCE	DESIGN COMPLEXITY PRODUCTION TIME	COST TO PRODUCE	EQUIPMENT REQUIRED
Flip charts	Informal	Fewer than 20	Drawing time	$10 (1 pad)	Flip chart Easel
Overheads	Informal	5 to 50	Drawing time plus use of office copier or laser printer	$20 (20 transparencies)	Overhead projector and screen or white wall
Slides	Formal	20 or more	Design, photography, plus 24 hours for service bureau	$120 (20 slides)	Slide projector and screen
Video	Moderate to formal	Depends on display	Days to weeks for scripting, production, duplication	$500 up (20-minute in-house video)	Videotape recorder and monitor
Multimedia	Informal to formal	Depends on display	Weeks to months for authoring, production, duplication	$5,000 up for CD master	CD-recorder/ player, multimedia computer, monitor

can keep selling—after my customer has forgotten many of the points I covered during my presentation.

CLIENT-CENTERED™ PRESENTATION TECHNIQUES

The primary objective of a sales presentation is to move business forward; it is not to educate your customers. The most effective way to move business forward is to ensure that your presentation facilitates an open dialogue.

The only way to maintain an open dialogue with customers is to give them an opportunity to discuss the ideas you have presented and to tell you whether you have overcome their concerns.

I have learned to ask lots of questions during my sales presentation and to *verify* that my customer understands what I have tried to communicate. Then, before closing my presentation, I verify that I have presented the information that my customer needs to make an informed purchasing decision; and I verify that my customer understands and agrees with any conclusions or recommendations I have presented.

- Use your sales presentation to help you arouse your customers' interest, provide information your customers need to help them make their purchasing decision, create a preference for your company's products and services, and maintain an open dialogue.

- Don't lose track of your presentation agenda; stay focused on topics that will enable you to help your customers make a purchasing decision.

- Your best chance of moving business forward is to keep your presentation as understandable, credible, reasonable, and simple as possible. Provide detailed information in response to your customers' questions.

- Don't lose track of the time. You are responsible for pacing your sales presentation so you have enough time to present your story and address your customers' questions.

- Use your customers' questions, responses, and nonverbal cues to help you evaluate their level of interest and agreement with your presentation. If necessary, adapt your presentation to address concerns or issues your customers raise during your presentation.

- Be prepared to reduce your sales presentation to a few minutes of "executive summary" in case your presentation time is cut short.

CHAPTER NINE

DEMONSTRATING SUCCESS

*"If we had had more time for discussion we should
probably have made a great many more mistakes."*
—**LEON TROTSKY**

In 1984, Microsoft began developing a graphical interface called
Windows for our MS-DOS operating system.

Digital Research, a competitor of Microsoft's, had already
developed a graphical interface that was beginning to attract the
interest of some of our OEM customers. And we were concerned
that they might be able to convince some of our largest OEMs to
begin selling their graphical interface with our operating system.

We realized that if any of our OEMs bundled Digital
Research's graphical interface with all of the PCs they shipped, it
could begin to build the momentum it needed to become a de
facto standard.

This admittedly worst-case scenario was unthinkable! But to
buy product development time for Windows, we needed to convince our OEMs that our upcoming Windows product was more
compelling than Digital Research's already shipping graphical
interface.

The Windows demonstration software our programmers developed to help us sell Windows could work with only a few miniapplications, such as a tic-tac-toe game and a clock, in different windows on a user's monitor. It could not work with any other programs.

Because our "smoke and Windows" demonstration was not really a functional prototype, we spent as much time as possible at our customer briefings talking about the future of graphical PC computing and about Microsoft's future plans for Windows.

I actually "invented" an imaginary software interface that I code-named "Magic" to help me explain how Windows would eventually enable different PC applications to share information.* Selling this future capability was critical because Digital Research's graphical interface was not designed to support this feature.

We worked very hard to position Windows as a viable alternative to Digital Research's product, and we ultimately prevailed. Our OEMs were tempted to ship Digital Research's graphical interface, but they trusted Microsoft to deliver the higher-performance product we previewed in our demonstration.

I believe that the main reason why our Windows demonstration was effective was that it provided an opportunity for our customers to *visualize* how using Windows could help them solve problems that Digital Research's graphical interface could not handle. But the primary objective of our demonstration was *not* to demonstrate that Windows could meet our customers' needs; it wasn't ready to do this. Our demonstration's primary objective was to help us maintain a positive working relationship with our OEMs and to continue to move our selling process forward, because we knew that if our OEMs believed our story— regardless of how little or how much of our product's functionality we could demonstrate—they would wait for us to complete our product.

---

* Windows' data-sharing capabilities became known as "DDE," which later evolved into "OLE" or Object Linking and Embedding. Over the past two years OLE has been reengineered into ActiveX components, which enable applications and data to be shared across global networks.

Which is exactly how Microsoft's now infamous "smoke and Windows" demonstration bought us the time we needed to ultimately win a multibillion-dollar revenue opportunity.

VISUALIZING YOUR SOLUTION

The main reason why demonstrations are such a powerful sales tool is that they provide an opportunity for your customers to see for themselves how your products can help them solve their problems. Once customers can visualize how using your product can help them solve their problems, they are usually well on the path to making a purchasing decision.

But demonstrations that involve complex technologies can be risky. If your demonstration is not convincing, you may lose the sale. And if your demonstration works properly, you may still "scare off" your customer if your products appear complex or difficult to manage.

This is why it is so important to learn your products "inside and out" and why it is so important to practice demonstrating your products until you are proficient enough to appear comfortable and relaxed during your demonstration.

The primary purpose of demonstrations and proposals is to support the recommendations you make to your customer.

DEMONSTRATIONS IN THE REAL WORLD

No matter how hard you prepare for a demonstration, it is impossible to predict everything that can go wrong.

I vividly remember demonstrating a computer application when a workman who was remodeling an office next door turned on an electric saw. The electrical noise caused by the workman's tool scrambled the memory in my computer. Each time I ran a report, the report was printed correctly, but the three times my customer touched the keyboard, the computer printed out pages of garbage, which is where my demonstration left my sale.

Every salesperson has experiences that teach them new lessons. I have learned, the hard way, to do demonstrations only when I am convinced that I absolutely need to do so to move business forward.

STEP 1: **KNOW YOUR OBJECTIVES**

Before you schedule a demonstration, you should determine what your objectives for doing the demonstration are.

I have made it a rule not to begin a demonstration until I understand exactly how my demonstration is going to move business forward.

STEP 2: **QUALIFY YOUR CUSTOMER**

I always qualify my customer's needs and analyze my user's requirements *before* I schedule a demonstration. And, whenever possible, I make sure that my customers understand exactly how my solution will solve their problem *before* demonstrating that my solution performs exactly as I have told them it would.

If you are not absolutely sure that your proposed solution can solve your customer's problem, you are not far enough along in the selling process to schedule a demonstration.

STEP 3: **EXPECT THE UNEXPECTED**

When I first joined IBM, I was invited to watch a demonstration for an important customer. One of our system engineers had set up a System/34 minicomputer to receive information from an IBM PC over a telephone connection. When the telephone connected to the minicomputer's modem began to ring, and ring—without being answered by the computer—the systems engineer calmly walked over to the telephone, picked it up, said "Hello," and pretended to have a brief conversation with a coworker.

This demonstration did not move business forward, but the systems engineer's quick thinking avoided a fiasco, and taught me to expect the unexpected.

The only practical solution I have come up with to avoid the unavoidable is to *practice* until I am convinced that my

DEMONSTRATION PLANNER

Presenter/salesperson: Terry Smith

Customer: Acme Corporation

Date: 9/23/97; **Time:** 9:45 A.M.

Location: Boardroom—234 Main St., Redmond, Wash.

Participants: Linda Harris, Tom Brown, and Peter Singer

Decisionmaker: Linda Harris

Objective for demonstration: Demonstrate AX-600 Internet server

Special interests: Acme wants to see how they can implement a commercial Internet server for their Catalog Sales Division. Acme is also interested in seeing our database connectivity options.

Products/equipment for demonstration: Bring notebook PC with remote access software and Internet browser.

Equipment checklist: Verify that our Web site is fully functional before performing demonstration.

Final checkout/run-through: Use the same procedure we used at Craft Publishing last week.

Support materials and personnel: Linda Baker will create a sample database of Acme Corporation's catalog items.

Special preparations: None

Fallback/disaster recovery: If our server goes down we can sign on to one of our customer's commercial Web servers. If our notebook PC isn't functional we can use one of Acme's PCs.

Solution/benefits to demonstrate:

Demonstrate advantage of Server Wizards to enable configuration.

Show how easy it is to build HTML pages from Acme's existing database files.

Show relative performance with 33.6 K modem and ISDN connection.

Action plan:

- Ask for commitment to purchase our server software.
- Schedule implementation planning meeting.
- Obtain permission to copy Acme's catalog database.
- Identify contact personnel.

demonstration really does work, and then to take a few minutes to *plan* my demonstration, which is how I developed my demonstration planner form.

STEP 4: **TRIAL CLOSE**

After I complete a demonstration, I *verify* that I have achieved my objectives and that my customer does not have any additional concerns.

If I have been able to address all of my customer's concerns, I feel that I have "earned" the right to ask for their business. But before I ask my customer for their business, I ask myself my five "keep myself honest" closing questions to verify where my customer is in the selling process:

1. Have I identified a real need?
2. Have I verified that my customers recognize this need?
3. Have I established the value of my proposed solution by demonstrating how it can help my customers improve operations, generate new business, reduce expenses, or develop new business opportunities?
4. Have I verified that my customers recognize this value?
5. Have I verified that my customers do not have any outstanding concerns that must be handled before they will be in a position to make an informed buying decision?

If I come up with five "yes" answers, I know that it is appropriate to do a trial close to move business forward.

My trial close often leads directly to a purchase decision, which is great. But in any case, my trial close helps me uncover any concerns my customer still has about the solution I have demonstrated, or about any other aspect of their purchasing process. Once I am aware of these concerns I can use Client-Centered™ communication skills to help me move the selling process forward.

STEP 5: **FOLLOW-UP**

After I complete a demonstration, I prepare a brief demonstration follow-up report, which describes any follow-up actions that must be handled to satisfy my customer's needs, and to move business forward.

DEMONSTRATION FOLLOW-UP

Customer: Acme Corporation

Date: 9/23/97

Presenter/salesman: Terry Smith

Demonstration objectives:

Acme wanted to see how they could implement a commercial Internet server for their Catalog Sales Division. Acme was also interested in seeing our database connectivity options.

Were objectives achieved?

The demonstration went very well. Acme was excited about our database Wizard feature.

Outstanding or unresolved concerns:

Acme is concerned that our server will not scale to support their database. Acme's database is about twice as large as that of Chrome Corporation (our largest installation).

Problems during the demonstration: Our original connection was very slow; however, everything worked well.

Follow-up Action:

Ask Chrome Corporation if we can use them as a reference.

If necessary, agree to implement system subject to performance requirements.

Customer commitment:

Expect commitment in 10 _X_ / 30 ___ / 60 ___ **days**

Purchase Agreement Signed: ___ / ___ / ___

What can be done to improve next demonstration?:

I would like to have at least one digital modem line dedicated to demonstrations to ensure maximum performance.

I like to transfer my demonstration follow-up action items into my daily planner to help me manage and prioritize my selling activities.

STEP 6: **PUT IT IN WRITING**

The more complex the information you need to communicate, the more beneficial it is to provide a written analysis, "white paper," or sales proposal to support your recommendations.

VERBAL COMMUNICATIONS	WRITTEN COMMUNICATIONS
Immediate action is required	No immediate action is required
Decisionmakers can attend a presentation	Difficult for decisionmakers to attend a presentation
Customer can make decisions with presented information	Customer needs time to consider facts before making a decision
Discussion is important	Discussion is not important at this stage
No permanent record is needed	A permanent record is necessary for legal reasons
The topic is controversial	The topic is routine
An emotional appeal will help convince decisionmakers	An emotional appeal is unnecessary
Can requalify customer as you present new ideas	Cannot requalify customer
Can verify your communication during your presentation	Cannot verify your communication

COMPELLING PROPOSALS

A sales proposal can help you document your recommendations, promises, and guarantees, and can help you provide the information and assurances your customer needs to help them make an informed purchase decision. But sales proposals are not magic bullets. A sales proposal will not move business forward unless it provides compelling business reasons for your customer to make a purchasing decision. And a proposal that is developed too early in the sales process can derail your selling efforts.

Experienced purchasers know that the more information they have about different vendors' pricing, delivery, and other purchasing factors, the better position they will be in to negotiate with suppliers. So most customers will greet a salesperson's offer to send them a proposal with an enthusiastic offer to "consider it." However, when a customer agrees to "consider" your proposal it does not necessarily mean that they are ready to make a purchasing decision.

20 TIPS FROM THE TRENCHES
FOR DOING EFFECTIVE DEMONSTRATIONS

It's impossible to summarize everything I have learned about doing demonstrations in a few pointers, but here are my favorites:

1. Practice presenting your demonstration. Practice error recovery. Practice handling common concerns.

2. Be prepared to answer detailed questions about your product's features and functionality, installation, implementation, management, and maintenance.

3. Verify that your customer's decisionmakers will be able to attend your demonstration.

4. Verify that you can demonstrate a solution to your customer's problem *before* beginning your demonstration.

5. Determine the best place to perform your demonstration—it may, for example, be more compelling to perform a demonstration at your customer's offices, or at a customer site, than at your sales office.

6. Verify your customer's interests and concerns before beginning your demonstration. Then use your customer's interests as a "flight plan."

7. Organize your demonstration to answer your customer's concerns in a logical manner.

8. If you cannot demonstrate the product or solution you are recommending, try to demonstrate a product or solution that is representative of the one you are proposing.

9. Keep your demonstration as short and as simple as possible.

10. Avoid overly technical explanations and industry jargon.

11. Don't use your customer's request to "show us everything" as an excuse to do a core dump of every product feature and fact you know.

12. Keep your demonstration on schedule, and don't ramble on.

13. When you discuss features, emphasize benefits.

14. Verify that you are addressing your customer's concerns as you proceed through your demonstration.

15. Maintain an open dialogue with your customer.

16. Stay calm and project confidence.

17. Verify that you have answered all of your customer's concerns before you complete your demonstration.

18. Use customer and industry references to help overcome any concerns your customer may have about your company's ability to deliver a solution that will meet their specific requirements.

19. Sell positive; don't attack your competitors. And don't discuss competitors' products unless you are absolutely sure that your information is correct and up-to-date.

20. Ask for your customer's business if your demonstration answers all of their purchasing concerns.

The better qualified your customer is, the easier it will be for you to create a compelling "win-win" proposal. So in most cases you should not create a proposal until you are prepared to do a trial close.

Drafting Proposals

All proposals are not created equal. *Compelling* proposals can move business forward and help you close sales. Poorly crafted proposals can introduce new concerns about your company's products or services and can disaffect a potential customer from wanting to do business with your company.

Proposals can be drafted in any style, but most proposals are based on one of three classic approaches:

- "We want to solve your problem."
- "We have the best product/service for your needs."
- "We can solve your problem as well as our competitors for less money."

Proposals typically include a summary of your customer's needs or requirements; information about products and services that are being recommended; information about installation, implementation, and after-sale support; an analysis of why a specific solution is being recommended; and information on pricing, cost justification, customer training, and product delivery.

Some companies use their proposal as a work order, which becomes a legally binding agreement when their customer signs it. I have always preferred to have my customers issue a separate purchase order, but it is common to use proposals as work orders in some industries.

You will probably not need to include everything in the sample proposal format in your own sales proposals, but the outline, below, which I developed at Microsoft, can help you get started.

Boilerplate Proposals

Boilerplate proposals are like form letters; to create one, you cut and paste your customer information into standard "boilerplate"

PROPOSAL FORMAT

Executive summary
Scope of work (need)
Proposed solution
- Summary of work and/or requirements planning to date

Explain solution
Financial benefits and cost justification
- Other benefits
- Potential risks

Product specifications
- Detail features
- Specify benefits
- Product reviews/comparisons

Company information
- Qualifications
- References
- Financial references

Terms of sale
- Price
- Delivery
- Default penalties
- Additional requirements and/or supplies
- Third-party work
- Deadlines for acceptance
- Guarantees and warranties

Follow-up action plan
- Installation, implementation, and support issues
- Customer resource and training requirements

Purchasing agreement or work order

text. Proposal boilerplate usually covers information about a company's experience and past success, product information, installation and implementation planning guidelines, service policies, customer agreements, and other information that is consistent from one proposal to another and is time-consuming to redraft.

At Microsoft, we had access to most of the marketing materials that were prepared and distributed by our product marketing groups, such as product specification sheets, comparative product analyses, independent analysts' reports, and published product reviews. We included these materials in our proposals to help us support any claims we made about our product's features, performance, and user satisfaction.

Developing proposals with boilerplate text saved us a great deal of time, helped ensure that we communicated a professional image to our customers, and helped us prevent problems that could result from omitting critical information, such as legal disclaimers.

If your company's products are targeted to solve a specific problem, it will be relatively easy for you to create proposal boilerplate. However, the more customized your company's solutions are, the less helpful boilerplate text will be.

Competitive Requests for Proposal

Most large companies use formal requests for proposals or "RFPs" to help them make important purchasing decisions. The format of different RFPs are as varied as the companies that send them out, but most RFPs request suppliers to propose a solution to one or more problems, and to explain why accepting their proposed solution is in the company's best interest.

Responding to an RFP can be very time-consuming. So it is frustrating to respond to an RFP unless you have a good chance of winning your customer's business.

Over the years, I have learned to qualify every RFP I receive. It is usually fairly easy for me to verify a customer's purchasing authority and time frame for their purchase by reviewing the purchasing process specified in their RFP. The harder task is qualifying a customer's needs and evaluating whether they have enough money budgeted to purchase my company's products.

To qualify my customer's needs, I match each requirement in their RFP with the products and services my company offers. If it is not completely obvious how my company can address their needs, I create a table or chart that maps my customer's specific requirements to my product's features and my company's services.

15 TIPS FOR PREPARING EFFECTIVE PROPOSALS (AT IT AGAIN!)

1. Do not draft a proposal until you have verified that you understand and can respond to all of your customer's needs.

2. Whenever possible, review key elements of your proposal with your customer before you submit it. This will help you avoid surprises such as "We had no idea your product wasn't compatible with our current system!"

3. Many business executives do not take the time to read long proposals—they "scan" them. To help ensure that your proposal is considered, you can include a brief, one- to five-page executive summary that describes your proposed solution, addresses your customer's primary concerns, and specifies costs and other important business terms.

4. At Microsoft, we often sent our customers detailed, personalized letters that covered the information that would normally be put in an executive summary, instead of creating formal proposals. It worked!

5. There is no point in putting detailed technical information into a proposal if the proposal is being sent to a business manager who does not have the technical background or the time to read it.

6. At Microsoft, we used "white papers" (reports) to provide the detailed information that our OEMs' technical personnel needed to understand and evaluate our products. Most of our white papers were created internally, but we would occasionally hire outside consultants or research companies to draft reports when it was more appropriate for our marketing materials to be developed by an objective source.

7. In some situations you can team up with your customer's personnel to develop product specifications for their proposal. Helping your customer specify their requirements requires extra work, but it can ensure that your products satisfy all of your customer's purchasing requirements. This process is very common with businesses that market to government agencies.

8. Make sure that a coworker who reads your proposal can understand your customer's problem, your proposed solution, and the logic behind your need analysis and cost justification.

9. Have someone double-check your arithmetic.

10. Avoid referencing any statistic, or making any product comparisons, unless you know exactly where your facts came from.

11. If your proposal requires any custom work to be done, or any "off the price list" services, have your proposal approved by your manager before submitting it to your customer.

12. Hand-deliver your proposal; you may have an opportunity to meet with your customer's decisionmakers.

13. Proposals can serve as legal contracts. If your proposal is a work order, include a time limit on acceptance.

14. Proposals that appear "custom"-written are more likely to be studied, and are more credible than less personalized proposals. Make references to your customer throughout your proposal, and delete any boilerplate that is not relevant.

15. Use a laser or high-quality ink-jet printer and attractive folders or binders to give your proposal a professional "published" image.

Next, I try to identify any requirement in the RFP that may eliminate my company from competition. For example, I might not be able to provide adequate financing terms, or to deliver specific brands of system components.

If I cannot meet one or more of my customer's requirements, I contact my customer to verify whether they have identified any suppliers who can meet all of their requirements, and whether my limitations will eliminate my products from consideration *before* drafting a response to their RFP.

Finally, if I have any doubt about my prospective customer's financial condition, I check their credit rating.

No Dialogue, No RFP

I like to contact my customer to verify receipt of their RFP and to clarify any issues, terms, or requirements I don't understand completely.

Then, depending on the situation, I try to schedule a meeting with the people who will be using my products or services, to help me better understand their needs and to get "inside" information about how my proposed solution compares to those of my competitors.

Qualify Your Competition

People are usually more comfortable doing business with people they have worked with in the past. So I always ask my customers whether they have a preferred supplier. If they do, I carefully evaluate my chance of winning their business before investing time responding to their RFP.

Don't Make Assumptions

RFPs are often evaluated by purchasing managers who are unfamiliar with my company's policies and who are unfamiliar with different suppliers' products. So I never expect my customer to "read between the lines" in my proposal, or to make any assumptions about whether my company will provide any products or services that are not specified in my proposed solution.

In other words, I strive to make my proposal as clear and as WYSIWYG as possible.*

If You Respond, Make It Compelling

A response to an RFP can help me move business forward by "proving" my company's success in similar situations. The best way I have found to do this is to supply written testimonials, and the names of customers who are willing to confirm the quality and value of my company's products and service.

Beating Competitive Proposals

I used to panic when I found out that one of my proposals was rejected in favor of a competitor's proposal. Now, I don't panic; I get back to work. I have learned that decisions can be changed!

When you get the big NO, the first thing to do is to ask your customer to explain why they chose your competitor's solution. It is possible that their analysis was in error and that your proposed solution is better suited to their needs.

Then ask your customer if you can review a copy of the winning proposal. You may find information that is incorrect, which you can use to change your customer's mind. And, in any case, you can use information from your competitor's proposal to help you compete with them for future business.

As a last resort, if you are absolutely convinced that your customer is making a serious mistake by choosing another supplier, you can go around your customer's decisionmaker. However, this course of action is risky. It is almost always better to give up a sale than to generate animosity with people you will need to work with in the future.

Over the years I have learned that any opportunity to sell into a company provides an opportunity to build personal relationships and to demonstrate my company's quality and service. So I like to check periodically to see if my "lost" prospect is sat-

---

* WYSIWYG is a common computer acronym that means "what you see is what you get." To the best of my knowledge, this term did not originate in Missouri.

isfied with my competitors' products and services. My tenacity has helped me uncover many selling opportunities.

Truth and Time

When you make a presentation, do a demonstration, or draft a proposal, you should avoid making any statement that can be easily challenged or is not completely true.

It is relatively painless to adopt this policy; however, being completely truthful can be tricky, because "truth" may be time-sensitive.

For example, if you are citing a quotation or a test report in a proposal, you might say: "According to a product comparison published by the Independent Testing Service *last June*, Microsoft's C++ compiler ran 15 percent faster than our competitor's C++ compiler." By "time-stamping" your reference you can ensure that your proposal is truthful, even if your competitor releases an improved version of their product after the product comparison you referenced in your proposal was published.

CLIENT-CENTERED™ DEMONSTRATIONS AND PROPOSALS

Demonstrations and proposals are just vehicles to move the dialogue you established with your customer forward. Not an end—just a means.

- Use your demonstrations and proposals to help arouse your customer's interest; provide information that your customer needs to help them make their purchasing decision; create a preference for your company's products and services; and most importantly, maintain an open, honest dialogue.
- Don't lose track of your agenda; stay focused on topics that will enable you to help your customer make a purchasing decision.
- Your best chance of moving business forward is to keep your demonstrations and proposals as understandable, credible, reasonable, and simple as possible. Provide

detailed information in response to your customer's specific concerns and questions.

- Use your executive summary and your closing statement to summarize the main points you have made and to provide a synopsis of your recommendations.

CHAPTER TEN

ADVANCED SELLING SKILLS

*"When I was young I observed that nine out of
ten things I did were failures, so I did ten
times more work."*

—BERNARD SHAW

At Microsoft, about 80 percent of our OEM revenues came from
fewer than 20 percent of our OEM customers. So to better
address our largest customers' needs, we divided our OEM
accounts between a regular OEM accounts sales team and a
strategic OEM accounts sales team. Our regular OEM account
managers handled five to twenty OEM accounts, while our
strategic OEM account managers spent all their time working
with just one or two of our largest OEMs.

Our strategic OEMs required more sales and marketing
resources than our regular OEM accounts, because they involved
more sales contacts, multiple sales locations, relationships with
third-party suppliers, and a more complex purchasing process.
And the cost of making a sale to one of our strategic OEMs was
many times greater than to one of our regular OEM customers.
But the larger profits earned from selling to our strategic OEM

accounts more than justified the extra resources and effort needed to provide pre- and postsales support.

Focusing your selling efforts on your own "major" customers can lead to greater profitability if you can meet larger customers' demands for pre- and postsales service and support.

In this chapter you will learn how to do a major account resource audit to determine whether you are ready to begin selling to major accounts. Then you will learn how major accounts make purchasing decisions, and learn some of my favorite techniques for selling to larger companies and facilitating sales meetings. It's a busy chapter, so get ready!

MAJOR ACCOUNT RESOURCE AUDIT

The strategic OEM accounts group at Microsoft had all the resources it needed to meet its customers' needs, and was extremely profitable. However, many companies do not have the selling resources they need to market successfully to large national or multinational accounts.

You can use the major account resource audit table to help you determine whether your company is ready to begin marketing to major accounts.

MAJOR ACCOUNT PURCHASE PROCESS

When you work with major accounts, you will have to take the time to understand and work through each customer's unique, and often circuitous, purchasing process.

Multiple Approval Levels
The purchasing process in larger companies usually includes multiple approval levels. For example, many large companies require a written purchase requisition to be approved before "routine" purchase orders can be released to an established supplier.

Multilevel Selling
Depending on your situation, you may need to work with people at all levels of your customer's organization to move the selling process forward.

MAJOR ACCOUNT RESOURCE AUDIT
• Do you have sufficient cash reserves or cash flow from other business activities to finance a long selling cycle?
• Do you have the cash reserves or the credit line you need to finance large purchases?
• Can you increase production or stock products fast enough to satisfy the needs of major accounts?
• Can you provide a broad enough range of support services to service major accounts?
• Can you provide competitive prices, volume discounts, financing, and other terms of sale to satisfy major accounts?
• Do your sales personnel have enough time to meet with multiple sales contacts within a major account's organization? If not, do you plan to hire additional major account sales and support personnel?
• Do you have a reliable source of referrals or marketing partners that can introduce you into major accounts?
• Do you have an efficient way to qualify major accounts?
• Do you have high-quality sales brochures and other presentation materials?
• Has your market research convinced you that marketing your products and services into major accounts is the best use of your selling time?
• Have you developed a business/marketing plan for your major account business?

It is common, for example, for decisionmakers in a large organization to delegate responsibility for the buying process to lower-level purchasing personnel who do not have the authority to "sign off" on purchase orders.

If you treat people the way you would like them to treat you, you will have advocates on every floor!

Formal Sales Proposals

Large companies often expect to get written sales proposals from their suppliers. In some situations you will need to prepare a written sales proposal and then present your proposal to your customer's decisionmakers at one or more formal sales presentations.

Commitment to Current Suppliers

Large customers are usually reluctant to adopt new products or technologies, and tend to remain with reliable suppliers. So you will need to present *compelling* reasons to convince your customers to replace established competitors.

Major accounts make three types of purchases: *replacement* purchases, *similar product* purchases, and purchases that require *new products* to solve problems that have not been addressed before.

A replacement purchase is made when a customer reorders the same product or service. For example, a company might reorder a disposable laser printer cartridge. If a company's current supplier has done a good job of meeting their needs, they have a good chance of maintaining an ongoing supplier relationship with their customer. If, however, the supplier's service level has been poor, or if they are not able to justify premium pricing, they may lose their account to competitors.

Customers can also order a product or service that is similar to other products or services they are currently using. For example, a company might want to upgrade their automated accounting system with a system that enables them to bar-code their inventory. If the new customer's requirements can be satisfied by their current accounting system supplier, and the supplier has provided good service and maintained a positive working relationship with them, they will usually be the preferred suppliers for similar products or services.

And lastly, customers can purchase new products and services that solve a problem, or replace or augment a task that has not been addressed before. For example, a company that does their bookkeeping using an outside service bureau may decide to implement an automated accounting system in-house. In this case, businesses typically look at several competitive solutions to help them determine which solution, and ultimately which supplier, is best able to satisfy their needs.

When I worked at Microsoft, almost all of our OEMs were new solution purchasers. But as the PC industry matured, we had the opportunity to renew our OEMs' software licensing

BUYING SITUATION	CURRENT SUPPLIER'S OBJECTIVES	NEW SUPPLIER'S OBJECTIVES
Repurchase	• Reinforce supplier relationship by providing good support and service • Maintain position as preferred supplier	• Most difficult new business opportunity • Provide lower-cost, higher-value solution • Use any selling opportunity to become preferred supplier
Similar purchase	• Rapid response to customer's new problems or concerns	• Offer cost-effective, high-value solution • Use any selling opportunity to become preferred supplier
New Solution	• Monitor changing needs in organization • Identify new selling opportunities • Provide leadership and coordinate task and/or problem resolution • Initiate requirement planning process	• Build positive relationship with buyer • Identify needs in organization • Participate in requirement planning process • Use any selling opportunity to become preferred supplier

agreements, and to sell them new software products we had developed, such as Microsoft Word, Excel, and PowerPoint.

Working with Multiple Contacts

Learning how to work with multiple sales contacts in your major accounts will have a profound impact on your selling success. Each sales contact you work with in your customer's organization can help you push the sales process forward, or can become an obstacle to making a sale.

You will need to learn how to identify each contact's role in your customer's decision process and how to encourage each contact to help you achieve your sales objectives for their business.

Your sales contacts may include the person who initiated contact with your customer, a technician or consultant who can

SALES CONTACT	TYPICAL JOB TITLE	INVOLVEMENT IN SALES PROCESS
Initiator	• President • General manager • Line manager implementation	• Recognizes need for product or service • Often "champions"
Decisionmaker	• President • VP of operations • Technical manager	• Approves purchase
Influencer	• Technical support • Outside consultant • Manager, information systems • C.P.A.	• Influence buying decision
Purchaser	• Purchasing manager • Administrative manager	• Administers purchasing procedure
Gatekeeper	• Administrative assistant • Corporate purchasing administrator	• Controls contact with influencer and decisionmaker
Users	• Personnel who use products or services • Support personnel	• Needs must be satisfied

influence the purchasing process, a "gatekeeper" who prevents you from reaching the company's decisionmakers, and people who use your products or services to help them achieve their work objectives.

Each sales contact in the purchasing process has specific professional and personal concerns. By understanding these concerns, you can encourage each contact to support your selling process.

If, for example, your sales contact is an influencer, they will be concerned about the quality and value of the solution they recommend, but they will also be concerned that a supplier or product they recommend might cause problems and tarnish their reputation.

The best way to address an influencer's personal agenda is to present compelling reasons why doing business with your company is a low-risk strategy with a very high likelihood of success.

SALES CONTACT	PROFESSIONAL AGENDA	PERSONAL AGENDA
Initiator	• Improve operations • Wants credit for successful implementation	• Doesn't want supplier or solution to reflect badly on his or her recommendation
Decisionmaker	• Responsible for • purchasing decision	• Wants solution to work well and provide a rapid payback on company's investment
Influencer	• Wants to appear informed and knowledgeable	• Doesn't want supplier or solution to reflect badly on his or her recommendation
Purchaser	• Wants to get the best deal possible for his or her company	• Doesn't want to be responsible for paying more for a solution than other purchasers
Gatekeeper	• Wants recognition of importance in selling situation before allowing contact with decisionmakers	• Doesn't want to be perceived as obstacle to business, once a decision has been made
Users	• Want solution that makes their work easier, faster, more enjoyable	• Concerned about learning new systems • Don't want job eliminated by solution

IDENTIFYING CUSTOMER CONTACTS

At Microsoft, we often worked with ten or twenty different people in a customer's organization. It was a challenge to remember the *names* of all of our customer's personnel, much less what their specific interests and concerns were.

I found it helpful to create simple customer contact tables, which included the name, title, role, primary objectives, and specific concerns of each individual involved in my accounts.

Taking the time to create these customer contacts tables enabled me to remember everyone's name, and their role in the selling process. This saved me a great deal of embarrassment

SALES CONTACT	SELLING OBJECTIVES	FOLLOW-UP
Initiator	• Maintain personal relationship with initiator • Encourage initiator to be proactive in the purchasing process	• Work with initiator to identify new selling opportunities • Cultivate to become a reference
Decisionmaker	• Sell on benefits of proposed solution, including increased profits, decreased operating costs, improved customer service and sales	• Review benefits that have resulted from implementing solution • Cultivate to become a reference
Influencer	• Sell the validity of your proposed solution • Reference sell support capabilities	• Cultivate to become a reference
Purchaser	• Convince that they are getting best possible deal	• Offer favorable terms as established customer
Gatekeeper	• Convince that they will be recognized for supporting proposed solution	• Encourage gatekeeper to become an initiator for new opportunities
Users	• Convince that solution is easy to implement • Sell ongoing training and support	• Encourage "user suggestions" to help improve new products and relationship

and helped me get a top-down view of the "people" side of my selling situation.

After I completed a customer contacts table, I would often realize that I was "forgetting" about one or more individuals who could help me move the selling process forward. For example, in the sample customer table, there is no attorney mentioned. Our OEM customer's in-house counsel was usually involved with the purchasing process. Completing this table could remind me to verify whether my customer's attorney had an opportunity to review our contracts.

NAME	TITLE	ROLE IN PROCESS	PRIMARY OBJECTIVES	SPECIFIC CONCERNS
Bob Smith	VP, software	Decisionmaker	• Provide best operating system environment	• Interoperability • Integration of ROM BIOS
Ana Main	Software manager	Technical influencer	• Integrate OS with hardware	• Documentation for OS
Loren Peters	Senior VP, sales and marketing	Decisionmaker	• Provide competitive, cost-effective products • Time to market	• Stability • Support for industry standards
Tom Baker	Controller	Contract administration	• Easy to administer royalty payments process	• OEM serial number

SELLING TO MAJOR ACCOUNTS

Selling to major accounts requires special communication and organizational skills.

Communication Skills

Major accounts often have poor internal communications. You cannot assume that your sales contacts are in communication with one another, or that they are aware of promises or commitments that have been made to you by other people in their organization.

I have learned to avoid problems that arise from this type of miscommunication by making it a habit to copy important information to each sales contact in my customer's organization.

Organizational Skills

Working with major accounts requires great attention to detail. You will need to maintain account files, including contact information, account analysis forms, meeting and telephone notes, and copies of all written communications and work orders.

Documenting your selling activities is time-consuming, but it is the only practical way to ensure effective communications between or among your sales team members, and continuity when major accounts are transferred to other account managers.

At Microsoft, our account managers maintained a file for each one of their OEM customers, which contained meeting reports, teleconference notes, and copies of all written communications, including copies of important E-mail messages.

This documentation was necessary because of the complexity of the OEM selling cycle. Many people were involved from different departments and divisions within our customers' organization, and negotiations often took place over the course of several weeks or months.

Vendor Relationships

Major accounts often have specific policies to control relationships with outside suppliers. For example, some companies allow their suppliers to work with as many individuals in their organization as necessary to expedite business, while other companies restrict suppliers' contact to specific purchasing personnel.

Similarly, some companies feel it is acceptable for a supplier to give small presents, or to purchase business lunches for their staff as long as they are not large enough to be seen as a bribe. Other companies will not allow their employees to accept any presents or free meals.

In today's information age it is frustrating to work with companies that do not allow suppliers access to their employees' direct telephone extensions and E-mail addresses; but many companies restrict access to these numbers to their own personnel.

I have found that it is best to respect my customers' policies regarding supplier relationships, regardless of how conservative or liberal they are.

If a customer learns that a salesperson is trying to "go around" their policies, they can become very reactive. But as the selling relationship progresses, and a customer begins to have confidence in their salesperson's honesty and judgment, they will usually be very open about sharing any information, including telephone extension numbers and E-mail access, that is relevant to maintaining their business relationship.

FACILITATING A SALES MEETING

Facilitating sales meetings with a large number of participants from your customer's company is the ultimate test for your Client-Centered™ communication skills. The stakes can be high, the people at your meeting may have varied or conflicting concerns and agendas, and it may be all but impossible to keep your customers focused on moving their purchasing process forward, rather than becoming sidetracked by unimportant details.

Introductions

If the people who are attending your meeting have not met before, you can save time and embarrassment by providing name tags or small table signs to identify everyone.

If there are more than twelve people at your meeting, you will need to use your judgment about whether to introduce each participant. You may, for example, just introduce senior personnel and presenters.

Rules of the Road

After your introductions, you should review your meeting's agenda and describe any rules you have for participation. For example, you might limit presentations to five minutes, or ask your customers to hold their questions until after your formal presentation has been made.

Stay Focused

It is your job to make sure that the discussion stays focused and that all of the essential information or ideas necessary to attain your meeting's objectives are introduced and discussed.

If important issues or topics are not being discussed, it may be necessary to review your meeting's objectives to refocus the discussion.

Watch the Time

You must also pay attention to how much time has passed. Depending on the situation, you may need to ask your presenters to move on to other topics if you feel that too much time has been spent on one issue.

You can often save time by summarizing long discussions and by asking customers who are becoming polarized in their views or deadlocked on one or more issues to hold their concerns until you can present additional information or schedule another meeting.

Keep It Moving

It is always a good idea to prepare questions in advance, to help you keep your meeting moving forward. If some of the participants are shy, or do not express themselves well, you can ask them questions to draw out their ideas and opinions.

For example, you might ask a customer what they think about a specific point that has been made, or how they think a specific action might impact their business. Or you might summarize the points that have been discussed, and then go around the table to verify how each customer feels about specific points or issues.

Similarly, after an outspoken individual or group has stated their position, it is helpful to ask the other participants if there is anyone who holds a different view.

Meeting Ergonomics

Conversations tend to go back and forth across a table, rather than around it. Round tables are ideal for encouraging peer-to-peer discussions, while rectangular tables allow more dominant individuals to take power positions at the end of the table, or in the middle of one side.

It may seem silly, but you can make your customers feel more comfortable by encouraging them to sit in power positions during your sales presentation.

Majority Rule

Some people will cling to an idea or position long after the rest of the people in the group have come to a decision. There is nothing wrong with holding a minority opinion, but at some point you will need to move your meeting from discussion to consensus to develop a plan of action and to move business forward.

Unfortunately, unless you have a strong advocate in your customer's company, it may be politically impossible for you to move business forward without appearing to be self-serving.

At Microsoft, I learned that one of the best ways to move a meeting toward consensus was to encourage one or more of my customer's personnel to restate supportive comments about my products or proposed solution at our meetings. This enabled me to restate my recommendations in a way that supported my customer's personnel's own position.

Leverage Your Communications

One of the best ways to leverage your selling time is to present multiple messages during your sales presentations. For example, if you make a sales presentation to discuss a new product, you might also discuss another issue, such as an upcoming training class, at the same time.

Similarly, if you send out a company newsletter that provides technical support information, you might use your newsletter to help introduce a new product your company is announcing or announce an upcoming sales promotion.

Delivering multiple communications can help you save time and provide a higher level of customer service.

MAJOR ACCOUNTS CAN YIELD MAJOR PROFITS

Focusing your selling efforts on large customers can help you generate greater profits than working with a larger number of smaller accounts. But to be successful, you will need to use your Client-Centered™ communication skills to help you work with multiple contacts within your customer's organization.

As you become experienced at major account selling, you will develop your own "creative" sales techniques. But over time, you will realize that the real "secret" of selling to major accounts is using Client-Centered™ communication skills to stay in sync with your customer's purchasing process.

In the next chapter you will learn how to find out what your competitors are up to, and learn how to leverage your existing customer base to help you build sales momentum.

STAYING COMPETITIVE— MARKET DOMINATION REVISITED

"A foot in the door is worth two on the desk."
—SALES MAXIM

Microsoft has become a very powerful company, but it still faces many challenges. Microsoft makes costly mistakes and is certainly not "unstoppable."

Intuit Software, for example, has been able to dominate the financial software category despite several attempts by Microsoft to break their control of this market. And Microsoft has been unsuccessful with a number of ill-conceived products, including the OS/2 operating system, which it codeveloped with IBM, and a "friendly" user interface program called "BOB" that most PC users found annoying.

A year ago, many industry pundits were predicting the "fall" of Microsoft to "open" Internet-based computing. But Microsoft has managed to change course, integrate Internet technologies across its entire product line, and emerge as a dominant force in the "network computing" era.

Microsoft's Internet success has not, despite some curmud-geons' claims, been based on unfair business practices. Microsoft's turnaround has resulted from hard work and the dedication to delivering new technologies and solutions that have enabled Microsoft to maintain its leadership position in the PC industry.*

To maintain its leadership position, Microsoft, like other successful businesses, has made difficult decisions about where to allocate its marketing resources. To help it make these decisions, it has invested millions of dollars in account management, market research, and planning.

Your business may not be in a position to invest millions of dollars in account planning and market research. But in this section you will learn how you can obtain valuable marketing information about your competitors, use the Internet to help you qualify prospective customers, and build a competitive matrix to help you focus your sales efforts, with little or no cost beyond the value of your time.

COMPETITIVE INTELLIGENCE

At Microsoft I learned that the best way to get information about my competitors was to stay "close" to the market I was selling into. I took time each month to talk with customers, suppliers, and industry consultants, to read industry newspapers and magazines, and to evaluate competitive software products.

---

* The computer industry is largely dependent on standards to facilitate interoper-ability between hardware and software components from different suppliers. And the success of software products in the market is largely a function of their ability to support these standards.

In some areas, such as PC operating systems, Microsoft (with its Windows operating systems) defines the industry standard and controls how other computer companies must design their products. But in other areas, such as Internet protocols and electronic commerce, independent standards committees are defining standards, and Microsoft's competitors have a good chance of dominating these markets.

**COMPETITIVE MARKET ANALYSIS
IS AN ONGOING SALES SUPPORT ACTIVITY**

Competitive Information Sources

- Local, regional, and national newspapers
- Business publications (*Business Week*, *Forbes*, etc.)
- Trade publications
- Trade associations
- Chambers of commerce
- Annual reports/stock prospectuses
- Bank/credit reports
- Academic institutions
- Government publications
- Standard & Poor's corporate record and industry surveys
- Dun & Bradstreet reference book of corporate management
- *Moody's Industrials* manual
- *Forbes* annual report on business
- *Encyclopedia of Business Information Sources*
- Private consulting and research firms
- Trade shows
- Personal contacts
- Company resources
- Past employees
- Job-seekers
- Suppliers
- On-line news sources
- Internet

There are many other information sources you can also use to gather intelligence about your competitors. And many of these information sources are free—for the cost of your research time.

For example, if your competitor's stock is publicly traded, you can request copies of their annual report and their 10-K. And a phone call to your trade association or to your local chamber of commerce can provide information on thousands of companies in your market.

Internet Magic

When I worked at Microsoft, the Internet was primarily used as a worldwide electronic mail system. Today, the Internet is the richest source of information in the world.

Before I make a sales call, I visit my customer's Internet site to get as much information as I can about my customer's business. Then I search additional Web sites for information that can help me understand my customer's needs.* For example, if my customer develops software for PCs, I might visit *PC Week* magazine's Web site to review copies of articles that reference my customer's products.

OVERCOMING COMPETITORS

Most businesses have both *direct* and *indirect* competitors. Direct competitors are in the same business and provide similar solutions; indirect competitors compete for business by providing alternative solutions. For example, a company that sells automated document management systems may have another document management systems supplier as a direct competitor, and a microfiche service bureau as an indirect competitor.

I have found it helpful to build a *competitive matrix* to help me analyze my competition and to help me focus my sales efforts to achieve the highest return on my investment of time and marketing resources.

The following example will help you understand how to use a competitive matrix to determine the best way to invest your sales and marketing resources.

In the example, product line 1 has a 25 percent share of a $15 million market, and product line 3 has a 25 percent share

---

* The easiest way to find information on the Internet is to use a Web search engine, such as AltaVista.

% CURRENT MARKET SHARE POTENTIAL REVENUE	STRENGTHS	WEAKNESSES
Product line 1 25% $15 million	Best products Good distribution Good technical support	Low margins Long, expensive sales cycle Many indirect competitors
Product line 2 5% $50 million	Reputation for reliability Good technical support Competitive prices	Poor name recognition Multiple distribution channel conflicts
Product line 3 25% $10 million	Highest-quality product Good distribution Market leader	Limited production capacity

of a $10 million market. Product line 2 has a 5 percent market share of a much larger $50 million market.

% MARKET SHARE	POTENTIAL DOLLARS CURRENT MARKET SHARE	DIRECT COMPETITOR "A"	INDIRECT COMPETITOR "B"	ALL OTHER COMPETITORS "C"
Product line 1	$15 million 25%	20%	25%	30%
Product line 2	$50 million 5%	10%	15%	70%
Product line 3	$10 million 25%	30%	25%	20%

The most successful competitor in product line 2's market has only a 15 percent market share. But product line 2 has suffered from poor brand-name recognition and from multiple distribution channel conflicts. These problems may be able to be resolved by increasing advertising and reducing the number of channel partners.

Based on this information, it appears that product line 2 has the greatest chance of winning new market share and increasing overall company revenues.

If you represented these product lines in your territory, it would make sense for you to focus your selling efforts on product line 2.

MAINTAINING YOUR MARKET MOMENTUM

Winning customers is hard work. In this section you will learn how to track the status of accounts in your territory to help you maintain a high level of customer satisfaction, and you will learn how to "map" your company's new products to your customers' needs.

Territory Maintenance

Established customers deserve the amount of time, attention, and service that is proportional to the percentage of business they provide your company. (This is, of course, why we created a strategic OEM accounts group at Microsoft.)

Satisfied customers are usually reluctant to court competitive suppliers. If they believe they are being treated well, they will reward you with repeat business. But to keep customers satisfied you must stay in touch with their emerging needs, and continually find new ways to add value to your selling relationship.

At Microsoft we invested a tremendous amount of time and money putting together OEM conferences, road shows, and technical workshops to enable us to stay as close to our customers as possible. This investment enabled us to stay in sync with our customers' emerging needs and helped ensure that our OEMs were informed about our new products and technologies.

We also endeavored to add value to our OEM relationships by providing a high level of after-sale support. For example, we gave our strategic OEMs advance information about new products we were developing, and offered them preferential business terms based on the volume of business they were doing with our company.

The best way I have found to add value to my customer relationships is by analyzing my customers' business periodically, to identify new opportunities for my company to help my customers improve their operations and profitability. And the best way to build "mind share" is to pay attention to my customers' needs and to communicate with them as often as possible.

Tracking Account Status

Tracking the status of your accounts on a weekly basis can help you maintain a high level of customer satisfaction.

At Microsoft I used a simple customer satisfaction tracking form to keep track of my customers' satisfaction with our company's service and support. You can use the sample customer satisfaction tracking form to help you develop a form that reflects your customer base and the type of products or services you represent.

ACCOUNT	SATISFACTION LEVEL (1 TO 5)	DATE OF LAST VISIT	SPECIAL SERVICE	OUTSTANDING PROBLEMS
Company A	1	4/14/97	2/7/97	BIOS errors in PC-400
Company B	4	3/12/97	10/3/97	NX machine keeps crashing SCSI drivers
Company C	2	4/17/97	8/25/97	A/R is 120 days overdue
Company D	2	3/10/97	3/10/97	Waiting for interim release of Internet server

Mapping Products to Your Customer's Needs

One of the keys to Microsoft's success has been its ability to articulate its future product strategy, and to map its product development plans to meet its customers' emerging needs. For example, when we developed our Windows story, we described Windows as part of the operating system "infrastructure" that our OEM customers needed to support their customers' evolving PC computing needs.

When I presented Windows to our OEMs, I emphasized that Windows was more than a fancy graphical user interface—it was an integral operating system component that was needed to support interapplication data sharing, and to make PCs easy enough for "normal" business users to use.

To help me present our Windows story, I created block diagrams (during my white board presentations) that represented the various components of Microsoft's operating systems. As I presented these diagrams, I described how MS-DOS and Windows worked together to support next-generation applications such as publishing electronic documents.

I believe this approach helped my customers visualize how Windows could add value to their customers' PC investment, and made it easier for them to justify Windows as an "added value" option for MS-DOS.

ACCOUNT MANAGEMENT SECRETS

Working with major accounts demands a high level of personal organization and careful attention to your customers' purchasing process.

In this section you will learn some of the Client-Centered™ account management techniques that enabled me to manage dozens of major OEM accounts and to close more than 40 percent of Microsoft's new OEM contracts.

Keep It Short and Simple

One of the most often repeated sales tips is "keep it short and simple" or "KISS." But it is not always obvious how much information you need to present to your customers to enable them to understand your products or to make an informed purchasing decision.

When, for example, Microsoft first developed a two-button mouse, its users' guide was several hundred pages long. I remember walking into our product manager's office with a mouse in one hand and a users' guide in the other. I told our product manager that I just couldn't believe that we needed to ship that much documentation with our mouse. Our product manager patiently explained that this information was necessary for software developers to mouse-enable their applications.

It didn't occur to me at the time to ask why we hadn't broken our documentation into two parts, one for software users, and one for developers. But fortunately, as Microsoft Windows became an industry standard, most PC software developers mouse-enabled their applications, and Microsoft no longer needed to disseminate so much technical information.

Today Microsoft supplies a simple six-page pictorial users' guide with their mouse. But most people don't even bother reading it! They learn how to use their mouse by "playing" with it, or by using an on-line tutorial program that is supplied with Microsoft Windows.

There is no "correct" amount of information to provide to a customer. It is the salesperson's job to determine how much information he or she needs to communicate to move business forward.

Limit Your Customers' Purchase Options

When I worked with OEMs at Microsoft, I was careful to limit the number of decision factors in my presentations. Whenever I broke my rule, and presented too many scenarios or tried to offer too many alternatives, I "forced" my customers to take their purchase decision under advisement, until they could analyze the information I had presented.

After unintentionally delaying several of my customers' purchasing decisions, I realized that the most direct way to move the selling process forward was to keep my sales presentations as simple and as brief as possible. Providing information that was too detailed, or that was confusing or contradictory, just delayed my customers' purchasing process.

Selling Positive

"Selling positive" means using your selling time to communicate your product's advantages, and the benefits of doing business with your company.

It is foolish to waste valuable selling time disparaging your competitors. Customers are skeptical of comments salespeople make about their competitors because salespeople are usually too biased to provide objective information. But if you need to discuss your competitors, make sure that your statements are absolutely accurate. If you make an inaccurate statement, you may appear to be lying to influence your customer's purchasing decision.

It is impossible for a customer to know whether you are lying or uninformed, and most customers will give you the benefit of any doubt. But you will appear unprofessional, and you will have to work hard to reestablish your credibility.

Sell Less Than You Can Deliver

Life is sweeter for optimists who see their glass as half full rather than half empty. But selling often requires proposing imperfect solutions to real-world problems.

One of the secrets of maintaining good relationships with customers is setting reasonable expectations for your products and services, and selling a bit less than you can deliver. If you sell less than you can deliver, your customers will appreciate the extra value you provide after you have taken their money.

When I was working at Microsoft, I had a nightmare that I had to go on a daytime television courtroom drama to explain why I had promised one of my customers a specific feature that would not be available until our next product update. The judge had no mercy. I was sentenced to work as an assembly language programmer for the next three years!

Don't Be Defensive

Microsoft's OEM customers depended on our ability to deliver new products to meet their own product release schedules. For example, there was no point in one of our OEMs including high-density 3.5" floppy disk drives in a new line of PCs unless their Microsoft-supplied operating system included device drivers that would enable their PC to read and write data to them.*

---

* A device driver is a software program that enables different hardware devices such as disk drives to work with a PC.

In most cases we met our scheduled product release dates, but in some cases we didn't. When our product schedules slipped, our customers usually called their account manager with a desperate plea for information about the delay, and their account manager called the appropriate product manager, who in turn consulted with the development manager. This flurry of activity invariably resulted in the "revelation" that our engineers were working on one problem or another, and that they would release their code when they felt it was ready.

Relaying this news to our customers was not an enjoyable experience. But after handling about a dozen "What's happening out there?" calls I realized that nothing I could say to my customers would make them feel much better about our internal problems. And I learned that the key to maintaining good customer relationships was timely, straightforward follow-up.

So the next time my customer asked me why a product was delayed, I didn't get defensive. I simply passed along whatever explanation I was given for the delay, and promised my customer that I would contact them as soon as any new information was available.

If You Can't Say "Yes," Say "When"

In most cases Microsoft provided exactly what our OEM customers demanded, but in some situations, such as when our customers wanted to connect their PCs together on a local area network, we were not able to provide a complete solution for their needs.*

If my customer needed a product we were developing but were not ready to deliver, I would usually provide information, under a signed nondisclosure agreement, about our product development strategy, and then would disclose specific information about when we expected to release our new products.

In many cases this disclosure provided sufficient assurance to convince our OEMs to wait for Microsoft to release its new

---

* Back in 1985 Novell emerged as the leading supplier of software for PC-based local area networks. Today Microsoft provides a compelling local area networking solution based on the Windows NT operating system.

product, rather than to develop the software themselves or to acquire a solution from another supplier. Of course if we were not working on a solution that would meet my customer's needs, I would try to suggest an alternative supplier that I felt could.

By disclosing our future development plans, we made it easy for our customers to get in sync with Microsoft's product development strategy, and we demonstrated that we were sincerely committed to working with our customers to help ensure their success.

Trust Your Customers, Not Your Contracts

Whenever I briefed my OEM customers about our future product plans, I asked them to sign a nondisclosure agreement, which we called an "NDA."

We had two reasons for asking our customers to sign an NDA. First, we wanted to keep our product plans as secret as possible. And second, we wanted to communicate to our OEMs that they were our trusted business partners.

Most of our OEMs were very careful not to reveal any confidential information we presented to them at our meetings, but some weren't. And time after time, we would read about our "secret" product plans in industry trade magazine columns.

The first time I had confidential information from one of my confidential briefings leaked to the press, I was pretty upset. But I got used to it. People love to gossip.

The funny thing, though, was that many times our "secret" plans were reported incorrectly. In fact, I realized that the PC industry's "sleuth" columns were the perfect way to disseminate misinformation. The only problem was that we didn't have time to play games. We were too busy developing new products and bringing them to market as fast as we could!

There always will be a few customers who take advantage of a special situation. But it is a mistake to let them determine your business policies. Most customers are honest, and are sincere about maintaining "win-win" relationships with their business partners.

FEAR, UNCERTAINTY, AND DOUBT

Just as Microsoft's OEMs must maintain an open dialogue with their customers to develop products that will meet their customers' needs and expectations, so Microsoft must maintain an open dialogue with the *entire computer industry* to enable it to develop products that will meet its customers' needs and expectations.

Some industry pundits have accused Microsoft of using "fear, uncertainty, and doubt" about its future product plans to coerce its customers into waiting for new products to be released (just as IBM was in the 1970s). But I do not believe that this has ever been the case.

Microsoft's customers and business partners, which include virtually every company in the computer, networking, and communications industries, are constantly asking Microsoft to disclose information about future products that are still in their preliminary design stage.

Early knowledge of Microsoft's product development plans enables Microsoft's business partners to share any ideas and concerns they have about Microsoft's product direction, and enables them to bring products that are based on Microsoft's new technologies to market as quickly as possible.

Premature disclosure of Microsoft's product development strategy has occasionally led to embarrassment, such as when Microsoft was caught unprepared for the impact of Internet technology on network computing. But while Microsoft's openness about its future product strategy has been a two-edged sword, I cannot think of a more appropriate and honest way for Microsoft to manage its relationships with its customers and business partners.

CLIENT-CENTERED™ ACCOUNT MANAGEMENT

Paying attention to your customers, and using Client-Centered™ communication skills to understand and respond to their concerns, are the keys to building sales momentum in your territory.

This sounds easy, but it's difficult to deliver your best effort day after day. So take it a step at a time. Be patient with yourself. And remember to thank your customers once in a while for the blessing of your livelihood.

CHAPTER TWELVE

LEVERAGING YOUR INTERNAL RESOURCES

"Surround yourself with the best people you can find, delegate authority, and don't interfere."
—RONALD REAGAN

The captain of an athletic team is responsible for coordinating the efforts of each member on the team and is ultimately responsible for the team's results. To be successful, a team captain must make the best use of each of his or her player's skills.

An account manager's job is *exactly* like a team captain's—he or she must learn how to delegate tasks and motivate coworkers to make their best effort. Otherwise they will not achieve their sales objectives.

Most of our sales at Microsoft were very straightforward, but some of our sales required a tremendous amount of pre- and postsale technical support. To be successful, our account managers had to learn how to manage the internal resources available to help them move business forward.

In this chapter you will learn how to use team selling and Client-Centered™ delegation techniques to help you manage your internal resources and maximize your selling potential.

TEAM SELLING AT MICROSOFT

Depending on the type of products and services you are representing, and on your customer's technical background, it may be necessary to have one or more support personnel involved in the selling process.

Team sales calls can help you leverage corporate resources, provide a higher customer service level, win more competitive sales, generate more revenue per customer, generate higher revenue per sales call, and develop a shorter sales cycle with fewer sales calls.

At Microsoft, our sales support personnel were responsible for various sales support functions, including:

- Prospecting
- Performing needs analysis
- Working on product configuration
- Custom application development
- Technical presentations
- Product demonstrations
- Pricing analysis
- Contract and negotiation support
- Tracking orders and delivery
- Customer support
- Customer training
- Scheduling internal resources

At Microsoft, we often held impromptu meetings in the hallways. These meetings gave us an opportunity to gossip about our coworkers and our customers, and to share information we needed to do our jobs. I loved these meetings because they enabled the people I worked with to share their energy and to bond together as a team.

Over the years, many of my consulting clients have asked me whether I ever miss working at Microsoft. To be honest, I don't miss the work, but I still miss the people!

ECONOMICS OF TEAM SELLING

Team selling is often the best way for technology-driven companies such as Microsoft to provide the combination of technical and marketing skills that are needed to solve their customers' problems.

To determine whether it is advantageous to implement team selling, you must evaluate the value that teaming people from different areas of your company will have on your ability to generate new business. Then you can compare the cost of making team sales calls with the cost of making sales calls on your own.

- AVERAGE COST OF "SOLO" SALES CALL = [COST OF SALESPERSON] / [NUMBER OF SALES CALLS]
- COST OF SALES SUPPORT PERSONNEL PER SALES CALL = [NUMBER OF HOURS SPENT BY TECHNICAL, MARKETING, FINANCIAL, ADMINISTRATIVE, AND MANAGEMENT PERSONNEL IN SUPPORT OF SALE] X [AVERAGE SALARY PER HOUR] X [NUMBER OF HOURS PER SALES CALL]
- COST OF TEAM SALES CALL = [COST OF "SOLO" SALES CALL] + [COST OF SALES SUPPORT PERSONNEL]

If your analysis indicates that the benefits of team selling justify the increase in direct selling expenses, you should consider implementing a team selling strategy.

PRE–SALES CALL PLANNING

The key to leveraging the selling efforts of the support personnel on your sales team is pre–sales call planning.

At Microsoft, I always had a pre–sales call meeting with any sales or support personnel who would be working with me at a customer meeting. Most of these pre–sales meetings were informal, and they often occurred in transit to our customer's office.

SAMPLE SALES CALL AGENDA

Greetings and introduction (5 minutes)

Linda Hopkins, product manager, will review resolution of high-pressure valve problem on customer's AX-90 machine. (15 minutes)

Don Howard, support engineer, will demonstrate the AX-200. Don will show how the AX-200 can handle multiple nodes and interface with customer's network management software. (20 minutes)

Marcia Sinclair, from Acme Bank, will present a leasing plan for our equipment. (10 minutes)

I will review our presentation, answer questions, and ask our customer to place an order for 20 AX-200s for delivery over the next four months. (10 minutes)

I used my pre–sales call meetings to prepare my team members to help me meet my sales call objectives, by reviewing my account situation and discussing my agenda for the sales call. I also discussed the contribution I expected each member of my team to make, to help me move business forward during our sales call. This helped my support people prepare for the meeting and made them feel more comfortable about "jumping in" to present information.

Credibility

The best way to build credibility on team sales calls is to respect the people you are working with and to be supportive of their expertise.

Open dialogue is critical to the success of a sales team. But arguing with a team member in front of your customer can destroy your credibility. If a team member says something you believe is incorrect, discuss it with that person after your sales call, unless it is imperative to clarify the point during your meeting.

Use the Client-Centered™ communication techniques you have learned to help you leverage your team members' skills and expertise.

CLIENT-CENTERED™ DELEGATION

When I was first promoted into a management position at Microsoft, I was used to getting things done myself, not delegating work to other people. But after a few months I began to understand the delegation process, and I developed a Client-Centered™ approach to delegation.

Define Your Delegation Goals

Take the time to determine which tasks you can delegate and which tasks you need to complete yourself.

If you take the time to delegate specific types of work to specific personnel, you will not have to assign each task on a case-by-case basis.

Communicate Clearly

Communicate the task (assignment) you are delegating to your coworker as clearly and precisely as you can.

If the task is time-critical, or if many steps are involved, put your assignment in writing, and verify that your coworker has all the training and resources needed to complete the task.

Include Your Coworkers in the Planning Process

People get a greater sense of accomplishment by doing work they have helped plan; and there is better communication when everyone is involved from the planning stage. Taking the sum of everyone's experience will also help ensure that the best plan is developed.

In addition to these benefits, people are more supportive and cooperative when they feel like equal team members, and it is easier to spot problems early on when everyone is working together.

Negotiate Deadlines

Discuss deadlines with the people you are delegating work to, and confirm that they can get their assigned tasks done in a reasonable time.

Follow Up All Assignments

Don't abdicate responsibility for assignments you delegate. If you are concerned about a delegated task being completed properly and on schedule, you should support the person you have delegated the task to, until the task is completed.

Don't Take Back Assignments

Taking back assignments wastes time, erodes your coworker's confidence in his or her abilities, and sets a precedent for failure. If you refuse to take back assignments, you can train your coworkers to be more self-sufficient and to bring you solutions, not problems.

I like to use "problem" situations as an opportunity to develop my coworkers' skills.

Make All Criticism Constructive

Demoralized people don't do better work. The only useful criticism is constructive criticism.

Reward Successful Efforts

Behavior that is rewarded persists. If your coworkers do a good job, you should reward them with praise, special recognition, the opportunity to work on more advanced jobs in the future, and financial remuneration.

Empower Your Sales Support Team

Delegation provides an opportunity for you to empower and develop people who work with you.

It is a mistake to assume that a coworker who has been doing one job for a long time cannot do other, more demanding tasks. Average workers who are given greater responsibility are often capable of delivering outstanding results.

At Microsoft, senior managers often delegated complex problems to less experienced managers, and then served as mentors to help build "next generation" experience within our organization.

THE 6 KEYS TO EFFECTIVE DELEGATION

1. Your coworkers must be capable and motivated
2. Training leverages performance
3. Verify your assignment and confirm deadlines
4. Establish checkpoints and be available to provide guidance
5. Be positive—implement rewards
6. Don't overmanage or take back assignments

For example, I was given responsibility for coordinating the pricing for our OEM products. I had never developed prices for OEM products before, and I needed some help along the way; but the experience gave me an opportunity to learn pricing theory and the confidence to help create the infrastructure we needed to support our sales team.

Don't Overload Your Best People

Rotate projects among your coworkers so they don't get burned out and so each person on your team has the opportunity to learn new job skills. And challenge yourself to offer new opportunities to everyone on your team—not just the people you like best.

Give Your Coworkers Latitude to Take Initiative

Give your coworkers the latitude to get tasks done their way, so they can learn to exercise their initiative and creativity.

You can grant your coworkers varying levels of authority to act independently, depending on your level of confidence in their ability to complete a delegated task.

THE SECRET OF MANAGING YOUR MANAGER

Sales managers are usually insulated from feedback because the people who work for them are afraid to tell them that their work needs improvement or that they are doing a bad job. Since most

---

DELEGATION PLANNER

Project: Demonstration Format for Interactive Web Database

Date: June 20. 1999

Project manager: Tom Brown

Priority: <u>A</u> / B / C

Do by: Time: _____ / Today / This week / <u>This month</u> / This quarter

Objectives: Create an interactive Web database system for new purchase orders

Accountability: Jenn Smith

    Key results: Beta program in two weeks

    Checkpoints: Weekly staff meetings

    Due dates: July 31, 1999

Follow-up actions: Beta test with Acme Company

    Comments: Use Microsoft Internt Explorer

    Evaluations: Robert Land

---

sales managers receive very little negative feedback from their salespeople, they assume they are doing a good job managing their sales team. But sales managers who are disorganized, compulsive procrastinators, poor communicators, or indecisive about their goals or priorities can bring havoc to their salespeople's work schedule.

If you have a bad manager, you have three choices. You can ignore the problem, which works pretty well if you and your manager will be working together for only a short time. You can resign yourself to your predicament and not worry about your wasted time. Or you can learn how to "manage" your manager.

If you decide to help your manager become well organized, you need to be sensitive to his or her personality and temperament. Some managers are open to suggestions about how they can improve; others are not.

6 TIPS FOR MANAGING YOUR MANAGER

1. Good communication is the key to a good working relationship. Discuss your objectives and key results, and your progress on the tasks you have been assigned, on a regular basis.

2. Be a team player. Try to make your manager look good to his or her manager.

3. Treat your manager the way you would like to be treated. Be patient and understanding, and accept his or her strengths and weaknesses.

4. Offer potential solutions whenever you discuss a problem.

5. Don't accept new assignments until you understand what you are responsible for, and what resources and authority you have been assigned or granted to accomplish your tasks.

6. Do your work with pride and enthusiasm.

Taking an indirect approach, such as making suggestions about how you can work together to improve your productivity, is often the best way to open a dialogue with your manager. You might, for example, ask your manager to help you prioritize the tasks you have been delegated, and then schedule periodic meetings to confirm that your activities are consistent with these objectives. By scheduling regular meetings you should be able to reduce your manager's interruptions.

If your manager constantly changes his or her objectives, or refuses to make decisions, it may be virtually impossible for you to manage your own time effectively. In this case you should verify your manager's objectives in writing, to help eliminate any possible miscommunication, and use your daily planner to record the time you spent with your manager, any new assignments you have been given, and any ongoing assignments that have been changed, postponed, or abandoned.

When you review your sales activities with your manager, you can document how you have spent your time. Then you

10 TIPS FOR MANAGING A NEW MANAGER

1. Be honest about your needs and your achievements.
2. Create a good first impression.
3. Don't gossip about your coworkers.
4. Be helpful, but don't become a pest.
5. Be prepared for change.
6. Don't assume that your new manager's objectives and priorities are the same as your old manager's.
7. Don't assume that your job will remain the same.
8. Do whatever you can to make your new manager look good.
9. Don't go behind your new manager's back.
10. Don't waste time comparing your new manager with your old manager.

can work together to set specific objectives, to enable you to focus your attention on completing the highest-priority tasks that you have been assigned—which in most cases should be spending more time with your customers!

The greatest time waster is poor interpersonal communications. But the most insidious time waster is often your own boss.

MANAGING YOUR SALES ASSISTANT

Delegating tasks to your administrative assistant can help you save time and be more productive.

One of the most difficult delegation challenges is learning how to help coworkers solve their own problems, rather than trying to solve their problems for them.

DELEGATION SUCCESS

Learning the art of delegation is the key to managing your sales team. But delegation, like any "art," takes time to master. You

14 TIPS FOR WORKING WITH SALES ASSISTANTS

1. Maintain a positive attitude and your sense of humor at all times

2. Schedule regular meetings in the morning or afternoon to help your assistant prioritize his or her work and to share information.

3. Avoid interrupting your assistant too often

4. Reward good performance.

5. Never reprimand your assistant (or anyone else) in public.

6. Don't overload your assistant with too many tasks at once.

7. Respect your assistant's advice and intuition.

8. Don't expect your assistant to read your mind.

9. Don't expect perfection.

10. Encourage your assistant to take on additional responsibilities, improve himself or herself, and join professional societies.

11. Make time to train your assistant.

12. Hire the best, expect the best, and pay the best.

13. Don't expect immediate attention if your assistant also supports other people.

14. Ask for help, don't demand it, and thank your assistant for work that is done for you.

will need to be patient with your sales team, and maintain your sense of humor when tasks are not completed properly or on time. Otherwise you will become stressed out, difficult to work with, and less able to motivate your coworkers.

CHAPTER THIRTEEN

THE SECRET OF EFFECTIVE SALES MANAGEMENT

"People ask the difference between a leader and a boss. The leader works in the open, and the boss in covert. The leader leads, and the boss drives."
—THEODORE ROOSEVELT

When I first left IBM to join Microsoft back in 1982, I was amazed by the difference in their cultures. There were superficial differences, such as IBM's passion for "dressing for success," and Microsoft's relaxed dress code. But there were also many deeper differences.

IBM was organized around a traditional hierarchical management structure. Communications were relatively formal, and it was unusual for salespeople to communicate with anyone above their line manager. At Microsoft, communications were "peer-to-peer," and it was not unusual to copy reports, send E-mail, or have sales meetings with Bill Gates, or anyone else in the company who could help move business forward.

The only one-on-one meeting that I had with my branch manager at IBM was when I told him I was leaving IBM to join

Microsoft. He told me he was sorry I was leaving, and he wished me good luck in my selling career. And then, as I was about to leave his office, he added that he felt that IBM, over the preceding ten years, had "engineered the creativity out of its people in the field." I was surprised by his candor, and impressed by his ability to understand the issue that would ultimately enable an "upstart" company such as Microsoft to foil IBM's attempt to dominate the fast-moving PC industry as it had the mainframe computer market.

Microsoft is organized into highly focused work groups, which are managed as independent business units. These work groups help Microsoft adapt to changing markets very rapidly and provide a significant competitive advantage against companies that are organized around a more traditional hierarchical management style.

MANAGING YOUR TEAM

Many companies today are in the process of reorganizing, downsizing, and restructuring their business to become more competitive and more profitable. These changes have eliminated layers of middle management and creating a flatter reporting structure.

Sales teams are a perfect example of work groups that do not have vertical lines of delegation. Different people on sales teams often report to managers in different business units, such as technical support and administration. And account managers must delegate tasks to team members over whom they have no direct hiring, firing, or rewarding power.

When I worked at Microsoft, we had very few layers of management. Our account managers reported to a sales manager, who reported to the vice president of our division, who in turn reported to the president of Microsoft and to Bill Gates, our CEO. Today Microsoft is a much larger company, but it has managed to maintain a relatively flat reporting structure by maintaining relatively small, interrelated business units.

OLD "GROUP" MANAGEMENT PHILOSOPHY	NEW "TEAM" MANAGEMENT PHILOSOPHY
People feel that work is inherently unpleasant	People enjoy working as much as playing if their work environment is supportive and positive
People are inherently lazy and irresponsible	People want to do a good job, and will accept responsibility if they are capable and motivated
People lack creativity	People are creative if given the chance to participate in the planning process
People must be motivated by external forces, such as money and fear of losing their job	People are motivated by internal factors, such as the need for acceptance by their coworkers
People must be closely controlled and supervised to accomplish their job	People are self-directed, and can motivate themselves to succeed if provided adequate incentives

GROUPS AND TEAMS

Many business organizations today are moving from a *group* management philosophy to a *team* management philosophy.

Being part of a group is very different from being part of a team. Groups work together. Teams cooperate, and rely on group collaboration to enable individual team members to achieve their goals. Microsoft is a relatively young company and has always had a team management philosophy.

When I worked at IBM, I felt that my sales group focused on individual achievement. At Microsoft I felt that my sales group focused on achieving our team's goals. Call me crazy, but it was sure a lot more fun to work at Microsoft!

Along with adopting a team-oriented management style, Microsoft has made a concerted effort to recruit the "best and the brightest" people in the computer industry. These people have helped Microsoft create one of the most successful marketing organizations in the world.

In the next section, you will learn how we recruited and selected account managers at Microsoft; but first, I will reveal the "secret" of effective sales management.

THE SECRET OF EFFECTIVE SALES MANAGEMENT

Managing salespeople ranks somewhere between "engineering" creativity and "controlling" an explosion. It is not a job for the faint of heart!

Most sales managers help their sales team by making suggestions, based on their own selling experience, about how to find prospects, close business, and fight the competition. And they use persuasion and motivational talks to support their leadership role.

However, very few sales managers have analyzed different selling skills, or can articulate a fundamental technology for successful selling. This limits most sales managers' ability to train their salespeople or to influence their sales team's efforts.

The "secret" to effective sales management is mastering a *selling technology*, such as Client-Centered™ selling, and then integrating the selling technology's techniques into your day-to-day interaction with your sales team.

Building on a common sales skills framework enables a sales team to communicate more effectively, and to work together to resolve problems and move business forward.

GETTING THE JOB DONE

In most companies, the sales manager's primary responsibility is to meet their business unit's revenue objectives, and to manage the day-to-day activities of their sales team. However, many sales managers are also expected to work their own territory, and to perform marketing, operations, and other duties as well.

At Microsoft, our sales managers did not have direct account responsibility, but they were responsible for coordinating OEM marketing programs and, of course, for meeting our division's business objectives.

How Sales Managers Spend Their Time

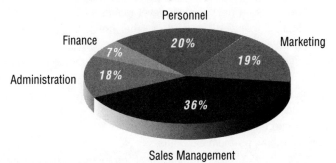

Sales Management

What Do Sales Managers Really Do?

If you ask most sales managers what they do for a living, they will probably tell you that they have four primary roles:

- *Coaching*—helping salespeople overcome problems
- *Training*—helping salespeople improve selling skills
- *Motivating*—providing incentives for reaching sales goals
- *Evaluating*—defining goals and measuring results

However, most sales managers actually spend a relatively small portion of their time working directly with their sales team.

In the early 1970s Rodney E. Evans conducted a study of how sales managers spent their time. The study's findings have been updated several times over the years. This is what Evans found:

Marketing Activities (19%)
- Analyzing sales data
- Communicating information to other salespeople
- Digesting information from management
- Summarizing sales and customer data for management
- Reviewing competitive activity
- Forecasting future sales
- Reviewing sales coverage and salespeople territory alignment

- Advising on changes in price, delivery, arrangements, products, or new product development
- Managing advertising and/or other nonselling promotional activities
- Participating in the formulation of overall marketing policy

Sales Management Activities (36%)
- Making sales calls with salespeople
- Personal selling to own accounts
- Handling problem accounts
- Deciding on customer's request for special terms of sale
- Expediting customer orders
- Working with dissatisfied customers

Administrative Activities (18%)
- Managing the office
- Keeping records
- Writing reports

Financial Activities (7%)
- Analyzing selling expenses
- Controlling inventory
- Controlling costs in relation to profits
- Preparing budgets
- Recommending additional capital expenditure

Personnel Activities (20%)
- Training salespeople
- Establishing performance standards
- Planning and holding sales meetings
- Advising salespersons on personal problems
- Handling problem salespeople
- Recruiting and selecting new salespeople
- Revising people specifications for field salespeople
- Reviewing compensation programs for salespeople
- Forecasting future personnel needs

According to Evans's study, only about half of an "average" sales manager's time is spent working with his or her sales force. The remaining half of a sales manager's time is dedicated to other responsibilities.

However, at Microsoft our sales managers were very proactive about working with their account managers. Our sales managers often went out on sales calls with their account managers, and helped them coordinate whatever internal resources were necessary to help them move business forward.

When I joined Microsoft, there were six people in the OEM group, including four OEM account managers. Three years later we had about twenty OEM account managers, divided between our strategic account and major account sales groups; and we had added an OEM technical support group and a sales support group.

I believe that there were two reasons why we were able to grow our sales force as rapidly as we did, without having major

SUCCESS FACTOR MATRIX	CANDIDATE'S PROFILE
Company size/culture	Likes informal environment Enjoys support and structure of large company
Products	Likes simple product story Challenged by complex/technical information
Customer mix	Enjoys "personal" side of selling smaller companies Enjoys complexities of major account selling
Sales cycle	Needs frequent sales Enjoys landing large orders
Compensation	Security-oriented Motivated by commission
Potential for advancement	Wants management experience Career salesperson
Level of supervision	Needs supervision Likes to work alone
Personal needs	People-oriented Task-oriented

JOBS REQUIREMENTS CHECK LIST

Educational Background

- High school
- College/graduate school
- Technical/trade school
- Professional certification/training
- Sales training

Work Experience

- Sales experience
- Sales support experience
- Outside sales
- Commission sales
- Remote territory sales
- Route sales
- Major account sales
- International sales
- Joint-marketing sales
- Specific industry experience
- Direct competitive sales experience
- Knowledge of customer base
- Knowledge of territory
- Existing customer relationships

Product Knowledge/Presentation Skills

- Verbal skills
- Writing ability
- Telemarketing skills
- Cold-call skills
- Foreign-languages skills (oral/written)
- General product knowledge
- Technical skills
- Analytical skills
- Organizational skills
- Office skills
- Computer skills

Management Skills

- Sales management experience
- Product marketing experience
- Other management experience
- Previous P&L responsibility

Personal Traits

- Honesty
- Loyalty
- Work ethic

- **Persistence**
- **Confidence**
- **Intelligence**
- **Creativity**
- **Problem-solving abilities**
- **Empathy/listening skills**
- **Professional appearance**

Other Qualifications

- **Desire to travel**
- **Conversational skills**
- **Relevant hobbies (e.g., golf)**
- **Other**
- **Other**

problems with our OEM customers. First, we hired only experienced sales professionals, and second, our sales managers worked very closely with our new account managers to help them get up to speed.

PICKING WINNERS

All of the account managers we hired at Microsoft were sales professionals with years of experience selling computer-related products to information technology professionals. And many of our account managers held engineering, computer science, or advanced business degrees.

But one of the first things I observed about our account managers was that there was very little correlation between our account managers' prior sales experience and their success at Microsoft. Our account managers' success was more closely related to a constellation of factors, including their ability to work with other people, their attitude about work, their desire to learn about the technology our products were based on, and their organizational skills.

Hiring the best people you can find is the best "prescription" for a successful business.

A GOOD FIT

There are many factors that determine whether a salesperson will be successful in a new sales job, including a salesperson's personality, maturity, previous experience, technical ability, communication skills, organizational skills, level of expectation for compensation, and outside hobbies and interests.

A salesperson who is comfortable representing nontechnical products and who enjoys a short selling cycle will not be happy representing a high-tech product that has a six-month sales cycle. Similarly, a salesperson who enjoys selling financial products will probably not be a good candidate to represent a line of fashion accessories.

JOB QUALIFICATION QUESTIONS

- Describe your last three sales jobs.
- What did you do during a typical day on your last sales job?
- Describe the products you used to sell.
- Describe your sales cycle.
- Describe your customer base.
- How many customers did you service?
- What percentage of your time did you spend cold-calling?
- What percentage of your time did you spend telemarketing?
- Were you involved with team selling?
- Did you work with a technical support team?
- Who did you report to?
- Did you have any direct reports?
- What was the dollar value of an average sale?
- What was your annual sales quota at your last job?
- What percentage of your salary was directly tied to commissions or to quota attainment?
- How much money did you make on your last job?
- Role-play a customer meeting based on products you represented in your last job.
- What did you like about your last job?
- Why do you think that working here will be a better opportunity for you?

PERSONAL CHARACTER QUESTIONS

- What were your most important achievements in your last job? Why were they important to you?
- What was your greatest business challenge? What did you learn from it?
- What was the most difficult problem you encountered? How did you handle it?
- Who was the most difficult person to work with at your last job? How did you overcome this problem?
- What was the most important course or project you completed in school? Why was it important to you?
- Why do you think someone with your experience should be chosen for a job that requires [fill in your own job requirement] experience?
- What are you looking for in a new job opportunity?
- Convince me that you have what it takes to do this job!

I have learned that it is difficult to recognize high-potential individuals unless you know exactly what you are looking for before you begin your interview. So the first step I take, before I begin the recruiting process, is to define my "ideal" candidate's previous work experience, educational background, technical skills, personality type, and management potential.

The way I identify the characteristics I am looking for in a salesperson is to create a success factor matrix for my sales position. Comparing my job candidate's profile with my success factors matrix helps me determine whether a salesperson is well suited to my specific selling situation.

Then I use a job requirements check list to help me screen potential job candidates.

During the interview process I try to ask questions that reveal my prospective salesperson's selling skills, industry background, and motivation for personal success.

I like to ask each candidate I interview the same basic questions. This enables me to be more objective, and it makes it easier for me to evaluate and compare different candidates I have screened over a period of time.

Then I make notes about a candidate right after I complete my interview, while they are fresh in my mind. If I wait until the end of the day, I have a difficult time remembering which candidate said what.

If I plan to interview several candidates, I have found that I can save time by creating a form to record my impressions.

NEW-HIRE DANGER SIGNALS

If you have any concerns about a person's honesty, or you just don't like him or her, don't hire that person. It is far easier to help someone you like and trust to become successful, than someone you are uncomfortable with.

Job History

If a person asks you not to check his or her references, that person may have had serious problems with his or her last employer or may have had difficulty getting along with coworkers.

If a person has had many jobs in a short time (unless just out of school), that person may not have chosen the right career path or may be burned out.

Job Burnout

If a person requires a period of time off when first hired, it may be because he or she has personal problems or because the person feels burned out from the last job.

Last Resort

If a person is very concerned about "low" compensation but is willing to take your job anyway, he or she may have lied about a prior salary or may leave as soon as he or she can find a better-paying job.

Poor Learner

If a person has poor verbal skills, that person may not be able to master your "story." Salespeople are first and foremost storytellers. If the person is having trouble telling his or her own "story," that person probably will have trouble telling yours.

MULTIPLE INTERVIEWS

At Microsoft, we never hired a salesperson without interviewing him or her at least twice. First impressions are very important and can be very revealing, but it is easier to assess personal qualities in another person after you are familiar with his or her personal presentation style.

Most of our account managers were referred to one of our sales managers as a potential new hire by someone in our group. But in any case, every job candidate's résumé was screened by a sales manager to determine whether that person was qualified for a position as an account manager based on his or her previous job experience.

Then, if the sales manager felt that the person would do a good job at Microsoft, the sales manager invited the person in for a series of interviews with the sales manager and several of the account managers on that team.

If after meeting with the person, the sales manager was convinced that the right person had been found for their team, the sales manager discussed the person's background with our vice president and asked him to interview the person he or she wanted to hire.

At this point, if everyone who interviewed the person was convinced that he or she could do a good job, the person usually was offered a position. But if there was no consensus about the strength of a candidate's sales experience, communication skills, personality, or technical acumen, we would continue searching for a better-qualified person.

TECHNICAL SALES

"Ideal" technical salespeople have good selling skills and a strong enough technical background to enable them to sell at a peer level. However, "ideal" candidates are not always available.

In many cases you will need to decide whether to hire an individual with a strong technical background, who has had little or no selling experience, or a professional salesperson who may not have the technical background to understand your customers' needs or explain how your products work.

Unfortunately, there is no formula for choosing between a person with a strong technical background and another person with proven selling skills. You will need to determine exactly what skills are necessary to be successful on your sales team, and make hiring decisions based on your instincts and your ability to provide on-the-job training.

It is easier for a job candidate with weak technical skills to succeed in an organization that relies on team selling and that maintains a presales technical support staff. In high-tech companies that require their sales representatives to close sales without technical support, it is usually necessary to recruit salespeople with strong technical backgrounds.

Some technical people are successful making the transition into technical sales positions; however, most technical people are uncomfortable moving away from their area of expertise.

I have found that technical people's selling success is directly related to their willingness to put aside their "expertise" so they can communicate effectively with their customers.

Depending on your selling situation, it may be necessary for your salespeople to have a thorough knowledge of their customers' business. In this case the only place to recruit salespeople may be from your customers' industry. For example, many salespeople who sell to the healthcare industry have previous experience as medical practitioners.

RECRUITING SALES PROFESSIONALS

The best place to look for new sales talent is often within your own organization. Personnel in sales support, training, customer service, and administration often have many of the skills and a great deal of the industry and product knowledge that are key to selling success.

If you must go outside your company to recruit salespeople, you can do your own search, or you can retain outside help.

If you do your own search, you can start by informing all your business contacts that you are looking for a new sales representative. Employees both past and current, customers, suppliers, and industry consultants are all good referral sources. Many of the account managers at Microsoft were recruited through referrals from people who worked at Microsoft.

Microsoft, like most technology-driven companies, invests a great deal of money in training its personnel, so it makes sense for Microsoft to promote from within whenever possible. People who are interested in moving from one business unit at Microsoft to another, or who feel that they are ready to move into more responsible positions, are encouraged to apply for any open position that is available.

Advertising in newspapers and industry trade publications is also a great way to find qualified candidates. The more general your advertisement is, the more résumés you will generate. But if you have very specific requirements, it usually pays to include them in your ad. The extra money you spend advertising will reduce your screening time by pulling better-qualified applicants.

Microsoft advertises for personnel in many industry publications, and posts open position notices on the Internet. Microsoft also receives tens of thousands of unsolicited résumés each year.

You can also use outside employment agencies and professional recruiters. Free employment agencies are usually sponsored by government organizations and by public and private high schools, colleges, and trade schools.

Employer-paid employment agencies can save you a great deal of time by screening job applicants. However, while some employment agencies do a good job of screening applicants, others will send over any "warm body" available.

Executive search firms, or "headhunters," who contract with your company to perform an exclusive job search, are usually the most professional and provide the best service. However, professional recruiters work on commission and often charge 30 to 80 percent of a candidate's yearly salary. Because of their expense, executive search firms usually are retained to recruit senior sales and marketing personnel.

Microsoft works with several executive search firms and is willing to pay large recruiting fees to hire senior-level personnel.

SALES TRAINING

After you hire a salesperson, you must provide the information and resources that person needs to be successful.

There are basically four types of sales training: seminars, workshops, one-on-one coaching, and field training.

Sales seminars are the least expensive way to train a group of new salespeople. However, passive sales training is also the least effective way to develop new selling skills.

Workshops can be more effective than seminars because they involve participants and can provide an opportunity to try out new skills. The main problem with workshops is that the sales situations that are studied are artificial; real-world situations are generally much more complex.

One-on-one coaching, where a senior person takes a new salesperson "under his or her wing," can be effective if the senior salesperson is a good teacher. However, if the senior salesperson just has the new salesperson perform sales support functions, the new salesperson will not have an opportunity to develop all the skills needed to be successful.

Field training, on "partnered" sales calls, is the most effective way to help a new salesperson develop selling skills. However, it is also the most expensive in terms of manpower and potential lost opportunities.

At Microsoft, I had the opportunity to create and staff the OEM training group. We used a combination of sales seminars, workshops, and field training with senior salespeople to help our new account managers get up to speed.

Sales training is most successful when it covers both basic selling skills and the product and industry information a new salesperson needs to represent the company's products.

EVALUATING YOUR STAFF

Many salespeople are evaluated on two simple criteria: Do they make quota? and Do they make trouble? If they make a great deal of trouble, they better excel at bringing in new business.

Although popular, this "binary" evaluation process does little to help a sales manager improve his or her sales team's performance.

To understand sales performance, a sales manager must consider a constellation of factors, including:

- Size of territory
- Product penetration (saturation level)
- History of sales territory
- Rate of sales growth
- Number of new accounts
- Number of lost accounts
- Percentage of business for "A"-, "B"-, and "C"-level accounts
- Number of sales calls, demonstrations, and proposals generated
- Spectrum of products sold
- Size of quota (attainment factors)
- Date of last sale
- Performance against other salespeople
- Customer relations/complaints
- Organizational skills
- Attitude about meetings/authority

Each one of these factors can signal a potential problem, which, if rectified, can help a weak salesperson get back on track.

WHAT YOU DON'T KNOW CAN HURT YOU

It is very important for sales managers to be informed about their company's personnel policies and their state's labor laws. Employees expect to be treated with respect and compassion, and will stand firm to ensure that their employee rights are upheld.

PROBLEM AREA	POSSIBLE CAUSE/SOLUTION
Size of territory	Salesperson cannot deal with so many prospects.
Product penetration	Salesperson may have to focus on selling secondary product line.
History of sales territory	Salesperson may have problem accounts that have "poisoned" the territory.
Rate of sales growth	If growth is slow and steady, it may be time for a new marketing campaign, or products may need to be updated or replaced.
Number of new accounts	No new accounts usually indicates strong competition, or that more time should be spent prospecting.
Number of lost accounts	Many lost accounts usually means customer service is low or products are obsolete.
Percentage of business from "A"-, "B"-, and "C"-level accounts	If all business is from "A"-level accounts, the salesperson may not have the time or energy to work smaller opportunities. You may need to reassign "B" and "C" opportunities to other salespeople.
Number of sales calls and demonstrations generated	If very few sales calls are being made, the salesperson may be burned out, or may be uncomfortable making cold calls.
Number of proposals generated	If very few proposals are being written, it may be time to put together a proposal "template," or a boilerplate proposal that can be used by all your salespeople.
Spectrum of products sold	If your salespeople are selling only a few of your company's products, you will need to evaluate whether market acceptance, lack of product knowledge, your sales compensation program, or other factors are responsible.
Size of quota (attainment factors)	If your salesperson has doubts about his or her quota, you may need to "resell" it to that person. If a quota is very low, it is not motivating; and if a quota is too high, it can also be demotivating.
Date of last sale	If it has been a long time since your salesperson's last big sale, he or she may be burned out, or may need a minimarketing campaign to put life back into his or her territory.

Performance against other salespeople	If one salesperson is doing poorly, it is probably the salesperson; if the entire sales force is having problems, it is time to reevaluate your marketing programs, product focus, and support infrastructure.
Customer relations/ complaints	If a salesperson is extremely well liked but is doing poorly, he or she may be socializing too much.
	If a salesperson is disliked, that person probably needs to work on his or her interpersonal communication skills.
	If a salesperson is despised but is consistently at the top of the sales charts, that person should be tolerated until you can replace him or her.
Organizational skills	If office work isn't getting done, you may need to change your compensation program to motivate your salespeople to complete their paperwork properly, or you can hire more support personnel so your salespeople can stay in front of their customers.
Attitude about meetings/authority	If a salesperson has difficulty showing up for meetings, he or she may have personal problems or be involved with substance abuse.

If you are in doubt about your company's compliance with employment laws, you should consult a human resources specialist or an attorney who specializes in this area. If your business does not have a clearly written employee policy handbook, you may have a great deal of legal exposure.

It is also important to become familiar with basic contract law. In that way you'll know when to consult your attorney and when to get out your checkbook!

WALK THE TALK

Sales managers are role models for their sales staff. If you are positive and enthusiastic, your salespeople will tend to be positive and enthusiastic; if you are pessimistic and cynical, your salespeople will tend to be curmudgeons as well.

Over the years I have learned that motivation equals positive energy and that positive energy sells!

MANAGING YOUR BUSINESS

One of the keys to Microsoft's success is the pervasive use of computers and electronic communications to support their sales and marketing programs.

In this section you will learn how to use your organizational skills, computers, and electronic communications to help you better manage your selling opportunities.

CHAPTER FOURTEEN

MAKING YOUR OFFICE A STRATEGIC WEAPON

"Early to bed, early to rise, work like hell and organize."
—ALBERT GORE, JR.

Microsoft's "recipe" for success is very simple. Microsoft hires the smartest people it can find, and provides them with the resources they need to channel their creative energy into building new business opportunities.

All account managers at Microsoft have their own private office, at least one computer, access to whatever clerical resources they need to support their selling efforts, and a corporate credit card to charge business expenses. They are also given access to the latest communications facilities, and to comfortable meeting rooms equipped with white boards, PC projection systems, and a never-ending supply of free coffee and soft drinks.

Microsoft's account managers are given the tools they need to work efficiently. And because of this, they give back their best effort.

It is not unusual for account managers to work several evenings and weekend days each month, and to spend a great deal of their time on the road, working with customers and attending industry sales events.

When I began working for Microsoft, I didn't feel that I had a new job, so much as that I had adopted a new lifestyle!

IS YOUR OFFICE A STRATEGIC WEAPON?

Account managers at Microsoft spend a great deal of their time on the road, but like most account managers, they spend at least part of their workweek in a "traditional" office setting.

Offices serve three key functions: a *work area* where you can perform your daily tasks, a *storage place* for the resources you need to do your work, and a *meeting place* where you can meet with your coworkers and customers.

In this chapter you will learn how to better manage the time you spend in your office, and you will learn several techniques you can use to help you overcome "information overload."

Taking the time to organize your office and eliminate time-wasting "info-distractions" will help you free up valuable selling time. And it will help you turn your office into a "strategic weapon" that will give you a competitive advantage against your less organized competitors.

ORGANIZING YOUR WORK AREA

The first step to organizing your office is to organize your personal work area.

At Microsoft, my desk used to be piled high with papers, never-filed folders, unsorted papers, out-of-date periodicals, and empty fast-food containers. My cluttered desk made it very difficult for me to work efficiently.

One day I realized that one of the easiest things I could do to improve my office productivity was to move everything off of my desk, and away from my field of view, that didn't need to be there.

Having piles of work in my field of view periodically interrupts my train of thought. When my "interrupts" are away from my field of vision, I find it easier to concentrate on the job that I am working on.*

Most people position their desk so it faces the front door of their office. This is appropriate for greeting customers and coworkers, but most people are less distracted if they position their desk so it faces a wall, or so it is angled away from distracting office traffic patterns.

At Microsoft, most of us positioned our desks so they faced a window or a wall. But to be honest, the glare on our computer monitors was a major consideration in how we arranged our offices. If we were on the sunny side of our building, facing our desk toward a window or having a window directly behind us was not an option.

I keep the tools I use on a regular basis, such as my telephone and computer keyboard, within arm's reach, and move less used objects outside of my personal work zone.

Austere offices look "professional," but they are not necessarily conducive to productivity. Having some personal objects around can liven up your workspace and can make it more enjoyable to work in. The trick is to draw the line when your office's "personality" metamorphoses into clutter.†

ORGANIZING YOUR PAPERWORK

One day I spent more than half an hour looking through papers on my desk to find a copy of a contract I was working on. I eventually found the contract on an office chair, where I had put it so I wouldn't lose it on my desk.

---

* Several years ago, I asked some of my coworkers to move their in-boxes off of their desks. They reported that their stress level decreased and that they found it easier to concentrate. This was not a scientific study, but I hope it encourages you to organize your work area.

† When I first went to work at Microsoft I was surprised to discover that a number of my coworkers kept birds and fish in their offices. But I soon discovered the reason. Your computer may turn against you, but your pets will always love you!

I spent the next half hour drafting four resolutions:

- I resolved to review papers once, and to make a decision about whether I needed to act on them at once, file them for future reference, or throw them away.

  I believe that this discipline has enabled me to recapture at least four hours of wasted time each month!

- I also resolved to no longer permit myself to stack up piles of paper. I reasoned that if my papers were important enough to keep, they were important enough to file.

  By eliminating the ten to fifteen minutes a day that I wasted resorting piles of paper, searching for lost correspondence, and moving stacks of paper away from my work area, I reclaimed another half of a workday each month.

- Since new paper usually means new work, I resolved to delegate as many office tasks to my sales support personnel as possible.

- And finally, I resolved to respect my own priorities. I realized that if I let myself become distracted by each piece of paper that was delivered to my office, I wouldn't have enough time to reach my sales objectives.

  This resolution has been the toughest one to keep. But I find that using my daily planner helps me stay focused on my high-priority selling activities and helps me limit the amount of time I spend on interruption-driven office tasks.

MANAGING YOUR MAIL

Most businesspeople are on hundreds of mailing lists. The more mailing lists you are on, the more unsolicited mail you will receive. I receive more than two *feet* of unsolicited mail each month.

Unsolicited "junk" mail is designed to be compelling. When I receive mail, something inside of me wants to open it up to discover if there is some valuable offer or free promotion inside. But the more unsolicited mail I receive, the more time I can waste sorting and reading it.

Before I developed a system to help me manage my junk mail, I allowed myself to waste about a half hour each day "sorting" my mail. At Microsoft I developed a simple technique I use to help me sort and prioritize my mail *before* I read it.

- First, if I can identify a piece of unsolicited mail without opening it up, and I know I do not need to read it, it goes into my paper recycling pail immediately. No point in risking a paper cut!
- Next, I sort my remaining mail into four "stacks."

Immediate action required. I try to handle at least 80 percent of my priority "A" mail when I open it. I define priority "A" mail as correspondence from my customers and from anyone in my company who can influence my job security.

I rarely send out formal business letters anymore, unless I am sending out a response to a prospective customer's request for information. My favorite way to respond to written communications is through Internet E-mail, or through quick handwritten notes on my stationery.

I also save time by keeping my old correspondence, marketing materials, and sales proposals on line, so I can use my word processor to cut and paste together new documents from my "boilerplate."

File for later use. My rule about unread mail is that if it's important enough to save, it's important enough to file. No stacks, no need for a paper chase.

Newspapers and trade periodicals. In the computer business, reading trade publications is the best way to keep up-to-date on new developments. I receive about fifteen different magazines a month to help me stay current in my field.

The text of most of these magazines is available on-line, and is accessible through the Internet. So it is no longer necessary for me to archive old magazines. I keep a few back issues of my favorite periodicals; the rest go into my recycling bin.

Financial statements and invoices. I use an on-line banking service to record transactions, draft checks, and pay many of my bills automatically by authorizing direct payments. This helps me save time and helps me keep accurate financial records.

Putting mail aside for further consideration is a time-wasting habit. In most cases, no new additional information ever comes along to help you make a better decision about how to handle it.

FILING SYSTEMS

Organizing paperwork by "activity" or "client" is a good way to ensure that you can find the information you need when you are working on a specific task.

At Microsoft, I created file folders for every customer, major task, administrative department notice, and information source, such as PC industry reports and newsletters, that I needed to store and reference.

Once I had created my files, I was able to reduce the time I spent organizing papers in my office to about five minutes a day.

JUST TO BE SAFE

Government regulations and our litigious society are compelling us to amass and store more information about our business operations than ever before.

More than half of the paper that I filed at Microsoft consisted of meeting notes, trip reports, nondisclosure agreements, customer letters, business proposals, reports, and other documents I felt might be needed to support my conduct if any legal actions were brought against Microsoft or myself.

As it turned out, the only legal actions I was involved with were bad-debt collections when a few of my OEMs decided not to pay the royalties they owed us!*

---

* It was at this point that I learned the legal term "restraining order."

TASK ANALYSIS

The key to improving office procedures is to analyze how your work is done and then to break each activity into separate steps. After you have identified each step, you can rethink how each step of the task is done and then develop new ways to save time or to make the work easier to accomplish.

Many companies bring in outside consultants to help them reengineer their operations; however, it is possible for most companies to improve their own productivity without using outside resources, by completing a simple *task analysis*.

I learned how to do a task analysis when my boss at Microsoft asked me to develop a procedure to resell prepackaged software products through our OEM division.

Developing this program could have been straightforward, but many people in different departments were involved, and it became very political. Everybody had an opinion about how we should set up the program, and a few managers, who wanted to have packaged product revenues continue to flow into their own department, didn't want the program set up at all.

It took about three weeks for me to figure out what I was doing, and another couple of months to get a pilot program for our new business up and running. This is how I did it:

STEP 1: **DEFINE THE WORK YOU WANT TO ANALYZE**

My first step was to define the tasks I wanted to restructure.

It is important to break complex tasks into manageable work processes. If the process you want to analyze is too complex, it will be difficult to visualize how different people (and computers) work together to complete each task, and you may get bogged down and discouraged.

STEP 2: **WRITE A BRIEF DESCRIPTION OF EACH TASK**

Pretend you are an investigative reporter, and get all the facts. Determine *who* is involved, *what* happens, *when* it happens, *why* it happens, and *how* each task is completed.

TASK ANALYSIS	EXAMPLE QUESTIONS
Who?	• Who is involved? • Are the correct people involved? • Should anyone else be involved?
What?	• What is being done? • What should be done? • Is there a better way to do the work?
Where?	• Where is the work being done? • Why is the work being done there? • Is that the best place to do the work? • Can the work be done somewhere else?
When?	• When is the work done? • Why is the work done at that time? • Is that the best time to do the work? • Is it better to do the work at a different time?
Why?	• Why is the work being done? • Is there any way to eliminate the work? • Should other work be done?
How?	• How is the work being done? • Can the work be done easier, faster, or with fewer resources? • Can these changes be implemented?

STEP 3: **IDENTIFY UNNECESSARY STEPS AND TIME WASTERS**

Be tenacious; don't assume that a process makes sense just because it has been in place for a long time. Look for bottle-necks, redundant steps, backtracking, transportation delays, lack of controls, and communication problems.

Some of my favorite time wasters are unnecessary reports, reports sent to managers who don't use the information, reports filed in multiple locations, detailed reports sent to busy managers without executive summaries, and my perennial favorite: detailed cover-your-backside reports for the "file."

STEP 4: **FLOW-CHART THE PROCESS**

You can illustrate each step of a process with standard workflow symbols, or you can just use labeled blocks connected with lines and arrows. The important thing is to make sure that every step in the process is included in your flow chart and that your diagram is easy to understand.

STEP 5: **ASK COWORKERS WHAT THEY THINK**

When your flow chart is complete, show it to the people involved with the work process you are analyzing to get their input. Each person in a work group usually has a slightly different perspective on the work being done by their group, and each person's perspective can help you identify specific steps or tasks that can be improved or eliminated.

STEP 6: **FIGURE OUT A BETTER SOLUTION**

At this point you can analyze each step in your flow chart to determine if any steps can be combined, rerouted, or eliminated. This is also a good time to consider the impact of replacing manual processing and routing steps with automated solutions.

STEP 7: **CONSIDER OFFICE AUTOMATION**

Implementing automated systems can help your company increase productivity, decrease operating expenses, provide a higher customer service level, and develop new business opportunities. However, automated systems can be very expensive to implement, and they may not provide a good return on your investment unless they are implemented and managed properly.

For example, if you route multipart paper forms through your company, you may be able to reduce your operating expenses by using a computer system to route electronic forms to different people who are working together to complete a specific task. But if your automated system is not implemented and managed properly, you can lose critical information, and you may need to return to your paper forms–based system to get your work done.

STEP 8: **REVIEW YOUR ANALYSIS, ASK FOR HELP**

After you have completed your task analysis you can put together an action plan to detail the steps you need to restructure to improve your group's productivity.

If you have already involved your coworkers in your task analysis, they should be ready to support your changes. If you haven't, you should be prepared to do some internal selling to convince your coworkers that the changes you are proposing will improve productivity and are worth implementing.

STEP 9: **IMPLEMENT YOUR CHANGES**

When your plan is complete, you should have it reviewed by your manager and approved by upper management (unless, of course, *you* are upper management).

When you have received final approval for your proposed changes, you should notify all the people involved, and verify that everyone understands your new procedures before they are implemented. This notification will help you avoid confusion and will help you anticipate any implementation issues that may arise.

STEP 10: **EVALUATE YOUR CHANGES**

After you have implemented your changes, you should determine whether your changes have improved productivity. If they have, your changes may become catalysts for you to invest time identifying other areas that can be improved. If they have not, you should review your task analysis to determine why your changes were ineffective.

Reasonable Expectations

Before you implement your proposed changes, you should make an effort to set your coworkers' expectations at a reasonable level. Many businesses operate on very small profit margins. The opportunity to increase productivity, even by a modest 2 or 3 percent, can make a significant difference on the bottom line.

You can use the task analysis process to help you reorganize your office, or restructure any business operation that has the potential to save your organization money and free up valuable selling time.

MANAGING INFORMATION OVERLOAD

Last month I became curious about how much time the average American spends processing information.

I learned that the average American will read more than a hundred newspapers and thirty-five magazines, watch more than twenty-five hundred hours of television, listen to more than seven hundred hours of radio, spend more than sixty hours on the telephone, and read three books this year. I have not been able to get any reliable data on how much time is consumed browsing the Internet, but I am sure it will have a tremendous impact as more information and services become available on-line.

Although we spend most of our waking hours processing information, most of this information has very little impact on our professional success or our personal happiness. And this information overload makes it very difficult to remain focused on high-priority sales activities.

To increase my sales productivity I have developed several strategies that enable me to reduce the amount of time I spend accessing and managing unnecessary information.

PRIORITIZE YOUR READING

I have found that one of the keys to managing information overload is to prioritize my reading materials. I have canceled all my unnecessary subscriptions, I only read articles when I believe that they are relevant to my work, and I encourage the people I work with to send me executive summaries instead of detailed reports whenever possible.

SPEED-READING SECRETS

Two of the most valuable courses I took in high school were my typing class and a short course on speed-reading techniques.

"HANDY" SPEED-READING TIPS

- Read selectively; concentrate on a few good information sources.

- Keep your objectives in mind when you are reading.

- Always scan reading material so you can identify the most important or interesting material and so you can get a "top-down" understanding of the information presented.

- Scan tables of contents and indexes before reading books and magazines to identify the most important articles and to enable you to avoid scanning hundreds of advertisements.

- Read articles or sections that are most important to you, rather than automatically starting at the "beginning" of the book or magazine.

- Concentrate on the first (topic) sentence in each paragraph; if it is not important to you, skip to the next paragraph.

- Don't move your lips when you read, and keep your eyes moving down and across the page. You can absorb written information at a much faster rate than you can read words silently to yourself.

- Practice reading groups of words together. After a while you will be comfortable reading large groups of words in the same time you used to read just one word.

- Don't reread lines. Once you have read a phrase or sentence, make yourself keep your eyes moving down and across the page.

- When you read at "high speed," pause after each section you read and rapidly summarize the most important points the author has made.

- Don't take the time to memorize text unless the information is vital to your work.

- Ignore any information you believe is trivial.

- Use a "highlighter" marking pen to identify important points, and take notes on material you think you will need to review at a later time.

- Look up new words to increase your vocabulary. The larger your vocabulary is, the easier it will be for you to understand what you are reading, and to read new material faster.

- Read important material when you are well rested and alert.

- Leverage your time by reading during meals eaten alone, commercial breaks on television, and waiting times during your workday.

- Keep important reading materials in a special "To Be Read" folder that you can take with you in your briefcase. Then, when you travel, or need to wait for a meeting to start, you can read the papers in your folder.

My speed-reading course relied on a machine that had an opaque shutter that moved down the page I was reading at a constant speed. The shutter helped me focus my attention, prevented me from rereading text, and forced me to read faster than I thought I could. As my reading comprehension improved, I programmed the machine's shutter to move down the page more quickly.

Most people in my class doubled or tripled their reading speed by practicing this "pacing" technique for a few weeks.

If you don't take a speed-reading course, you can use your hand or a piece of cardboard to help yourself pace your reading, and you can practice my "handy" speed-reading tips.

MANAGING YOUR NEWS SOURCES

Many businesspeople spend more than an hour a day watching news broadcasts and reading daily local and financial newspapers.

You can save hours each week by subscribing to an on-line news service that scans, collates, and "filters" news, weather, sports, investment, and technical information based on your interests and then faxes or electronically mails the information to you each morning. Or you can spend a few minutes each morning on-line viewing MSNBC's Internet Web site, as I do.

VERBAL REPORTS

In many cases, it is faster and just as effective to provide a concise verbal report, rather than a more comprehensive written report. However, when you deliver a verbal report, it is important to be concise, organized, and specific, and to *verify* your communication.

MEMORY SKILLS

Most salespeople have a difficult time remembering the names of people they meet at business meetings and conferences. This can be a serious problem, because many people are offended when someone they are considering doing business with forgets their name.

Some people learn best through visual cues; other people learn best with audio or kinesthetic cues. I am a very visual person, so it helps me to write down the names of people I meet at meetings as soon as possible.

Over the years, I have learned a few tricks that may help you improve your memory:

- Concentrate on what you want to remember.
- Form a mental picture of what you want to remember.
- Write down what you want to remember.
- Use mnemonic devices such as "spring forward—fall backward" to remember how to switch from standard to daylight saving time.
- Use acronyms and abbreviations to help you remember phrases or sequences of instructions.
- Associate the names of people you have just met with unusual objects that remind you of them. For example, you might associate the name of a fast-talking woman who has red hair with a fire engine.
- Eliminate clutter; the better organized you are, the easier it is to remember things.
- Break out of your routines; it is easier to remember things that are unusual or out of the ordinary.

THINK GREEN

It's easy to become self-absorbed and forget about "the rest of the world." But we are the custodians of our planet. If we take responsibility for helping to conserve our natural resources, we can help ensure that the earth will remain a beautiful place to live for future generations.

At Microsoft we made a sincere effort to "reduce, reuse, and recycle" paper and office supplies to help preserve our environment. I hope you encourage your business to make a similar commitment.

FIRST THE PAPER, THEN THE ELECTRONS

In this chapter you learned how to turn your office into a "strategic weapon." In the next two chapters you will learn how to use computers and electronic communications to help you leverage your selling efforts.

Take a deep breath, and get ready for the future....

CHAPTER FIFTEEN

LEVERAGING YOUR COMMUNICATIONS

"This is an exciting time in the Information Age. It is the very beginning."
—**BILL GATES**

The key to successful selling in today's information-driven markets is communication. Any technology that improves communication between you and your customer can help you move the selling process forward.

In most selling situations your telephone and facsimile machine are the two most powerful tools you have for leveraging your selling time. Telephones enable you to communicate with your customers instantaneously, without taking the time to commute to face-to-face meetings. And facsimile or "fax" machines enable your documents to be transmitted digitally over a telephone connection.

At Microsoft we relied on telephones and fax machines to help us leverage our selling time so we could stay in touch with our OEMs—regardless of where we were, what time zone we were in, or how late we had been out partying the night before!

6 TIPS FOR MANAGING INCOMING CALLS

1. Screen your business calls using voice mail or a receptionist.
2. Notify frequent callers if you will be out of the office for the day.
3. Return your calls promptly.
4. Be courteous at all times.
5. Avoid taking calls when you have visitors in your office.
6. Inform frequent callers of the best time to call you.

MANAGING YOUR TELEPHONE

At Microsoft, I learned that the best way to eliminate unnecessary telephone interruptions was to stop answering my phone and to delegate the responsibility for routing my incoming phone calls to our telephone receptionist or our voice mail system.

My customers expect me to be responsive when they call, but they don't expect me to be sitting at my desk waiting to talk with them.

Returning Your Calls

There is no formula for how often you should return your calls throughout the day. When I worked at Microsoft, I made it a habit to return my telephone calls twice a day, once in the morning and once late in the afternoon. But you may need to return your calls more or less frequently than this.

In any case, when you are busy with a project, or if you have visitors in your office, you will be more productive if you have your receptionist or voice mail system record your messages, and then return your telephone calls between your other activities. This will save you from unnecessary interruptions and will allow you time to prepare for your calls before returning them.

Create a "Flight Plan"

If you take the time to create an agenda or "flight plan" for your telephone calls, you will save time, and you will be better prepared to move business forward with your customers.

10 TIME-SAVING TIPS FOR PLACING CALLS

1. Time your calls to track how much time you spend on the phone.

2. Schedule important calls in your daily calendar, like any other business meeting.

3. Keep a record of the best times to call frequently called business associates.

4. Place calls early in the morning if they require some action to be taken later that day.

5. Use a speed dialing system for your most frequently called numbers.

6. Use three-way conference calling to share information with multiple customer contacts and to eliminate the need to make additional "for your information" calls.

7. Use call forwarding to have your calls automatically forwarded to you from your office phone.

8. Don't spend too much time socializing; the person you are calling may be politely waiting to get back to his or her own work.

9. Install additional telephones, or use a cordless telephone to eliminate the need to run between rooms to take calls.

10. I prefer to use a 900 MHz wireless phone because it is more secure, has better sound quality, and can transmit farther without becoming too noisy.

In 1989 AT&T did a study indicating that unplanned business telephone calls averaged eleven minutes, while planned telephone calls averaged seven minutes. When AT&T mandated that their employees keep a log of why they made each long-distance call, the company was able to reduce their own long-distance telephone charges by 30 percent.

Telephone Tag

Our OEM account managers spent a significant percentage of their workday on the telephone. Unfortunately, a great deal of this time was wasted playing "telephone tag."

According to a study done by Adia Personnel, in Menlo Park, New Jersey, only 17 percent of business calls are completed on

10 TIPS FOR MANAGING VOICE MAIL

1. Record a short, polite message in your own voice so a caller has instant verification that they have reached your voice mail. Humorous messages are rarely funny after the first listen.

2. Ask your callers to identify themselves, record their telephone number, and state the time and purpose of their call. If possible use a voice mail system that time-stamps your callers' messages.

3. If you are going to be away from your office for more than a day, specify in your answer message when you will be returning your calls.

4. If you will be gone for an extended time, record in your answer message the name and extension of a person your caller can contact for immediate help, and arrange to have someone return "urgent" calls while you are away.

5. If your voice mail system or your access numbers are being changed, inform your key customers and contacts as soon as possible.

6. Try to limit the number of different mailbox selections for your callers.

7. If possible, allow repeat callers to bypass automated voice mail prompts and go directly to your voice mailbox.

8. If possible, program your voice mail system to enable a caller to reach a live operator by dialing "0" on their phone.

9. If you return your calls promptly, your customers will be happy to leave messages for you.

10. Don't be frustrated by other people's cumbersome voice mail systems; leaving a message is better than wasting time playing telephone tag.

the first try; 26 percent are completed after two tries; and 47 percent are completed after three tries. In 1990 AT&T reported that the chances of reaching the businessperson you were calling on the first try was only one in six.

VOICE MAIL

Voice mail systems are great time-savers. They can record messages more quickly and accurately than a receptionist, and they can help you reduce the number of interruptions during your workday.

Voice mail can also help you prioritize your messages by allowing callers to specify whether their call is urgent, and can provide access to your messages from any telephone, using a secure password that restricts unauthorized access.

If your company uses a paging system, voice mail can reduce the need to page people to the telephone and can be programmed to forward messages to a wireless pager system or to an Internet voice mail account.

But the main reason I'm sold on voice mail is that voice mail messages are usually much *shorter* than regular phone messages.

If your customers avoid using your voice mail system, your system may be too difficult to work with, or you may not be returning your calls as quickly as your customers expect you to.

TELEPHONE LOGS

Keeping a telephone log of every call you make or receive can help you track where new business is coming from. A telephone log can also come to the rescue if an important contact's name or phone number is misplaced.

The only downside of keeping a telephone log is the time necessary to maintain it. But if you spend most of your workday at a desk, a PC-based contact manager such as Symantec's ACT!™ can automatically track each phone call you make using the program's telephone interface.

As PCs become more functional and easier to use, it is becoming easier to maintain an "audit trail" of the entire selling process.

CLIENT-CENTERED™ TELEMARKETING

At Microsoft, we did not need to make telemarketing calls to OEMs to identify new prospects. But most companies must rely on telemarketing to help them identify qualified prospects for their products and services.

Many salespeople feel that telemarketing calls are difficult to make, because many of the people who are contacted are either unqualified or don't want to be bothered. But telemarketing is a great way to qualify prospective customers.

Over the years I have learned that the key to making effective telemarketing calls is careful planning. The seven-step Client-Centered™ telemarketing process is effective, and it is *almost* painless:

STEP 1: **DEFINE REASONABLE OBJECTIVES**

Before you make your first telemarketing call, you should define objectives for your calls that are *reasonable.*

For example, in most situations it is unrealistic to try to close a high-ticket sale on your first "cold" call. A more logical objective is to establish a dialogue with your customer, and to use your dialogue to move your customer's purchasing process forward by qualifying his or her need, and presenting enough information about your products and services to position yourself as a viable solution provider.

I like to set objectives that are achievable in at least 20 percent of the calls I make. I have found that when I spend hours of time on the phone without achieving my objectives, it is almost always because I am attempting to move the selling process forward too quickly by setting unrealistic objectives.

STEP 2: **DEVELOP AN AGENDA**

Many salespeople find it helpful to create a script that outlines the information they would like to present during their sales call, and then to memorize their "pitch" to make it easier for them to rapidly qualify the people they call.

Memorizing a sales pitch can help telephone marketers present a simple marketing "story." However, I have never been comfortable with this approach. I have found that when I repeat memorized lines, I stop listening to my customers, and that it is difficult for me to respond to their questions or concerns until I "play back" the appropriate point from my script.

I prefer to develop a simple agenda or "road map" for my telemarketing call that includes a brief *introduction*, a few *general qualification questions*, time to respond to my *customer's questions*, and a *request for action*.

STEP 3: **DEVELOP A COMPELLING INTRODUCTION**

The first twenty seconds of a telephone call are the most important. During this time you must introduce yourself and begin to establish a productive dialogue with the person you are calling.

The first step toward establishing a dialogue is to identify yourself, and then explain why you are calling and how your information will benefit the person you are talking to.

I like to cover this information in two or three sentences. For example, I might say, "Hi, my name is Doug Dayton. I work with Client-Centered™ Training. We're doing a free seminar on Internet marketing next month and wanted to know if anyone in your company might be interested in attending."

One of the secrets of effective telemarketing is making it as easy as possible for your customer to get in sync with your objectives.

STEP 4: **QUALIFY YOUR CUSTOMER**

After I have introduced myself, I like to open a dialogue with the person I have called by asking them a few general qualification questions.*

The rhythm and flow of the conversation I have with the person I have called is as important as the information that is communicated. If I can involve my customer in a dialogue, I know I am well on the way to building the trust and rapport I will need to establish myself as a problem-solver and supplier.

STEP 5: **ANSWER YOUR CUSTOMER'S QUESTIONS**

After you have established a dialogue with your customer, you should be prepared to answer any questions your prospective

---

* If you have forgotten how to qualify a customer, refer back to the chapter on Client-Centered™ selling skills.

customer has about your company, your products, and any other issues they wish to discuss with you.

If your product line is technical or very broad, you should have background material available that covers the details potential customers will be interested in.

It is very important to take the time to figure out how to handle each customer concern you think may come up during your sales calls before you pick up your telephone. If you don't know exactly what you want to communicate to your customer, you may wind up making your "cold" calls from the "hot" seat.

STEP 6: **REQUEST AN ACTION**

Before you end your call, you should verify whatever action plan you have developed with your customer. For example, if you and your prospective customer agree that it is worthwhile to schedule a product demonstration, you should verify the time and place of your meeting.

STEP 7: **THANK YOUR CUSTOMER FOR HIS OR HER TIME AND CONSIDERATION**

The last thing you should do before you hang up the receiver and record your contact qualification information in your contact database, and any action items you need to follow up in your daily planner, is to thank your customer for his or her time and consideration.

Prospective customers are not obligated to talk to salespeople. If a person is courteous enough to take your call, it's only fair to thank that person for his or her time.

Commitment, Discipline, and a Sense of Humor

Successful telephone selling takes commitment, discipline, and a sense of humor.

All salespeople face the same frustrations when they try to reach their customers and prospects on the phone. The people you want to reach are often unavailable; your call may reach them at a bad time; they may not want to talk with you; or they may not have voice mail or a receptionist to take your message.

The biggest challenge of telephone selling is learning to overcome setbacks, and to maintain a positive attitude when you make each new call.

PERSONAL SELLING STYLE

Many salespeople believe they must adopt a special telephone selling style to be effective telemarketers. But after working with hundreds of account managers over the years, I have realized that there is no "correct" telephone selling style.

The key to successful telephone selling is learning how to *flex* your selling style to accommodate your customer's needs and concerns—in other words, to view the sales process from your customer's perspective and to use your telephone call to initiate a dialogue that will help your customer make an informed purchasing decision.

The key to telemarketing success is not to "make more calls"; it is to use your Client-Centered™ communication skills to enable you to help each customers you talk with move their purchasing process forward.

Telemarketing Energy = Results

Telemarketing is a great way to qualify prospective customers. However, successful telemarketing, like other sales activities, requires you to prepare for your sales call, to pay careful attention to your customer, to establish a dialogue, and to verify your communications.

When you plan a telemarketing campaign, it is helpful to put together a call agenda or script to make sure you obtain all the information you need to qualify your prospects. And if your product line is technical or very broad, you should have background material available that provides the information you will need to answer prospective customers' questions.

After each telemarketing call you can enter contact qualification information into a prospect database. Over time your prospect database will become a valuable marketing resource.

Most salespeople keep their prospect and customer contact databases on index cards. These are easy to file alphabetically, and convenient to keep on a desk. However, the best way to manage a large number of prospects or customers is with an automated sales management system.*

Telemarketing Problems

It is more difficult to communicate over the telephone than face-to-face. And in most cases, you cannot move the selling process forward over the telephone as quickly as you can in a face-to-face sales meeting. But telemarketing can help you leverage your selling time, and the telephone may be the only way to contact some of your best prospects.

Unfortunately, many salespeople have a difficult time making telemarketing calls. There are several reasons for this:

- Telemarketing calls are "real" sales calls. You should not pick up your telephone to call a prospective customer until you are ready to handle his or her questions and concerns. Depending on your situation, you may need to attend product training, memorize information from your company's product brochures, or make other preparations to ensure that you are prepared to help your customer move his or her purchasing process forward when you call.

- You should not make a telemarketing call until you know exactly how you plan to introduce yourself and your products, and how you plan to qualify your prospective customers' needs. As noted above, it is helpful to develop an agenda or "script" for your sales calls to help you qualify the people you contact.

- If you are discouraged because you have not achieved your telemarketing objectives in the past, you may need to set more reasonable objectives, and practice handling customer concerns, before you will be ready to make telemarketing calls again with a revitalized attitude.

---

* We will discuss sales management systems in the next chapter.

Many salespeople feel that telemarketing is a "low-level" sales activity that should be done by entry-level sales support personnel. But the truth is, the better prepared a telemarketing salesperson is, the easier it will be for that person to qualify prospective customers.

If your telemarketing objective is to acquire basic contact information, such as a purchaser's name and job title, an entry-level sales assistant should be able to handle the call. But qualifying a customer's need for a technical product often requires a product specialist's knowledge and experience.

In any case, before you ask your sales support staff to make telemarketing calls, you should make a few calls yourself to determine whether your telemarketing objectives are reasonable and to evaluate whether your staff has the information and expertise they need to handle prospective customers' concerns.

ROLE-PLAYING

One of the best ways to improve your telephone skills is to role-play different types of sales calls with a coworker. For example, you might pretend to make a "cold" call to prospect for new sales leads, or to handle a "problem" account situation, such as responding to a call from a customer upset about a delay in your delivery schedule.*

Nonverbal Cues

Most salespeople are unaware of how much they rely on nonverbal cues during a sales call. After role-playing telemarketing calls at Microsoft, we had our account managers "replay" the same sales call "face-to-face" with a coworker so they could experience the dramatic difference in their ability to communicate when they could rely on visual cues.

---

* The easiest way to role-play a telephone sales call is to simulate a telephone call with a coworker by simply avoiding looking at each other during your conversation.

Sales Call Checklist

What you say during your sales call is very important, but how you say it will ultimately determine whether you can establish an effective dialogue with your customer, and whether your customer will be inclined to do business with you in the future.

After you role-play your telemarketing call with your partner, you should discuss your call with that person to find out how he or she felt and what that person was thinking during and after your call.

DIRECT MAIL/TELEMARKETING

One of the most effective ways to prospect for new business is to combine a direct-mail campaign with telemarketing.

The cost of prospecting with a direct-mail/telemarketing campaign is incremental. If you do not have enough active prospects to work with, you can increase your telemarketing efforts, or send out more direct-mail pieces. Then, as soon you have generated enough prospects to keep yourself busy, you can reduce the amount of telemarketing and direct mailings you are doing.

If you initiate a direct-mail/telemarketing campaign, you should be sure that everyone who answers your phone knows how to qualify a caller's needs, and how to answer specific questions about your program or promotion, such as where and when a seminar is being held.

Pilot-Test Your Program

One of my more interesting consulting assignments was with a company that had recently announced a new software package for executive "decisionmakers."

At our meeting my client told me they had used a direct-mail program to market their products but that they had not had much success.

I was surprised to learn that my client had mailed about fifty thousand pieces, at a cost of more than $4 per mailer. They received fewer than a hundred requests for information, and subsequently sold about fifteen copies of their $300 software

SALES CALL CHECK LIST

I have developed a simple check list to help evaluate how effective
role-played telemarketing sales calls were:

- Did you identify yourself and state why you were calling?
- Did you verify the name of the person you were talking with and, if necessary, establish that person's position in his or her company?
- Was your introduction interesting, informative, and compelling?
- Did your introduction help you build a positive rapport with your customer?
- Did you say anything that was confusing or that might cause a future misunderstanding?
- How would you change your introduction?
- Were you able to qualify your customer's need for your products?
- Were you able to qualify your customer's purchasing authority?
- Were you able to qualify your customer's time frame for a purchase?
- Were you able to determine whether your customer had budgeted funds to purchase the type of products that you sell?
- Did you feel that you qualified your customer well enough to determine whether it was worthwhile for you to commit additional selling time to helping the customer move their purchasing process forward?
- Did you ask your customer for some type of commitment to move the selling process forward?
- Did you and your customer agree on an action plan to move business forward?
- Did you verify this action plan with your customer during your call?
- Do you feel that you achieved your objective for your call?
- Are you optimistic that you can move business forward with this customer?
- What questions do you wish you had asked to better qualify your customer?
- Were you prepared to answer your customer's questions?
- Did you enjoy your sales call?
- What would you do differently with the advantage of hindsight?
- What additional steps do you feel you need to include in your telemarketing agenda?
- What do you plan to do to prepare for your next telemarketing sales call?

package to companies that responded to their promotion. The mailing cost the company more than 75 percent of its $300,000 annual marketing budget.

When I reviewed my client's marketing program it was evident that they had never done a direct-mail campaign before and that they had made almost every conceivable error.

First, they produced a very expensive brochure, which did not clearly explain what their product did, or how it would be of value to prospective customers. It focused on describing the "how" of their product story—rather than focusing on customer benefits.

Then they purchased mailing lists that were inexpensive but that were poorly qualified and did not include recipients' telephone numbers.

More than 15 percent of the mailers my client sent out were returned for incorrect addresses. And since there were no telephone numbers included with their mailing list, it was extremely difficult to follow up with any recipients to determine whether they had received their mailer and what they thought about it.

Although these were serious problems, my client would have been able to overcome them if they had *tested* their program before committing so much of their marketing resources to it.

To test their program, my client could have sent copies of the mailer to a small sample of the names on their mailing list and then followed up with telemarketing calls to determine whether their story was compelling.

As it turned out, my client had invested more than three-quarters of their marketing budget without making a significant number of sales, and most importantly, without ever discovering exactly *why* their campaign was unsuccessful.

SPEAKERPHONES AND HEADSETS

Speakerphones allow you to free up your hands during a telephone call, or to participate in a teleconference along with other people in your office. Although speakerphones are convenient to use, many people think that the "boom in a barrel" sound is obnoxious.

Higher-quality speakerphones, which are designed for conference rooms, provide sound quality that is comparable to a traditional telephone handset. However, these units cost from $250 to $1,500.

Most of the technical support people, and many account managers at Microsoft use telephone headsets when they are working at their computers.

Telephone headsets are inexpensive, they free up your hands to type or to take notes, and their sound quality is comparable to a standard telephone handset.

PAGERS

Millions of people use wireless pagers to enable their friends and business contacts to reach them when they are away from their home or office phone. To page someone, a caller dials a special access phone number, and then enters their own phone number to alert the person to call that person back.

One of the main reasons for the popularity of pagers is their low cost. Pagers are available for about $30, and monthly service fees are nominal. Motorola is the leader in this technology, but competitive products are available from Seiko and other manufacturers.

New paging services that support digitally recorded messages and Internet mail services are being introduced. But the advantages of these "next generation" paging systems may be obviated if the cost of other wireless communication services continues to decline.

CELLULAR TELEPHONES

Cellular telephones are great time-savers for salespeople who spend time away from their office, or in their car commuting.

Pocket-sized, wireless cellular phones perform well in most urban areas. However, car phones have more transmit power, and perform better in rural areas.

The prices on cellular phones have dropped rapidly. Most cellular communications companies subsidize "free" cellular phones for customers who sign a one-year service contract. And high-usage customers pay about twenty-five cents per minute for access charges during normal business hours. However, in addition to these charges, callers pay "roaming" fees if they leave their assigned cellular area.

Digital (PCS) cellular phone service is becoming more widely available and offers less expensive connection time, advanced features such as caller ID, and better security. Digital cellular connections do not yet provide the same quality of sound as analog connections, but they are acceptable.

The easiest way to manage cellular connection time is to restrict access to your cellular telephone number to your assistant at work and the members of your family. Your assistant can screen your calls so you only have to return high-priority messages while you are out of your office.

MANAGING YOUR FAX

The power of fax machines to provide instantaneous "mail" service has literally revolutionized how many businesses operate.

Fax machines used to be costly, but over the past decade they have become much less expensive. Stand-alone fax machines are available for about $125, and fax/modem cards for PCs cost about $40. Most fax machines include an automatic line switch so that the fax machine can share a single telephone line with a standard telephone; and many fax machines feature automatic document feeders and sheet cutters.

High-end fax machines can be programmed to designate multiple recipients for a fax transmission, and can delay document transmission to save telephone line charges by placing calls after standard work hours. They can also be programmed to block reception of "junk" faxes from specific phone numbers and provide extra memory chips to store incoming faxes when they run out of paper.

Most fax machines use thermal paper, but more expensive fax machines feature laser or ink-jet printers that can produce high-quality plain-paper output.

Fax transmission is usually very reliable, but fax machines are not perfect. Fax transmission problems usually result from incorrectly dialed telephone numbers, or when faxes are received properly but are routed to the wrong person.

Fax machines do a fair job of transmitting graphic information. However, signatures on faxed documents may not be legally binding.

Automated Fax Distribution

You can use automated fax distribution to eliminate the need to manually fax your message to multiple contacts.

To automatically distribute faxes to a list of recipients, you must first create an electronic "address book" that contains your sales contact's fax numbers using PC-based fax software, such as the Fax software included with Microsoft Office.

After your electronic "address book" is compiled, you can put your sales contacts on different fax distribution lists based on their product interest, location, previous sales history, or any other selection criteria you choose. Then you can "broadcast" newsletters, product and service updates, and other time-sensitive messages automatically by selecting the appropriate fax distribution list.

Fax-on-Demand

Microsoft uses programmable fax servers to enable their customers to request that information, such as technical support documents stored in a special database, be automatically faxed back to them by selecting different buttons on their telephone in response to automated voice prompts.

Fax-on-demand is easy to cost-justify if the volume of calls for information you receive is very high.

Junk Faxes

Over the past decade, most businesspeople thought of fax transmissions as high-priority communications. However, as fax transmission has become more commonplace, and since direct marketers have begun sending millions of unsolicited "junk" faxes, most businesspeople no longer greet faxes with the same sense of urgency they used to.

I have found that in many situations, I have a better chance of getting my customers' attention by sending them a personal letter via snail mail (the post office), or an E-mail message on the Internet, than by sending them a fax.

Fax and the Internet

At Microsoft, I relied on faxed communications for most of my contract negotiations. Faxing documents to my customers helped me save delivery time and enabled me to draft briefer, less formal fax-cover letters. But today I rarely fax documents to my customers, because almost all of my customers can receive E-mail through the Internet.

WHAT'S NEXT?

In this chapter you learned how to use your telephone and fax machine to help you leverage your selling time. In the next chapter you will learn how to use emerging PC-based technologies to help you manage your territory and focus your selling efforts.

CHAPTER SIXTEEN

SALES FORCE AUTOMATION

"There is always a better way to do everything. It's up to you to find it."

—THOMAS EDISON

One of the first things I noticed when I left IBM to join Microsoft back in 1982 was that there were PCs on virtually everyone's desk. Microsoft's early investment in PCs and networking technologies gave Microsoft a significant competitive advantage against less automated competitors by lowering its operating costs and by increasing the productivity of its sales and marketing teams. Every hour our account managers saved using PC-based office productivity applications such as electronic mail, spreadsheets, and word processing was an hour they could invest in making sales calls and building awareness of our products.

Microsoft still invests heavily in PC-based office automation to improve their sales and marketing employees' productivity—because it's a formula that works!

DIGITAL HELPERS

PCs have become inexpensive enough for almost every company to afford, but many companies are reluctant to automate their sales force because they think that PCs will be too complicated for their salespeople to use. And despite the obvious value of using PCs, their salespeople still rely on paper and pencils to help them manage their territories.

But fortunately, PCs have become easy enough for almost anyone to master. The latest word processing and E-mail programs from Microsoft, for example, feature onscreen "wizards" that can have a new user doing productive work in just a few minutes. And Microsoft's Internet Explorer provides "point and click" navigation to Internet Web sites around the world.

Just as an average salesperson today is comfortable using voice mail and fax, over the next five years, virtually every salesperson will be using electronic mail, videoconferencing, the Internet, and other emerging PC-based technologies to help them manage their sales territories.

In this chapter you will learn about some of these new technologies. It will only take a few minutes, and the rewards are well worth the investment of your time. So be confident, and jump in. You'll be working with these "digital helpers" before you know it.

SALES MANAGEMENT SYSTEMS

When you invest selling time to qualify prospects, you acquire valuable information. Each fact you collect, such as a buyer's name, or the type and age of installed equipment, can be used to help you market your products and services.

You can store this information on index cards or in some other paper-based system. But paper-based databases are not very efficient.

The primary limitation of paper-based systems is that the information stored is difficult to find. If, for example, you store contact information on index cards, you can only locate information using an "index" (such as contact name or company) that you use to file each contact card. And you cannot use the information you have collected in computer-based tools, such as word processors and appointment schedulers, without reentering the information into your computer system.

The most efficient way to keep track of sales contacts and account information is with an automated sales management system. Using an automated sales management system for *database marketing* enables you to "save" all the information you have spent your marketing resources to acquire, and then "borrow" that information to help you achieve your sales objectives. When your company develops new products, introduces special promotions, or initiates a new sales campaign, your sales contact database can help you target your selling efforts to your best-qualified prospects.

Sales management systems such as TeleMagic™ from the Sage Group, PLC, are usually implemented at the departmental or corporate level, and enable authorized system users to generate sales status reports on demand. Simpler personal information managers usually include a contact database, an appointment scheduler, and basic reporting features. Most personal information managers are designed to work on stand-alone PCs, but some, such as Microsoft's Outlook and ACT!™ from Symantec Corporation, can also work on a local area network.

At Microsoft, we used databases to track almost every aspect of our OEM customer relationships. We tracked customer contacts, software contracts (payment schedules and renewal issues), and technical support issues. And we used a database to help us keep track of product ideas and new feature requests, which were suggested by our OEMs.

OFFICE PRODUCTIVITY SOFTWARE

Salespeople can also leverage their selling time with an integrated office application "suite" such as Microsoft Office. Microsoft Office includes a word processor, an electronic worksheet, presentation graphics tools, a powerful database, scheduling and electronic mail software, seamless Internet connectivity, and a simple personal information manager.

ADVANTAGES OF E-MAIL	DISADVANTAGES OF E-MAIL
E-mail enables you to send messages almost instantaneously to other E-mail users.	Once you've sent an E-mail message, it's "gone"—you can't edit it or take it back.
E-mail recipients do not have to be present when their mail is received.	There is no guarantee that a recipient will respond to your E-mail.
E-mail tends to be brief and less formal than other business correspondence.	E-mail can present a poor image to your customers and coworkers if it includes typographical errors, misspelled words, sentence fragments, bad grammar, or nonsequiturs.
E-mail is a convenient way to communicate with mobile and remote coworkers.	E-mail cannot replace "in person" communications.
E-mail systems enable you to "carbon copy" a message to multiple recipients on a mailing list.	It's easy to get en-"listed" on other people's mailing lists.
E-mail is a very inexpensive way to communicate.	Many people "abuse" E-mail and waste time sending unnecessary messages.
If you are using an on-line service such as America Online or Microsoft Network, or if your company's electronic mail system has a gateway to the Internet, you can send E-mail to millions of people around the world, using their Internet E-mail address.	If you don't respond to your E-mail in a timely way, the phone on your desk will start ringing again.

Microsoft Office is relatively easy to learn, and includes on-line tutorials, and easy-to-follow "wizards" that enable new users to begin doing useful work almost immediately.*

ELECTRONIC MAIL

More than one hundred million workers—connected to local and wide-area networks—use electronic mail or "E-mail" to communicate with their coworkers, customers, and suppliers.

---

* I used Microsoft Word, which is one of the office productivity applications in Microsoft Office 97, to write this book.

The primary advantage of E-mail is that it is an almost instantaneous "store and forward" technology, like voice mail, so the person you are communicating with does not have to be available at the time you send your message.

E-mail Etiquette

People interpret things they read differently from things said to them in person. So when you send E-mail, you need to be especially careful you do not "flame" anyone (be rude or obnoxious).

My rule about sarcasm, or any mean-spirited comment in my E-mail correspondence, is simple: I leave it out.

Your E-mail Address

Many people include their E-mail address on their business cards and letterhead. Encouraging customers and coworkers to send you E-mail, instead of calling you on the phone or dropping by your office, will reduce the number of interruptions in your workday, help you focus your attention on your highest-priority activities, and lower your telephone bills.

VIDEOCONFERENCING

Videoconferencing systems enable users to view each other as they talk over a standard telephone or computer network connection.

Today's desktop videoconferencing technology enables users to connect two or more PC-based videoconferencing systems together over standard (analog) or high-bandwidth (digital) telephone connections. Each videoconference participant must have a high-speed PC, specialized software, a videocamera, and access to a videoconferencing network—if they need to connect up more than two participants at one time. The videoconference connection may be local, or it may be remote over leased or dial-up telephone lines.

High-bandwidth ISDN or faster DSL and cable-modem-based videoconferencing systems can achieve VHS-quality transmission. But videoconferencing using standard analog (plain old telephone system) telephone lines results in a picture that falls short of broadcast television—it is a bit fuzzy; motion is jerky; and small movements, such as facial expressions when someone is talking, are out of sync.

High-bandwidth digital communications lines are available in most major cities but are more expensive than analog telephone connections.

Although desktop videoconferencing is not yet perfected, many of my clients are using it to help them communicate with customers and sales personnel who work in distant locations. My clients justify the cost of videoconferencing with saved travel time and expenses.

DOCUMENT CONFERENCING

Document conferencing enables PC users in different locations to look at a common image, such as an electronic spreadsheet model, or a slide presentation, while they discuss it over a telephone connection.

Document conferencing systems transfer images of drawings, slides, or documents, using a "white board" metaphor, by delivering an image on their computer's monitor that is analogous to the image you would see on a white board during a meeting. This enables two people to view and manipulate documents and images while they discuss them over the telephone.

Most document conferencing systems operate in real time, using a high-speed modem, which "echoes" the screens from the user in control to the other people who are connected together.*

Microsoft and Intel have announced electronic messaging and document conferencing standards that will help ensure that Internet-based "electronic meetings" become commonplace over the next five years.

---

* Document conferencing systems use simultaneous voice/data modems (SVDM), which share some of the telephone line's bandwidth for the audio portion of the conference.

ELECTRONIC FORMS

The paper form is the most common and proven business tool, but paper forms–based office systems can be very inefficient.

Paper forms are expensive to print, store, and distribute, and must be updated constantly to reflect the changing needs of an organization. Inaccurate information and incomplete forms often result in incorrect data; reentering information that is common to multiple forms wastes time; and circulating paper forms through an organization often results in important information not being available when needed.

Saving information in electronic forms that are linked to computer databases makes critical information accessible to those who need it in real time. And integrating electronic mail services with electronic forms automates the process of transferring information between users in an organization and can remedy the problems that are inherent with paper forms–based systems.*

ELECTRONIC DATA INTERCHANGE

Electronic Data Interchange (EDI) enables different computers to send data back and forth electronically, across telephone lines, without user intervention.

Many companies are implementing EDI to help them automate their inventory tracking and ordering process. EDI systems can, for example, enable low- or out-of-stock items in inventory to automatically generate electronic purchase orders, and can post those orders directly into a supplier's order entry system. EDI systems can also generate invoices and post accounts receivables automatically.

In the future, as communication standards, data security, and other implementation issues are resolved, more companies will use EDI on the Internet to help them buy and sell products and services electronically.†

---

* Doug Dayton, "Using Electronic Forms to Improve Office Operations," *The Office* (June 1989).
† According to Forrester Research, on-line sales transactions will exceed $2.5 billion by the year 2000.

THE INTERNET

Microsoft believes that the Internet is the most important "platform" since the IBM PC was introduced in 1981, and predicts that virtually every PC will be connected to the Internet within the next ten years.*

Tens of thousands of businesses are using the Internet for electronic mail, market research, digital marketing, customer support, electronic commerce, and a constellation of other applications. However, despite widespread enthusiasm and support for the Internet's World Wide Web, private computer networks will support most electronic commerce for the next few years, until data integrity, security, and system reliability issues are addressed.†

If you have never "surfed" the Internet, it's time to try it out! All you need is a PC, a modem, and an account with an Internet service provider such as Microsoft Network or America Online.

COMPUTER ERGONOMICS

Studies have shown that ergonomically designed office furniture, and computer monitors that are treated to reduce glare, can help you reduce fatigue and stress. If you are comfortable when you work, you will feel better, have more energy, and be more productive.

If you spend a lot of time using a computer, you should also be aware of the risks of repetitive stress disorders such as carpal tunnel syndrome. Repetitive stress disorders can be prevented by regular exercise; taking periodic breaks for stretching and rest; and using ergonomic work stations, keyboards, and monitors.

If you are experiencing any symptoms of a repetitive stress disorder such as tingling, numbness, or pain in your wrist joints,

---

* Microsoft Seminar for Independent Software Vendors (October 1995).

† According to a report published by Novell, over 40 million users in 159 countries are already connected to the Internet. This number is expected to grow to 100 million to 200 million people by the end of the century.

you should contact a physician immediately. Do not take pain pills and hope the problem will go away. Repetitive stress disorders can lead to lifelong disabilities if not treated promptly.

THE VIRTUAL OFFICE

Many salespeople maintain "virtual" offices by using computers and telephones to help them manage information and stay in contact with their customers and coworkers. For these salespeople, their "office" is any convenient place they agree to meet with their customers and coworkers.

Real-estate salespeople, for example, often use their automobile as a mobile office, by relying on cellular telephones to stay in contact with their buyers and sellers, and portable computers with modems to access their real-estate listing service.

If you generally meet your customers outside of your office, and are comfortable using a portable computer, you should take the time to evaluate whether you need to maintain a "physical" office. You may be ready for a virtual office of the future today!

PORTABLE COMPUTING

I was very excited when I got a Tandy® M-100 computer at Microsoft back in 1984. It ran on disposable batteries, and had a built-in text editor and an eight-line monochrome LCD display. The screen was almost impossible to read if there was too much or too little light. But I took it with me to sales meetings to take notes, and used it on airplanes and in hotel rooms to write up trip reports and to keep track of my travel expenses.

My M-100 had many limitations, but it weighed about twenty pounds less than the "transportable" Compaq computer I kept on my desk, and it helped me save time and do a better job of serving my customers.

Portable computer technology has improved dramatically over the past thirteen years. Notebook computers have become more powerful, smaller, and much less expensive than they used to be. But in one sense, portable computing hasn't changed at all.

I remember thinking, when I first started using my M-100, that I couldn't think of any tool, other than the telephone, that had such a profound impact on how I did my job. I still can't!

PART FOUR

MANAGING PERSONAL PRODUCTIVITY

Selling at Microsoft is really no different from selling anywhere else—it requires commitment, dedication, discipline, and the right attitude.

Most salespeople are aware of the commitment, dedication, and discipline necessary to be successful in professional sales. But it is equally important to maintain a positive attitude about your life, and a balance between your professional and your personal objectives.

In this section you will learn how to achieve this balance to help you achieve greater selling success.

CHAPTER SEVENTEEN

ATTITUDE, COMMITMENT, AND SUCCESS

"If we did half of what we know we should do, we'd be twice as well off as we are."

—**WILL ROGERS**

THE SECRET TO SELLING SUCCESS

I have always wanted to believe that there was a simple key to successful selling. But my experience has taught me that the selling process is anything but simple—selling is a *people* business.

If there is a secret to successful selling, it is that you must commit yourself to understanding the selling process and to paying attention to yourself and to your customer. By observing exactly what you are doing, and by observing the effect your communications have on your customer's decision process, you can refine your selling techniques to become a more effective salesperson.

But paying attention to the selling process is a tremendous challenge. I have learned that I cannot observe my customers objectively until I forget any preconceived notions I have about their needs and concerns. And I cannot be a good listener unless I focus my attention on exactly what my customer is trying to communicate to me.

The ability to achieve this objectivity—and to pay attention to the selling process—is dependent on how I feel about myself and on my personal energy level. When I am comfortable with who I am, and I can forget my own problems, I am a good listener. When I am a good listener, I can be a good problem-solver. And when I am a good problem-solver, I am able to move business forward with my customers almost effortlessly.

But when my personal energy level is low, because I am concerned about personal issues, or frustrated with my work, I can easily become preoccupied with these concerns and lose my ability to listen to my customers with an open mind. When I can't see the world from my customers' point of view, I impair my ability to help them move their purchasing process forward.

The only way I have found to ensure that my personal energy stays high, so I can maintain the level of attention I need to keep my "objectivity," is to maintain a balance between my business objectives and my social, physical, and spiritual needs.

BALANCING YOUR OBJECTIVES

Everyone has their own thoughts about the meaning and value of each activity in their life. And everyone has their own perception of the value of spending their time doing different things.

I have learned that the most effective way for me to achieve my goals is to be honest about what I want and about what is important to me, and then to make a conscious effort to balance how I spend my time between the business and personal tasks I have prioritized for myself.

Like most businesspeople, I have periods when I am so involved with business activities that I "forget" about my other obligations and objectives. Being a workaholic for short periods certainly has its rewards. But I have learned that when I become too focused on work, I begin to develop a negative attitude about my life.

AREA OF LIFE	EXAMPLE GOALS
Family	Coach children's soccer team Do a home improvement project with family
Social	Spend two nights each month with friends Join gourmet dinner club
Spiritual	Go to church Sunday morning Teach Yoga class every other week Write poetry
Physical	Do aerobic workout three days a week Play on company softball team Climb Mount Rainier
Business	Make sales quota Open 5 new accounts each month Earn top salesperson award
Educational	Take a self-improvement class Learn to speed-read Earn an M.B.A. degree
Financial/Retirement	Put aside 10% of salary for retirement Contribute to college fund Purchase lot for retirement home

To prevent myself from "burning out," I have learned to block out vacation periods, spiritual activities, family gatherings, and social occasions in my daily planner. I no longer allow my business objectives to undermine my resolve to maintain a balance among the different areas of my life.

BIORHYTHMS

One of the best ways I have found to leverage my productivity is to schedule my most important tasks at the time of day when I have the most energy.

I am a morning person. My mind is clearest and I have the most physical energy early in the day. But each person has his or her own unique biorhythm. Different people tend to be "morning," "evening," or "up all the time" people.

MY 10 FAVORITE TIME MANAGEMENT TIPS

1. When you wake up in the morning, get out of bed!

2. Plan a prebreakfast activity such as meditation, an exercise routine, or checking your E-mail.

3. Choose clothing that is easy to coordinate.

4. Organize your closet and drawers so you don't waste time looking for clothes.

5. Keep a box on your dresser for easily misplaced items such as keys, sunglasses, tickets, and coins.

6. Eliminate unnecessary items from your wallet or handbag.

7. Limit yourself to one or two credit cards; this will save you hours of time reconciling statements each year.

8. Organize your kitchen and bathroom to facilitate your morning preparations, systematize your breakfast preparations, and put your vitamins on the counter so you remember to take them.

9. If you are a coffee drinker (do you live in Seattle?), use a timed drip coffeemaker; the smell of the coffee will help get you out of bed.

10. Take 5 minutes at the same time each day, in the morning or before going to bed, to review what you have done, record your expenses and important action items, and plan your next day's activities.

To determine your own biorhythm you will need to chart your energy level at different times during the day. Over a period of a few days you should be able to determine the high- and low-energy periods during your day.

The easiest way to do this is to put a +, =, or − sign in your daily planner every hour to record your subjective feeling about how energized you feel. If you feel tired, enter a − sign; if you feel "normal" enter an = sign; and if you feel energized, enter a + sign.

In most cases you will be able to recognize your "energy" pattern after a few days. However, if you are going through an especially stressful period, you may need to track your biorhythm for a week or two to get an accurate chart of your biorhythm, because stress can temporarily change your normal energy patterns.

10 STEPS TO BETTER HEALTH

1. Develop specific goals and milestones to motivate yourself to attain the peak physical condition for a person of your age and abilities.

2. Schedule a time and place for your workouts, and prioritize your personal workout time.

3. If you are having a difficult time getting motivated, or do not know how to put together an exercise program for yourself, hire a personal trainer to help get you started. A personal trainer can make sure that you are exercising properly to prevent injury, and can help you maximize the benefits you receive from your workouts.

4. Start slowly, and increase the difficulty of your exercise program gradually so you don't injure yourself.

5. Do several different types of exercise (this is called "cross-training") to help you build strength and endurance.

6. If part of your health plan is to lose weight, learn how to reduce your fat intake and eat a well-balanced diet.

7. Use relaxation techniques such as massage and meditation to help you manage your stress.

8. Utilize new advances in exercise shoes and sports equipment to help prevent injuries while you get into shape.

9. Keep a record of your progress in an exercise journal.

10. Reward yourself when you attain your exercise and fitness milestones.

Once you have identified your high-energy periods, you can use these times for creative thinking, problem-solving, accomplishing unpleasant but necessary tasks, or completing "A"-level tasks you have prioritized for your day. During lower-energy periods you can concentrate on accomplishing your lower-priority tasks, such as sorting your mail or returning routine telephone calls.

Although my biorhythm is consistent from one day to the next, I have found that I can change my energy levels during the day by changing my exercise level and my diet. For example, I can increase my energy level in the afternoon by doing an aerobic exercise in the morning; and I can avoid my lowest-energy periods, and negative mood swings, by getting enough sleep, and by eating healthy snacks to avoid getting low-blood-sugar levels.

MANAGING YOUR HEALTH

Healthy people have more energy, and they get more done during the workday. Unfortunately, the majority of Americans are overweight, out of shape, and uninspired to take the steps necessary to bring themselves into peak physical condition.

Most health and fitness experts agree that the simplest route to good health is to eat a balanced diet, get enough sleep, and exercise moderately at least three times a week.

Heaven knows I'm not as fit as I would like to be, but my "10 Steps to Better Health" have helped me stay in reasonably good shape for a man with a receding hairline!

MANAGING STRESS

The pressure to meet sales quotas can lead to stress, and stress can cause both psychological and physical problems. Symptoms of stress such as nervousness, headache, fatigue, depression, and anger are very common in salespeople.

One of the most insidious aspects of stress is that it can drain the personal energy you need to overcome the source of your stress, leading to a debilitating slide into depression. So it is

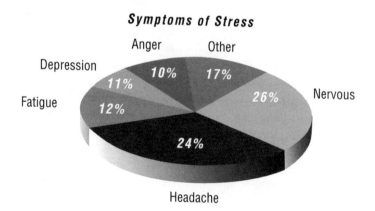

Symptoms of Stress

very important to recognize the symptoms of stress in yourself, and in your coworkers, so you can take action to reduce the factors that are causing stress before they become destructive.

Any challenging job, such as professional sales, will be stressful at times, and experiencing a moderate level of stress is normal. But if you are experiencing more serious symptoms of stress, such as frequent headaches or depression, you should consult a physician or other health professional.

What's Really Important

Many people get caught up trying to do things they think are expected of them, rather than just living life on their own terms. But the secret to selling success doesn't have very much at all to do with how you dress, or whether you have had a formal education.

Bill Gates, the richest man in the United States and one of the most successful entrepreneurs of the twentieth century, used to go to sales meetings with executives from *Fortune* 50 companies wearing a sweater with a hole in the sleeve. And Bill was a college dropout—from Harvard—after deciding to live his life on his own terms.

So the next time you become concerned about your business "assets," take a deep breath, remember Bill's sweater, and *just do it.**

DEVELOPING YOUR "PEOPLE SKILLS"

One of my best customers at Microsoft once made me wait almost an hour before he would see me, and seemed anxious to end our meeting as quickly as possible. Thinking that I had done something wrong, I searched my memory to figure out what I could have done to upset my customer. Weeks later, I found out that my customer's child had been taken to the hospital the day of our meeting.

---

* "Just do it!" was a piece of advice I got from a Zen monk when I was in college, twenty-five years ago. I do not know if a famous sport shoe manufacturer also received this advice.

NEGATIVE THOUGHTS . . .	CAN BECOME POSITIVE AFFIRMATIONS
• The economy is bad, so I can't sell anything.	• I can sell more by learning how to arrange financing for new business.
• Our product is not state-of-the-art, so no one wants it anymore.	• Our product is reliable and has proven itself in the field.
• New customers just waste my time.	• New customers will grow into major accounts and will enable me to meet my sales objectives.
• No one wants to talk to me.	• I am a likable person and people are interested in what I have to say.
• I can't sell to Republicans/ Democrats/Libertarians.	• I can work with everybody.

Most customers are open and communicative, but some are very difficult to work with. It is not always possible to understand your customers' concerns or motivations, and it is not always possible to help your customers find a solution to their problems.

If you are having difficulty communicating with your customers, ask them if they can help you identify their concerns. And if you don't feel that you will be able to help them through their purchasing process, ask your manager for help.

Mastering the "people" side of selling is a lifelong process. Be patient with yourself.

WHY SALESPEOPLE FAIL

Most businesses fail because their fundamental business model is flawed, or because their business fails to maintain good customer relations.

Most salespeople fail because they have a negative attitude about their work, or because they convince themselves to accept negative assumptions, which makes it difficult for them to take the actions necessary to achieve selling success.

It is hard to identify when or why people develop their attitudes about work. Different theories suggest that it is genetic, or that our preschool, adolescent years, early work experiences, or

NEGATIVE PERSONAL FACTORS THAT CAN INFLUENCE SUCCESS	POSITIVE PERSONAL FACTORS THAT CAN INFLUENCE SUCCESS
• Negative attitude	• Positive attitude
• Low self-confidence	• Optimistic personality
• Abrasive personality	• Team player—good communicator
• Lacks enthusiasm	• Ambitious
• Lacks initiative	• Dedicated and persistent
• Lacks personal or professional goals	• Goal-oriented—interested in learning new skills
• Poor self-discipline	• Motivated to succeed
• Poor organizational skills	• Well organized
• No respect for employer or manager	• Respects manager and coworkers
• Desire for different type of work	• Loves job
• No interest in self-improvement	• Constantly strives to improve performance
• Dishonest	• Honest and ethical
• Unacceptable personal appearance	• Pays attention to personal grooming
• Problems with family, friends, or coworkers	• Stable personal life
• Philandering, gambling addiction, substance abuse	• Stable personal life

some combination of genetic predisposition and life experience may be the culprits.

I have found that regardless of where attitudes about work come from, the most effective way to overcome a negative attitude is to identify negative thoughts and purposely change them into positive affirmations.

I have spent years identifying the positive and negative personal factors that can influence a salesperson's motivation and selling success. This is the list I have come up with:

I make a conscious effort to cultivate positive attitudes in myself and in the people I work with.

10 STEPS TO ETHICAL CLIENT-CENTERED™ SELLING

1. Never misrepresent your products.
2. Answer your customer's concerns honestly and completely.
3. Provide accurate, timely information.
4. Inform your customers of issues that are critical to their success.
5. Don't pursue business that is bad for your customers.
6. Don't pursue business that is bad for your company.
7. Don't disparage your competitors.
8. Work with people you believe are ethical.
9. Take responsibility for your customers' satisfaction.
10. Honor the "Golden Rule."

WORK FOR A COMPANY YOU BELIEVE IN

It is easy to be enthusiastic about selling when you are proud of the company you represent.

I was proud to work for Microsoft, because Microsoft has a Client-Centered™ approach to marketing and customer service. Like Nordstrom, Eddie Bauer, and McDonald's, Microsoft realized early on that the best way to grow their business was to develop a large base of satisfied customers.

Today, Microsoft generates huge sales revenues by selling product upgrades and enhancements. This "repeat" business enables Microsoft to develop and market new products and to maintain its position on the leading edge of computer technology.

As long as Microsoft maintains their Client-Centered™ attitude, I am confident they will maintain their leadership position in the PC market. And I will continue to recommend Microsoft stock to all my friends!

HONESTY AND CANDOR

Most salespeople are fundamentally honest and will not lie or misrepresent their products to make a sale. But it is almost impossible for a salesperson to be completely candid.

It is unreasonable, for example, to expect computer sales-people to provide the names of every dissatisfied customer their company has ever had, when prospective customers ask for a referral. But it is reasonable and legally required for pharmaceutical salespeople to inform physicians that use of their products may cause specific side effects.

If you are asked to do something you feel is unethical, don't panic. First, discuss it with your manager, and outline why you believe the action is wrong. Then, if your manager won't back down, ask that person to put his or her request in writing to document that person's responsibility. If your manager is willing to assume responsibility but you are still uncomfortable with the situation, ask your manager to take you off the account.

Taking the "moral high ground" may make you unpopular and may cost you commissions, but it can save your reputation and your conscience, and it may keep you out of court.

Ethics start at the top of an organization. If a company believes in a code of conduct, it should be proud to publish it. If a company believes that its employees are acting in an unethical manner, it should strive to rectify the situation as quickly as possible. And if a company harms their customers, the company should act decisively to mitigate the problem.

Many companies have suffered public relations nightmares when they refused to acknowledge product design flaws, environmental problems, or other mistakes. If you are involved in this type of situation, you should strive to maintain open, honest communication with your customers. When you overcome your problems, your honesty and candor will help restore faith in your products and in your company's brand.

SELLING IS A ZERO-SUM GAME

The difference between a salesperson with twenty years of experience and a rookie salesperson is the sum of their professional selling skills and their attitude. But sales is a zero-sum game; a rookie salesperson with a positive attitude can easily outsell an "old shoe" who has become a know-it-all curmudgeon.

I have learned that to be effective, regardless of my previous selling experience, I must demonstrate a caring attitude, strength of character, determination, persistence, responsibility for my actions, and the ability to plan and analyze selling situations objectively and honestly.

I try to encourage these traits in myself and in the people who work with me.

CREATIVITY DRIVES SUCCESS

It is normal to experience some ups and downs in any sales job. Every salesperson I have worked with has had days when their "get up and go, got up and went." But, over the years, I have learned that *creativity* is the key to regaining and retaining selling enthusiasm.

Many years ago I had a job selling electronic cash registers to fast-food restaurants. During that time, the country went into a recession, and very few fast-food stores were built. Bob, my company's sales representative in Texas, was the only salesman in the entire company who was achieving his sales quota.

When I asked my manager to tell me Bob's secret, my manager replied that Bob was selling systems to fine-dining restaurants. When I pointed out that the system wasn't designed for fine-dining restaurants, my manager replied, "Don't tell Bob!"

By making a conscious effort to improve your selling style, and by being proactive about developing and implementing new prospecting and qualifying techniques, you can make your work more challenging, more enjoyable, and more financially rewarding.

Creativity equals motivation, motivation equals positive energy, and positive energy sells!

PUT TOGETHER YOUR ACTION PLAN

The most effective way I have found to increase my personal energy level is to make a check list of the things I can do to increase my personal self-esteem and self-confidence, and then to create an action plan to help me achieve each of my goals.

After I have created my list, I take the time to "visualize" myself achieving my goals, and I encourage myself to focus on the activities I have prioritized.

When I am ready to implement my action plan, I use my daily planner to help me plan and prioritize the activities I believe will help me achieve my goals.

By taking time to plan my day, I know that each action I take will bring me a step closer to realizing my goals and to enjoying the rewards I have put in place to motivate myself.

The key to maintaining a positive attitude about yourself and about your work is challenging yourself with goals, and rewarding yourself for your achievements.

WHAT DOES SUCCESS MEAN TO YOU?

Success means very different things to different people. To one person, success means being promoted to a new job; to another person, it means earning a diploma, or saving up enough money to buy a new house.

In any case, to feel successful, you must first define what success means to you; otherwise you may not recognize success when it arrives!

So go ahead—try on a mental image of success.

If you take advantage of the power of your own ideas, and stay focused on achieving the objectives you have prioritized, you will have a great chance to succeed in everything you do.

YOUR EFFORT = YOUR SUCCESS

Throughout this book I have shared the Client-Centered™ selling techniques I developed at Microsoft and throughout my career as a consultant. These techniques can enable you to get a fresh perspective on your selling process and to maximize your potential as a sales professional.

But to be honest, my techniques will not help you become more successful unless you are ready to make a *conscious effort* to change your ineffective selling habits and to understand the purchasing process from your customers' perspective. That's what Client-Centered™ selling is really about.

My hope is that you will make a sincere effort to master Client-Centered™ selling, that you will experience even greater selling success than I have, and that you will pass this knowledge along.

We have the blessing of living in a universe that expands with the curiosity and courage we bring to our lives; so don't worry, there's plenty of success to go around!

INDEX

CLIENT-CENTERED™ TRAINING SEMINARS

Client-Centered™ training seminars present all of the core selling skills needed to develop an effective, professional sales force.

For information on in-house seminars, consulting services, and custom program development, contact:

Client-Centered™ Training, Inc.
477 123rd Place NE, Bellevue, WA 98005-8419
Internet E-mail: info@daytonassociates.com

Visit the home page at
www.daytonassociates.com